THE HISTORIAN'S
BUSINESS
AND OTHER ESSAYS

RICHARD PARES IN 1950

THE HISTORIAN'S BUSINESS

AND OTHER ESSAYS

BY

RICHARD PARES

Edited by
R. A. and Elisabeth Humphreys

With an introduction by
Lucy S. Sutherland

OXFORD
AT THE CLARENDON PRESS
1961

Oxford University Press, Amen House, London E.C.4

GLASGOW NEW YORK TORONTO MELBOURNE WELLINGTON
BOMBAY CALCUTTA MADRAS KARACHI KUALA LUMPUR
CAPE TOWN IBADAN NAIROBI ACCRA

PRINTED IN GREAT BRITAIN
AT THE UNIVERSITY PRESS, OXFORD
BY VIVIAN RIDLER
PRINTER TO THE UNIVERSITY

PREFATORY NOTE

THREE of the articles and lectures included in this volume were printed in the 1930's. The others were all published between 1951 and 1957. For permission to reprint them here it is a pleasure to acknowledge the kindness of the Council of the Royal Historical Society, of the editors of the *Economic History Review*, the *English Historical Review*, *History*, the *Listener*, and the *University of Edinburgh Journal*, of Jonathan Cape Ltd., and of Messrs. Macmillan & Co. Full particulars of the original place and date of publication are given in the headnotes.

My wife and I wish also to acknowledge with gratitude all the help and encouragement we have had, in making this selection of her brother's papers, from Janet Pares, his widow, from Professor John Bromley, and, above all, from Dr. Lucy S. Sutherland, to whom we are still further indebted for the introductory memoir.

R. A. H.

CONTENTS

INTRODUCTION

RICHARD PARES, historian, died in Oxford on 3 May 1958 at the age of 55, completely paralysed in body, but at the height of his intellectual powers. A Fellow of the British Academy, a Fellow of All Souls College, an honorary Fellow of Balliol College, an honorary LL.D. and former Professor of the University of Edinburgh, and for nearly twenty years joint editor of the *English Historical Review*, he had gained many academic honours and, had fate been kinder to him, would have gained many more; and, after fighting for more than ten years with all the courage and intelligence of which he was capable against the mortal disease which was advancing on him, he retained even in defeat something of the mien of a conqueror.

He was, and prided himself on being, before everything else, a professional historian, a detached and expert observer who knew that 'the sense that historians make is an increasingly complicated sense' and whose recognition of this fact was 'a matter of scientific conscience'.[1] His claims for the practical value of his chosen field of study to the society in which he lived were scrupulously moderate and even a little wry. 'Good history', he said, 'cannot do as much service as money or science; but bad history can do almost as much harm as the most disastrous scientific discovery in the world.'[2] But of its deeper though less tangible value he had no doubt. Among the papers found after his death was a note, dated (with characteristic precision) 3.9.46: '*The historian in the modern world*—one thing at least that he can do is to dispel the stupor and allay the anguish with which our older and feebler society views the rise of newer, and, for the purpose, more efficient social and political forms, whose ideas of right and wrong so baffle us.' And to the discovery, analysis, and re-creation of the past he systematically and absorbedly dedicated his life.

He was nevertheless the least solemn of men. Though a man of so lively an intelligence that his friends said of him (with pardonable exaggeration) that 'he could understand anything', whose mind was so individual that he was incapable of treating a topic in a commonplace way, and whose sense of style was so nice that,

---

[1] See below, p. 10.   [2] See below, p. 82.

while he might be intricate, he could never be obscure, he submitted himself to an unwavering self-discipline for the perfection of his highly sophisticated and meticulously unspectacular art. 'The historical process', he wrote, 'is very complicated: it has its laws and its uniformities, but it can only be explained in terms of itself.'[1]

The events of his life can be briefly narrated. He was born at Colchester on 25 August 1902, the eldest of the five children of a remarkable father, Bernard (afterwards Sir Bernard) Pares, and of Margaret, daughter of Edward Dixon of Colchester. A precocious and delicate child (he was to grow up both active and wiry, but his strength was always more moral than physical), he early developed the habit of omnivorous reading. A scholarship to Winchester opened up to him a peculiarly happy and successful school career, to be followed by an equally brilliant four years at Oxford; beginning with a scholarship to Balliol, going on to a first class in Greats, and culminating in his election to a Fellowship at All Souls in November 1924, an election which cut short an intention to read also for the Honour School of Modern History.

Though an archaeological expedition to Turkey with Professor (later Sir William) Calder in the summer of 1926 might have confirmed his interest in the study of the ancient world, and in 1926-7 a brief excursion into journalism[2] might have seemed to be leading him away from his life work, the lines of his future were already laid down. When in 1927 he was appointed to an Assistant Lectureship at University College, London, he had already chosen his period of study, the eighteenth century, and his approach to it, an examination of British imperial problems with special reference to the West Indian islands, in that century the most prized of English possessions. It has been suggested that his interest in questions of empire was first aroused by his undergraduate studies in the Roman colonate (and one of the 'two great teachers of history' to whom he dedicated his first book was C. G. Stone, with whom he had read Roman history at Balliol). It is certain that another Balliol historian, Kenneth Bell, had drawn his attention to the significance of the West Indian interest in the political life of eighteenth-century England. But he owed little

[1] See below, p. 10.

[2] He spent some months on the *Liverpool Daily Post and Mercury* as a preparation for work on *The Times*. As a schoolboy he had edited *The Wykehamist*, and as an undergraduate *The Cherwell*.

to the direct assistance of any teacher in his apprenticeship to modern history. He himself claimed that it was the 'library, traditions, and conversation' of All Souls which had formed his mind as a historian.[1]

A year later he resigned his Lectureship to take up a Laura Spelman Rockefeller Memorial Studentship which enabled him to travel throughout the West Indies and in New England, examining the manuscript sources preserved there and gaining first-hand knowledge of the regions. On his return in 1929 he settled in Oxford, where, as Fellow of All Souls and Lecturer of New College, he spent ten years of concentrated and fruitful labour, tutoring and lecturing for the History and P.P.E. schools, taking his share in College and University administration (he served his turn as Proctor in 1938–9), and, above all, laying the basis of his historical learning by extensive and systematic reading and research. In this period he wrote his first two books—*War and Trade in the West Indies, 1739–1763* (1936), an authoritative work of many-sided learning and confident judgement, though it suffers in presentation from a young scholar's desire to do too many things at once, and *Colonial Blockade and Neutral Rights, 1739–1763* (1938), a by-product of the first, and the original and lucid study of a subject more usually treated by international lawyers. He also made several contributions to learned periodicals and began the long series of admirable reviews which, particularly after 1939, when he became, with Professor J. G. (now Sir Goronwy) Edwards, joint editor of the *English Historical Review*,[2] were to be one of his major contributions to historical studies.

In 1937 he married Janet, younger daughter of Sir Maurice Powicke (then Regius Professor of History at Oxford), by whom he had four daughters. The marriage brought him the encouragement of a supremely happy home life, and the companionship of a devoted and courageous wife.

The outbreak of the Second World War cut through this pattern of academic achievement and private content, and brought, as with most scholars of his generation, an interruption of more than five years in his career. He was one of the earliest academic recruits to the Administrative Civil Service and one of the last to be

[1] In the foreword to *King George III and the Politicians* (1953).
[2] In 1937–8 he was Review Editor of *The Oxford Magazine* and during several years wrote many reviews for it.

released. He entered the Board of Trade as a Temporary Principal in 1939 and left it at the end of 1945 with the rank of Principal Assistant Secretary and the post of Principal Priority Officer of the Department.[1] In 1945 he was awarded the C.B.E. for his services. The qualities of mind and character which were leading him to distinction in the academic sphere served him equally well in that of higher administration. But although he enjoyed his mastery of this new and unfamiliar world and made many friends in it, he remained a stranger there, solacing his rare moments of leisure with his editorial duties for the *English Historical Review*[2] and the reading of the voluminous literature of the history of exploration.

In 1945 he was elected to the Chair of History at the University of Edinburgh and, no more than a fortnight after his release from the Board of Trade, took up his new duties. In the City and University of Edinburgh he at once felt at home—the beauty of the city never ceased to move him—and he undertook with lively zest and outstanding success the work of a Professor and Head of a Department. As soon as he could he picked up the threads of his interrupted research, beginning with a West Indian study on which he had already worked a good deal before the war and which was published in 1950 under the title of *A West-India Fortune*. In this he used with great skill the correspondence and business records of a single family to elucidate the West Indian economy between 1685 and 1852.[3] The study also displayed for the first time his remarkable gifts as a biographer. He had also undertaken late in the war to write the volume of the Oxford History of England covering the years 1760 to 1815, and he seems to have intended to use this project as the occasion for a shift of emphasis in his historical studies, and for the move from the periphery to the centre of the empire towards which much in his earlier works had already pointed the way. Everything seemed set for the production of the work of his maturity.

---

[1] He described the duties of a Principal Priority Officer in 'The Work of a Departmental Priority Officer' in *Lessons of the British War Economy*, ed. D. N. Chester (1951).

[2] Despite his almost overwhelming official duties, he continued to contribute reviews to the journal.

[3] The value of this type of approach to historical problems was much in his mind at this time, as may be seen from his 'Recent British Works on Modern British History', *Bulletin* of the Institute of Historical Research, xxi (1948), 116–27.

But it was here that his fortune failed him. Hardly had he assumed his new duties when the first signs appeared of the rare and incurable disease, progressive muscular atrophy, which was first to incapacitate and then to destroy him, and though he wasted no energy in self-pity or useless revolt, the rest of his life was a defensive and inevitably losing battle. By 1954 he had decided that he could no longer carry out his professorial duties, and, All Souls offering him a Special Research Fellowship, he returned to Oxford. Here, in Holywell Street, the last four years of his life were spent, surrounded by his family and by friends whose idiosyncrasies he observed with a pleasure quite unmixed with malice; watching the University cricket in the Parks and the succession of the seasons in College gardens; reading, writing (or rather dictating), lecturing, supervising research students, and managing the affairs of the *English Historical Review*. His advice was much sought after in private, and never in vain, and even when he knew that death stood at his elbow he would discuss, with all his accustomed wit and incisiveness, but also with a deeply impressive serenity and detachment, the historical problems which were the constant subject of his thoughts.

For a historian who conceived his task as did Richard Pares, one whose systematic studies had to depend on his own examination and subjugation of a vast variety of detailed first-hand material, the incapacity to seek out and, when found, to annotate this material was a handicap which no effort of his own could more than partially overcome. Though his output during these years would have done credit both in quality and volume to a historian suffering under none of his disabilities, this limitation was inevitably reflected in his published work. He had to abandon the volume for the Oxford History, though before his incapacities became too crippling he was able to complete the remarkable tour de force of his Ford Lectures, delivered from a wheeled chair to a large and delighted audience in 1952, and published in the following year under the title of *King George III and the Politicians*. It was an independent, masterly, and highly allusive examination of the major political problems of the period. Four years later he wrote for the Historical Association a pamphlet on *Limited Monarchy in Great Britain in the Eighteenth Century*. But otherwise he confined himself to the writing of reviews, to the further development of his colonial studies, and the exploitation of material amassed before 1939. Two books, *Yankees and Creoles. The trade between North America and the West Indies before the American Revolution* (1956) and *Merchants and Planters* (comprising his Chichele Lectures of 1956–7 and appearing posthumously in 1960), as well as several articles, bear tribute to the range and thoroughness of this early research.

Notable though his achievements were, however, his historical writings stand as a fine but unfinished torso; the longer works which would have done full justice to the range of his knowledge and contemplation could never be written. It is therefore fortunate that we have, in addition to the more systematic works of his maturity, his occasional writings of the same period in the composition of which he felt less severely the limitation imposed by physical helplessness. The present volume is designed partly to bring together for the use of scholars the most important of the learned articles he wrote in the course of his career. It is also, however, intended to provide some illustration of the quality of his writing on a wide variety of subjects during the years when his powers were at their height.

L. S. SUTHERLAND

I

THE HISTORIAN'S BUSINESS

[A lecture given at the City Chambers, Edinburgh, on 19 January 1953. *University of Edinburgh Journal*, xvii (1953), pp. 32–38]

IN one of the early works of my favourite English novelist, the hero and heroine are taking a walk not far from the city of Bath. They discuss, among other things, history and historians. The heroine—who, I must confess, is one of the silliest girls I have ever met with, even as a heroine—expresses her dislike of history. 'I read it a little as a duty, but it tells me nothing that does not either vex or weary me. The quarrels of popes and kings, with wars and pestilences, in every page; the men all so good for nothing, and hardly any women at all—it is very tiresome: and yet I often think it odd that it should be so dull, for a great deal of it must be invention.'

The hero and his sister have more sense. The latter says a few words in defence of the historians, and the heroine, being already in love though she does not know it, immediately changes sides. 'At this rate, I shall not pity the writers of history any longer. If people like to read their books, it is all very well, but to be at so much trouble in filling great volumes, which, as I used to think, nobody would ever willingly look into, to be labouring only for the torment of little boys and girls, always struck me as a hard fate; and though I know it is all very right and necessary, I have often wondered at the person's courage that could sit down on purpose to do it.'

'That little boys and girls should be tormented,' the hero replies, 'is what no one at all acquainted with human nature in a civilized state can deny; but in behalf of our most distinguished historians, I must observe, that they might well be offended at being supposed to have no higher aim.'

I have undertaken to discuss 'The Historian's Business'; but first let me ask, for whom the historians do that business: let me discuss the professional, or perhaps I ought to say, professorial historian's relation to the general public. There is at present a misunderstanding between them: they are hardly on speaking

B

terms. It was not always so. Gibbon's *Decline and Fall of the Roman Empire* was something like a best seller, by the standard of the times, though even then there were, according to the testimony of Miss Catherine Morland, some historians who were no more than 'tormentors'. In modern times this closer relation between the historian and the general public has disappeared; the professionals and the general public have drifted apart, and nearly all professional historians nowadays are tormentors—a phrase which, as the Rev. Henry Tilney pointed out, is synonymous with instructors—of boys and girls, big or little. Why is this so?

It is partly the general public's own doing: its tastes have changed, and not only in history. The general public is much less interested in politics than it was in the days of Gibbon or of Bishop Stubbs. I believe it was the late Lord Northcliffe who made the great discovery that what the general public likes is private life. Perhaps this is one reason why the general public dislikes the professional historians, who are still aware of the importance of politics and try to remind it of that importance.

But this is not the whole explanation. The historians themselves write less politics than they used to write—many of them are concerned with economic history, with the history of art, of science, of ideas, and so forth; and still the general public does not much like them, though there are some exceptions such as the popularity of G. M. Trevelyan's *English Social History*. Perhaps, however, this too can be explained. These kinds of history do not usually tell a story. They discuss questions. The general public does not like questions, but does like a story. Moreover, even when they are discussing social and economic history, professional historians do not portray private life so wholeheartedly as the general public would like. It is very hard to do so, for private life leaves comparatively few records just because it is private.

For all these reasons the professional historians are not supplying what the general public wants. This is not a matter of style. The general reader believes that he cannot endure the works of professional historians because they are so badly written. I may be biased, but I think the style of professional historians is generally good, sometimes very good. Style is not the reason why the general public cannot read their books. The reason is a much graver one: they are the wrong kind of books, written about the wrong kind of subject.

But the professional historians are also partly responsible for this rift. They too are changing. I said, a few minutes ago, that I was in doubt whether I ought to use the word 'professional', or 'professorial'. History, like other sciences, has been getting into the hands of the professors—a very important change, for better or worse. Some people do not think that the professors are professional historians at all: for example, the late Philip Guedalla used to contend that he was a professional historian and they were not, because he lived by writing history books and they lived by doing something else, namely, teaching. It is a fact, however, that most professors do write books; and the present state of historical writing is largely explained by the fact that it is in the hands of university teachers. These are the people whom I call professional historians.

What results from this? In order to answer that question we must consider what a teacher does when he uses history as a discipline for university students. In the first place, it goes without saying that he must insist on having any historical statement which is wholly verifiable 100 per cent. right—not merely 99 or 98 per cent. This involves constant corrections and complications, for the truth about human beings is seldom simple. But the general public does not like corrections and complications. Still more important than corrections of fact is the constant refinement and supersession of interpretation. There is a perennial dialectic between each generation of historians and its predecessor, not only because new information is brought into use, but still more because new emphases and new patterns take the place of old.

At this point it will occur to the general public that historians must be very tiresome fellows, since it is evident that they write in order to show how clever they are. It is quite true that they do so: the best way to get a university job in history is to write a book or an article, successfully undermining some interpretation which passes current. But there is more excuse than that for the refinement and the supersession of interpretation: it is necessary for the discipline of the students; they only begin to think, or to produce their own interpretation, when they see other people's interpretations compared with each other.

That is a valid justification; but it is very annoying for the general reader, who would have wished to read history for pleasure or inspiration. In history, as in scenery, the general reader likes a bold outline of peaks and valleys—great events, great characters, great movements, great mistakes. The professional historian is always moving the peaks about and, what is still worse, scaling them down. Let us take, for example, the idea of the 'Renaissance of the fifteenth century'. You find one professional historian saying, 'The Renaissance of the fifteenth century was not a really important renaissance: it is the Renaissance of the fourteenth or the thirteenth or the twelfth century that matters.' Another will say, 'There was no such thing as the Renaissance of the fifteenth century: you cannot isolate a single episode in a great process like that.' A third will admit that the Renaissance of the fifteenth century existed, but will tell you that such a renaissance was not at all important: the really important development, according to him, is the scientific revolution of the seventeenth century. All this is very tiresome for the general reader, who finds that the Alpine peaks and valleys which he expected have been moved about or ground down to something like the scenery of West Lothian, with which he is all too well acquainted already. And yet the professors are right: their version is more lifelike than the older version.

What use, then, is the professional historian to the general public—how can he even get at the general public at all? He does so chiefly at schools and universities—especially universities: and this is a pity, since everybody goes to school and not everybody to the university. The work of professional historians takes too long a time to get into the school textbooks: they are not revised often enough in the light of the latest knowledge; even when new ones are written they tend to say much the same things as the old ones, as if the professional historian had never written at all. Perhaps there is a reason for this. The teaching of history in schools is dominated by consideration of the kind of thing that can be taught at all at a certain age. The right age to start reading history is about twenty-five, and those who have to study it at fifteen must obviously be studying something which is not in the full sense history at all. Still more is the teaching of history in schools dominated by consideration of the kind of examination question that you can ask. The kind of history in which modern professional writers delight does not suit these requirements. For example, how can you examine a child of fourteen on the question whether there was a Renaissance, when it was, whether it was important, and so forth? You could not get the child's own judgement on these questions, nor would they even very successfully test its memory. These, I think, are the reasons why much of the discussion among professional historians never gets into the school books at all. I am told that these things happen differently in Russia; but perhaps this is because the correction of accepted versions takes the form of modifications of the party line, which nobody can ignore. If so, perhaps the Russians pay too high a price for having their history books kept up to date.

The professional historian is of most use to the general public if the general public goes to the university. Many professors—for example my great predecessor Sir Richard Lodge—made their chief contribution to history in the form of their old students, some of whom, I hope, are in the room tonight.

When, therefore, I talk about the historian's business, I am thinking of teaching rather than of writing, and of interpretation rather than fact-finding.

The finding of facts is, no doubt, much discussed. What is a historical fact? How does the historian know it? What does he mean when he generalizes or infers? These things are more discussed by philosophers than by historians: the philosophers are much readier to say what the historians ought to be doing than the historians are to say what they are doing. Historians are clearly the worse for that: I should not like to say how much worse, for there are other artists, such as practitioners of the art of war, who are allowed to practise their arts without theorizing about it. Perhaps the historians may have some of the same latitude.

I do not discuss these questions tonight. But we must beware of thinking that historians can interpret without any relation to fact-finding. Very often it is the interpretation that makes the fact. For example, we often have to decide what must have happened from knowing the character of the actors, at the same time as we decide what the actors were like from knowing what they are known to have done. Sometimes we do both these things at once! We say that X must have done this because he was that kind of man and that he was that kind of man because he did certain actions, including, probably, this action. A circular argument? Perhaps so, but that is how we build up our knowledge of people in history and in real life. Perhaps there is a parallel in textual criticism (a discipline which is of extreme value to historians).

We establish a doubtful text, partly by what it looks like, and partly by what it must have been; and that, in turn, is based on other texts, some themselves doubtful, reinforced by the probability that this is one of them. By these means textual critics develop a sixth sense for what must have been written and historians can likewise develop a sixth sense for what must have happened.

Historians, then, as teachers, interpret. What does that mean? It means partly that they inculcate historical judgement by publicly judging, as the mother cat inculcates the principles of mousing by catching mice in the presence of her young. But what does the historian do when he judges or interprets? It is hard to define; but perhaps I can give some examples.

He is reading the biography of a statesman, and he comes upon an incident which makes him say to himself, 'So that is why this statesman said, three years later, something which I have never been able to understand: evidently he was thinking of this experience.' Or he looks at a graph showing the rise and fall of the value of money: he notices that at a certain point it ceases to fall and he remembers that about the same time the economic theorists began to worry about the nation's money supply. He says to himself, 'So that is why they bothered about it: of course they had every motive for doing so when money was becoming harder to get.' It may appear from these examples that history is simply a series of bright ideas. So it is; but that kind of intuition is only the first stage; it has to be tested against other bright ideas. The historian must call to mind similar effects which were not produced by similar causes. He must carry in his mind several alternative explanations of an action. Sometimes he is slow to decide between them and perhaps he never does so, for they may all be true. In some kinds of history it is certainly easier to assign causes than in others. Perhaps it is hardest in economic history and easiest in diplomatic history: but even there it is not always easy—we know much more about what Bismarck or Neville Chamberlain did than about his reasons for doing it.

The historian is always saying to himself, 'So that is why'. He asks why, why, why, all the time. Why were the Tudors successful? Why was Lord Shelburne so unpopular? Why did the Industrial Revolution start in Great Britain? Not only why, but also why not? Why did the Industrial Revolution not start at some other time and place? Why did the Romans make so few scientific inventions? Why was there no revolution in Great Britain in 1848? Very often the answer to the question 'why not' is even more illuminating than the answer to the question 'why', for it shows what people took for granted and what they thought important. (Sometimes, however, the question 'why not' only serves to point to the limitation of human endeavour and human attention, especially in politics, where it must always be true that because certain things are attended to, others must be neglected; as, for example, attention is often distracted from internal reform by war, less often from war by internal reform.) Historians, in asking why and why not, are seeking for a coherent system of explanations, and above all of causation, for history is especially a study of causality.

There is another characteristic activity of historians which shows, in a different way, their need and their quest for coherence. Among a miscellaneous series of facts, a historian comes upon one which causes him to prick up his ears and to say, 'I have seen that before', or alternatively, 'I have never seen that before.' He notices a fact either because it is exactly what he expected, or because it is exactly what he did not expect. Why is this? His interest is not purely statistical. The historians wish to establish a norm—what is, and what is not, the kind of thing that happens. Events are indeed unique; but historians would have little interest in them if they could not tentatively classify them. The historian who notices a fact because he has seen it before, or because he has not, is trying to establish his system of coherence—the familiar facts confirming his system, and the unfamiliar ones pointing to the necessity of a more elaborate system of coherence, of a more elaborate system of uniformity. Above all there is the uniformity which we call 'human nature'. There is a paradox about this: no human beings are so unlike us that we cannot understand them at all—if they were so, they would not be human beings—yet it is hard to be sure what, if any, are the points at which they must resemble us if they are to be human beings. If there were no such thing as human nature (a doctrine which the late Professor Collingwood came very near to holding) no general laws could safely be laid down, nothing could be predicted, nothing even could be detected, in history. Yet human nature itself varies in time, as a result of the historical process, and failure to treat it as doing so renders history unlifelike. For example, there were many nineteenth-century historians who thought that thirteenth-century politicians were just like nineteenth-century politicians. We can now see that they were not, for they were not thinking about the same kind of things at all. It is this kind of treatment that makes the history books of the nineteenth-century so unlifelike for us— they are just like the portraits of the kings of Scotland in the galleries of Holyrood House which were all painted from imagination by the same artists in the reign of Charles II. Sometimes the failure to recognize the effect of the historical process itself upon human character reduces history to a mere repertory of moral and prudential examples such as were so popular in the sixteenth and seventeenth centuries. The authors of these compilations say, for example, 'Alexander the Great did this, and it was a great success', or 'I should not advise you to do that, for Alfonso the Wise did it and it did not pay him at all'; they never think of mentioning the fact that Alfonso the Wise lived more than a thousand years after Alexander the Great, and several hundred years before the prince to whom they are giving the advice. This is not history at all.

It is a question not only of understanding how far every age is unique, but of translating what is admittedly unique into terms which make it recognizable for us. For example, it does help us if we can realize that Charlemagne was just like an enlightened American millionaire, for this recognition brings him into a class about which we may know something. But we cannot be sure of being able to make the translation at all. There are some things for which there is no translation and therefore no perfect recognition. The historian has to accept the fact that the unique is unique at the same time that he tries to classify the classifiable. The recognition of the unique is therefore a stumbling-block in the search for uniformity.

But what are these uniformities for which historians look? Ought they to look for a single systematic uniformity? Many have searched for it and some have found it in cyclical theories of history, in theories of challenge and response, in laws of successive economic and political stages, and in Marxism, which reduces all to the social, political, and intellectual effects of 'conditions of production'.

Some of these are only drawing-room fads; Marxism is certainly more than that. But none of them is a complete success—not even Marxism. There is much very superior Marxist criticism, but it only applies well to certain things, and the things to which it does not so easily apply are apt to be comparatively neglected by Marxists. It is fair, however, to say that all historians neglect certain things as unimportant, and the things which they neglect are nearly always those which do not confirm views they have already begun to form.

I doubt whether any historian will succeed in reducing everything to one system. It seems to me that there are at least four or five independent variables—climate, war, religion (I am not quite sure of that one), technology and science, and 'conditions of production' (which are not the same thing as technology and science). Attempts to explain one wholly in terms of another are generally unsuccessful—for example, the attempt to explain scientific invention in terms of material needs or class interests. It is true that scientific inventions are not used if they are not profitable, but I doubt if we can affirm that they are always forthcoming when they would be profitable. It is argued, for example, that Sir Isaac Newton was a bourgeois—a member of a class which wanted certain improvements in transport and production—and that he discovered the principles that are associated with his name because they would be practically useful in this way. But other historians have pointed out, in the first place, that Newton was not a bourgeois (one might retort that 'bourgeois is as bourgeois does', but that would result in giving the whole case away); furthermore, it is said that Newton's optics, the most important of all his discoveries, are not related to any practical need. Yet, in putting forward this explanation of Newton's discoveries, the Marxists are only using a type of explanation which historians often use: we find ourselves saying, 'A said this because he was a strong Protestant', or 'B thought that because he was an ex-civil servant', or 'C voted this way because he and his constituents grew cider apples', or 'D took a risk in politics because he was a gambler in private life'.

Again, the attempt to interpret war in terms of economics is not wholly successful. It has been said that all wars are due to economic causes, but there have been wars, for example the Spanish-American war of 1898, which are very hard indeed to interpret in terms of any business interests. Moreover, even if all wars were due to economic causes, that would not explain why one side won rather than the other—often a very momentous thing—nor would it explain why some wars are more destructive than others: the difference between the effects of a walk-over and those of a long, even struggle is often highly important. Nor would an economic interpretation of war wholly account for the distraction from other activities, the strain upon some institutions and the incentives to create others, which all in varying ways arise from the stress of war.

I doubt even if all these independent or semi-independent variables taken together would explain everything—for example, would they explain the change which came over the character of western European monarchy round about 1300? Yet it is wrong to blame the Marxists or anybody else for trying to construct their system. They are only doing what all historians do: they are trying to make sense of history. One can only blame them if they make it too quickly and too easily. (One could also, of course, blame them, if they used political power in order to avoid the unpleasantness of admitting the failure of their explanations.) The sense that historians make is an increasingly complicated sense. It may perhaps be suggested that professional classes always create complications in order to make themselves indispensable. But I think that such an explanation would do the professional historians less than justice. It is a matter of scientific conscience. The historical process is very complicated: it has its laws and its uniformities, but it can only be explained in terms of itself.

II

'A STUDY OF HISTORY'

[Review of ARNOLD J. TOYNBEE, *A Study of History* (10 vols., London, 1933–54). *English Historical Review*, lxxi (1956), pp. 256–72]

ANY man who plans and undertakes a work of this size and range deserves our admiration; he who pursues and completes the plan in the course of twenty years, amid the duties of a full professional life, and with a world war thrown in, deserves it even better. Professor Toynbee has many wonderful accomplishments. He appears to have a reading knowledge of several Asiatic languages and most of the chief European ones. His ecumenical outlook is especially admirable in an age when historians are relapsing into patriotism all over the world. The width of his reading is enough to make any ordinary historian feel ashamed of having read so little and so narrowly, though, on a closer inspection, one can discern an inner field within which Dr. Toynbee writes as an expert, not feeling himself at a loss when his authorities differ: this inner field may be described, very roughly, as the history of Greece and the Near East, with special concentration on certain periods, such as the fifth century B.C., the early centuries of Byzantine history, and the movement for Greek independence at the beginning of the nineteenth century. Even this inner field is a wide one; and, outside it, Dr. Toynbee's acquaintance with secondary historical writings is remarkable; although he brings forward many odd ideas, I could find very few things which one could describe as crude mistakes of fact. In addition, Dr. Toynbee has a mind of the utmost liveliness, darting hither and thither in search of new things and surprisingly retentive of what it has found. Anecdotes of conversations in Lithuania, in Anatolia, and in Chicago are retained and appreciated at their proper value. When the train crosses a river or a mountain of historic interest, Dr. Toynbee is at the window, ready to make the most of what he can see and to use it in order to explain things which have puzzled him in the writings of historians; and how many of the thousands of people who have seen performances of

Mozart's *Cosi fan Tutte* have ever troubled to ask themselves, still more to find out, as Dr. Toynbee has found out, what a couple of Albanians could plausibly be supposed to be doing in Naples in the 1780's? Dr. Toynbee has seen, heard, and read much, and has garnered a great deal of it. His mind retains not only facts but even the echoes of words. This is sometimes a handicap: he evidently cannot forget a word of the Authorized Version of the Bible or of the Book of Common Prayer, upon which he was brought up, and too often uses what one can only describe as a bible jargon, which is the more noticeable because he gives chapter and verse for every phrase (in vol. x he justifies this practice by the example of Clarendon; but surely, when Clarendon gave chapter and verse from the Bible, he did so because he used the Bible as an authority, whereas Dr. Toynbee does so whenever he uses it as a repertory of words or phrases; and the resulting effect reminds one not so much of Clarendon as of the school of the late C. H. Spurgeon). In other ways too, Dr. Toynbee's style is open to objection: his passion for periphrasis (which he attributes rather surprisingly to the example of Lucretius) and for dependent clauses makes heavy reading.

Dr. Toynbee's original theme, as set out in the early volumes, can be very roughly characterized as follows. The smallest 'intelligible field of study' is not the 'parochial' national state but the society or the civilization. The history of such societies or civilizations is found to arrange itself in a pattern. The society first arises in response to the stimulus of a 'challenge', and, provided it overcomes the first challenge by its response, it can continue to undergo an indefinite number of challenges until it 'breaks down'. This breakdown he appears to ascribe to more than one cause; the commonest is 'militarism', but (what is not necessarily quite the same thing) it can also be described in terms of the deterioration of a 'creative minority'. In the stages of growth and harmony, this creative minority attracts 'mimesis' by its charm, but when it goes dead it is content to dominate without charming, and so alienates certain elements within and without the society, which Dr. Toynbee describes as the 'internal' and the 'external proletariat'. The breakdown is followed by a period, often a long one, of 'disintegration', which is not a uniform decline but allows for alternate 'beats' of 'rout' and 'rally'—Dr. Toynbee tells us the precise number of these beats, viz. $3\frac{1}{2}$. The last rally takes the form of a 'universal state', which comprehends the whole, or very nearly the whole, of the disintegrating society. This state itself comes to an end, and the society dissolves; but this is only the end of the dominant minority. The internal proletariat has secreted a 'universal church'—indeed, it may have given birth, in favourable circumstances, to something which Dr. Toynbee classifies as a 'higher religion'. (There have only been four perfect examples of higher religions in the history of the world, viz. Christianity, Mahayana Buddhism, Hinduism, and Islam.) The external proletariat also makes contributions of an inferior order—the chief of them appears to be 'heroic poetry'. From these contributions a new civilization may arise: in particular, the universal church secreted by the internal proletariat may become a 'chrysalis' within which a new civilization or society develops. The relation between the new society and the dead one is described as 'apparentation and affiliation'. The new society now launches upon a life-cycle of its own, in which the uniform pattern described above is repeated. After its demise this second society may give birth to a third. Dr. Toynbee does not discern any genealogical trees of more than three generations—grandmother, mother, and daughter. (Two additional grandmothers have been exhumed by archaeologists between the publication of vols. vi and vii; but these do not affect the argument materially.)

This (if I have not misunderstood it) is Dr. Toynbee's original scheme; and it seems to me to be open to many serious objections.

In the first place I cannot accept his practice of hypostatizing societies or civilizations. Early in vol. i he makes legitimate fun of those who hypostatize a national state; later, he devotes much effort and learning to deriding the conceptions of 'Europe' and 'Asia'. The objections to treating civilizations or societies in the same way do not seem to have occurred to him. He does not appear to be fully aware that he is doing so. In vol. iii he rightly rebukes Spengler for treating a civilization as an organism; but he himself cannot claim to have treated it consistently as a mere field of study. Sometimes he calls it a personality; once a 'living soul'; and he frequently describes it, and still more frequently treats it, as having a life of its own. For him, far from being a mere concept, it is a highly active and combative personality, trying to impose its will on others of the same species, and to resist the imposition of their wills, by fair means or foul—one civilization will attack another with a military conquest, and the other will retort with a heresy or an art-style. (For example, the doctrinal content of the Monophysite and the Donatist heresies is never explained at all, but Dr. Toynbee describes them, at least half a dozen times, solely in terms of the will of the Syriac civilization to resist a dose of Hellenism by expurgating Hellenistic elements from Christianity; likewise, the Stalinist phase of Russian communism is treated solely as a device of the 'Orthodox Christian society in its Russian offshoot' to protect itself against 'Western Christendom' and get its own back upon Western Christendom's aggression, by the ingenious device of retorting Western 'heresy', viz. Marxism, against the West.) In short, these societies, or civilizations, quarrel with each other like cat and dog; and each of them, like a robin, has a pitch of its own, within which its achievements are 'historically legitimate', whereas, outside this pitch, they rank as aggression. Even their ghosts bicker: for example, in discussing the Gothic revival in architecture, Dr. Toynbee (who believes that the pointed arch was first introduced into western Europe from Lesser Armenia by the crusaders) sees in it a 'successful revenge' for the ghost of the Syriac society against that of the Hellenic society.

I can only see one possible justification for this kind of thing. Dr. Toynbee has been much influenced by the psychological theories of Jung; indeed, he treats them as though they were the only modern theories which held the field.[1] According to his interpretation of these theories, the wills and intellects of individuals are all trifling matters compared with the Collective Sub-conscious Psyche; and he believes that each society may in some way represent, or correspond to, a 'layer' of this Psyche. (Dr. Toynbee is too much given to splitting the human mind into 'layers' and 'flakes', each one supposed to correspond to some department of human activity.) The exact relation of the Psyche to the society is not made clear: for example, on one occasion Dr. Toynbee denies that the 'primordial images' have changed in historical time, but more often he assumes that they have changed, though very slowly, and that these changes affect the development of the societies. According to this interpretation, even when individuals believe that they are acting for reasons which they apprehend consciously, in fact they are expressing the reactions of the Psyche to its needs. For example, when he discusses the history of shipbuild-

[1] For example, the name of Freud is not found in the indexes.

ing (a subject upon which, thanks to the schooling of a nautical great-uncle, he displays great learning), he suggests that important developments in the fifteenth century are to be accounted for by the Sub-conscious Psyche's reaction to the Western Christian society's danger from the Ottoman Turks, and awareness of the need for evading it by oceanic voyages.[2] Whether all this is a warrantable deduction from Jung's theories or a mere fantasy upon them, I am not qualified to say. The idea that one regional Collective Sub-conscious Psyche might differ from another, and that either of them might develop in time, does not appear to be foreign to Jung's system. I cannot, however, understand how the idea of apparentation and affiliation could be fitted into this system. Moreover, when Dr. Toynbee describes the mutual hostilities of these entities, I think he may have misjudged what Jung means by the word 'collective' in the phrase 'Collective Sub-conscious Psyche'. However, obscure and doubtful as all this appears to be, it is the only justification which Dr. Toynbee provides for his habit of personifying societies.

He seems to have first perceived the pattern which I have been describing in the relation of modern Western society to its ancestors: the genealogical tree consists of the Minoan society (grandmother), the Hellenic society (mother), and the twin daughters, the Western Christian society and the Orthodox Christian society with its 'offshoot' in Russia. This is the 'master copy' from which the pattern is imposed upon the rest of human history. One may therefore expect that Dr. Toynbee's account of these societies and their relations should be as convincing and consistent as anything else in the book. Yet it contains some very questionable things.

He tells us very little about these societies' stages of growth; nearly all his attention is given to their breakdowns and disintegrations. Periods of growth are represented as periods of health and harmony, but hardly any evidence is given for this. Even if it were generally agreed (as it is not) to admire primitive forms of art—the archaic sculptures of sixth-century Greece and the Romanesque art of tenth-century Europe—more than the developed art of the periods which followed, I know of no reason to

[2] He does not seem to have noticed that, when he treats the nineteenth-century developments, he does so entirely in terms of the conscious response of individuals to stimuli presented by the economic needs of society as economic opportunities for them.

believe that the times in which these primitive arts flourished
were times of exceptional social harmony. For example, there were
in sixth-century Miletus political parties whose names can be
rendered roughly as 'Capital' and 'Labour'. But, whatever their
quality, these periods of growth were soon brought to an end. The
people whom W. S. Gilbert satirized for believing that 'Art
stopped short at the cultivated court of the Empress Josephine'
were nothing to Dr. Toynbee. The breakdown of the Hellenic
society is placed (with surprising exactness) at the Peloponnesian
War, and the whole remainder of this society's history (which
includes, by another disputable interpretation, the Roman empire)
is described as disintegration. It seems to me that this is over-
stating the case. The Peloponnesian War is represented as showing the failure of the Greek society to master the 'challenge' of
international anarchy which was itself intensified, if not created,
by the development of exporting economies, in Athens and other
cities, under the leadership of Solon, in order to support an ex-
panding population. But, in the first place, was this solution of the
over-population problem really invented by Solon? Other cities
besides Athens, such as Chalcis and Eretria, had adopted it before
Solon's time, and it did not solve their population problems to the
point of rendering colonization unnecessary. Moreover, was the
Peloponnesian War the first or the last breakdown in the Greek
international society? Why not the Lelantine War, in which
many states were mixed up, before it, or the wars of the fourth
century after it? This seems to me a good example of Dr. Toynbee's habit of pinning a long and complicated process to one or
two salient events or dates in order to dramatize it.

Equally questionable is Dr. Toynbee's treatment of the relation
of the Roman empire (the 'universal state' of the Hellenic society)
and the barbarians. Indeed, the whole idea of the 'external proletariat' seems rather dubious, if only because external proletariats
(especially in the Roman empire) tended to get inextricably mixed
up with internal ones. Moreover, I doubt whether Dr. Toynbee is
right in treating the character and the very existence of the external proletariat as things for which the 'universal state' is itself
responsible. Dr. Toynbee believes that the political ideas of the
barbarians of north-west Europe were influenced (in the direction
of greater 'democracy') by Hellenic examples; that the existence
of the Romans on the other side of the *Limes* militarized German

society and religion, discouraged agriculture, and diminished the power of the kings. I can see no warrant for this except some very daring speculations in H. M. Chadwick's *The Heroic Age*; and, even so, Dr. Toynbee has given Chadwick's hints a definiteness which Chadwick may not have intended.

One could also question some things which Dr. Toynbee says about the relation between the Hellenic and the Western Christian societies, even if one were to accept the (not universally agreed) assumption that they are two separate societies at all, with separate souls of their own. When Dr. Toynbee treats 'universal churches' as a kind of chrysalis out of which new societies emerge, this is indeed a recognizable description of the role of the Christian church in western Europe during the 'Dark Ages'. Even so, it is surely an exaggeration to suggest that Western, or even Italian, agriculture was revived solely by the example or the labours of Benedictine monks. Dr. Toynbee also seems to exaggerate the role and even the claims of the church, and especially of the papacy. Again, although some popes may have claimed great authority, was there ever, in reality, as Dr. Toynbee represents, a *Respublica Christiana* in western Europe?

Dr. Toynbee seems to me, moreover, to exaggerate and to over-dramatize the contribution of Hellenic theories and examples to the political ideas and practices of Western Christendom. To begin with, it is doubtful whether absolute monarchy ought to be treated as a culture-trait, handed down by one society to another, rather than a spontaneous reaction to a frequently recurring situation. Furthermore, Dr. Toynbee suggests that it was the Emperor Frederick II, and he alone, who effected this translation. This seems to be another exaggeration. Surely there was already a tendency towards greater 'absolutism' in some parts of Europe before Frederick: for example, King John of England cannot, for chronological reasons, have learnt anything from him; nor does it seem reasonable to ascribe the strengthening of this tendency after Frederick's death to his example, which was neither universally known nor admired. Here again, Dr. Toynbee seems to have mistaken a portent for a cause. It is the same thing, a little later, with his handling of the influence of the Italian Renaissance. It seems to be an exaggeration to suggest that absolutism, or effective government, were unknown in north-western Europe before they were introduced there from Italy in the fifteenth century. In the history, for example, of England, nobody who studies the household of Henry II can suppose that there was no bureaucracy and no concern for efficiency; and the dose of 'Italian' efficiency introduced in the reign of the early Tudors was only one of a series —in Victoria's time, or even in George III's, the institutions set up by Henry VIII looked just as archaic as the institutions of Henry II's time must have appeared to Henry VIII.

Dr. Toynbee's whole treatment of renaissances is rather hard to follow. He distinguishes a renaissance from archaism: the latter is an attempt to reproduce a former state of the same civilization, and must always be futile, whereas the former is an attempt to reproduce a corresponding stage of an earlier (apparented) civilization. This, he suggests, is more respectable, for psychological reasons, but it may also be mere 'necromancy', and one is left with the impression that it would be better if renaissances did not take place at all. But the whole distinction is slightly absurd, and in some instances (especially Byzantium and China) Dr. Toynbee fails to make it clear why a certain phenomenon should be classed as a renaissance rather than a case of archaism, and even whether it is either of them, rather than a continuation of the same thing. In any case, renaissances are not the only means by which one society can influence a successor. In vol. viii Dr. Toynbee discusses a mysterious phenomenon called 'cultural radiation', of which he gives an extraordinary example: the Spanish attempt to exclude other nations from the Caribbean Sea in the sixteenth century is represented as an evocation, by some kind of sub-conscious echo, of the Carthaginian attempt to exclude other navies and traders from the western Mediterranean 1,800 years earlier. I can only say that I do not believe this.

The history of the Minoan civilization and its descendants is the norm; it may or may not be a properly chosen norm, but it is a natural one for Dr. Toynbee to use. This 'normal pattern' is imposed on other societies by a free use of analogy. Dr. Toynbee's mind runs very readily to analogies: besides the main structural ones upon which the argument depends, he indulges in unnecessary but fascinating *fioriture* of analogy in the footnotes. It goes without saying that no one man could know whether all these analogies are good ones. Sometimes his zeal out-runs his good sense; for example, when, in vol. v, he attempts to construct an analogy between the position of the Romans in 168 B.C. and that of Napoleon in 1810, he is forced to conclude that the existence of Russia and England in 1810 without anything to correspond to them in 168 B.C. renders the comparison unworkable—then was it worth attempting at all? His reliance on analogy is made easier for him by his readiness to disregard exceptions. He often uses the phrase 'the exception which proves the rule' as though it were the same thing as an exception, pure and simple; indeed, in vol. viii, pp. 506–7, he goes so far as to imply that the existence of a single exception never disproves any rule. Thus reassured, Dr. Toynbee's method of operations, when he wishes to analyse any problem, is to take the first convenient example he can find and impose the pattern by force on all the rest of the material. He looks only for what his analogy requires; he pursues it with eager and partial credulity; and, since he generally has several hundred years in which to look for it, he always finds it. This method he describes as 'empirical', but I do not think that this is what most people understand by the term.

Sometimes the facts have to be squeezed pretty hard to get them into the pattern. For example, in the table in vol. ix, p. 255, Dr. Toynbee is trying to detect a rhythm between war and peace, and between particular kinds of wars, in the history of the European balance of power since the beginning of the sixteenth century: in order to make the facts fit, he has to treat the Thirty Years War as a mere 'epilogue' of the earlier wars of religion and, still more surprisingly, the Second World War as an epilogue of the first; in addition, he runs wars together even though the combatants were by no means the same throughout (for example, Spain changed sides between the war of the League of Augsburg and the war of the Spanish Succession), and suppresses wars, even important ones like the war of the American Revolution and the Russo-Turkish war of 1768, in order to produce a period of 'general peace'. He divides the whole story into a number of cycles, of which each appears to be meant to correspond to a particular 'aggressor', but, as he recognizes himself, the fourth of these cycles does not correspond to any one aggressor, unless one over-rates the French danger, and ignores the Russian danger, between 1815 and 1870. In a corresponding table for the ancient world on page 268 the argument is even more sketchy: in some of the cycles hardly any of the necessary items are present at all, and the Roman political disturbances of 133–111 B.C. are made to do duty as a war.

Even with such high-handed methods, Dr. Toynbee still meets with difficulties. He starts with a given number of 'societies', but he soon finds that they do not include everything, and he is forced, like other makers of systems, to supplement them by new categories which shall not invalidate the old ones. Thus he adds 'fossils' (one of them—Judaism—a surprisingly lively fossil) and 'ghosts', arrested and abortive civilizations. Moreover, the pattern sometimes fits even the main examples awkwardly. Why, for example, does Dr. Toynbee resist the common-sense view that 'Islamic Society' (if there was such a thing) begins with the Abbasid Caliphate? He argues that conversions to Islam were only beginning to be widespread during the period of this Caliphate, but one may also suspect that he was influenced by the feeling that if Islamic society began as soon as that, the 'universal state' would come in the wrong place. He divides what most people would regard as a unitary Indian history into the 'Indic' and the 'Hindu' societies, and a unitary Chinese history into the 'Sinic' and the 'Far Eastern' societies, each with a soul of its own. I wonder if this is justified, but presumably he had to do it because, had he not done so, in India the same society would have given birth to two 'higher religions', which would be contrary to the system, and it would be hard to fit Mahayana Buddhism, for which he feels particular affection, into Chinese history in the proper manner. Lastly, the reader will probably be struck by Dr. Toynbee's evident animosity against the 'Egyptiac' society; is this to be accounted for by sub-conscious resentment against a society which would not lie down and die according to the formula?

Dr. Toynbee would have been more than human if he had not sometimes fallen into inconsistencies in the course of a work occupying 5,938 pages and twenty years of his life. Most of these inconsistencies are small ones, with which it would be unworthy to twit him. Somewhat more serious are the changes of tone in which he refers to important events, according to the argument. For example, the Italian *Risorgimento* and, still more, the Kemalist revolution in Turkey are disparaged or praised according to the purpose to be served: in 1935 Mustapha Kemal's change of alphabet was compared in wickedness with Hitler's burning of the books, but in 1954 the Kemalist revolution is almost praised for discarding Islam in favour of Western technology. There are also some awkward border-line cases. Parthia is one of them and modern Russia is a much more important one. Dr. Toynbee finds himself unable to decide what is the society of which these peoples are members and, in the case of Russia, this leads to some absurdity, since every theme and every class in Russian history is valued differently, according as Russia is treated as 'Orthodox Christian' or 'Western'. The Ottoman Turks also present some difficulty: Dr. Toynbee treats them as providing Orthodox Christian society (excluding Russia) with its 'universal state', which is ingenious and, in some respects, illuminating; but at other times he describes them as constituting an 'Iranic society' which is a, perhaps rather unnecessary, sub-division of the Islamic society.

Three still greater inconsistencies call for comment. Dr. Toynbee appears to be impressed and perplexed by the difficulty of placing modern Western civilization in the world-scheme. Since every civilization must have a breakdown, it is natural enough to ask whether this civilization has already broken down (an event which, if it has taken place at all, might be expected, by analogy, to have happened quite early in the society's history). Dr. Toynbee cannot pronounce on this point. Part of the reason is obvious: according to his theory the final stage of breakdown, in every society, takes the form of a universal state, and it is clear that no such state has yet been set up in Western society. But Dr. Toynbee's embarrassment and, I think, his inconsistency go deeper than this. In dealing with all the other civilizations, Dr. Toynbee has treated the universal state as the inevitable climax of the 'time of troubles', but now, in vol. ix, he says that before the establishment of a universal state no breakdown is irreversible (after that, it is). He has given no example of a time of troubles which did not end in a universal state, but he now says that this does not matter, as he has not enough specimens of civilizations to prove anything. From a man who, for the last 5,500 pages, has been acting on the assumption that he has enough examples, this seems to be inconsistent indeed.

A second inconsistency is still more important. Throughout the first half of the book Dr. Toynbee treats the emergence of 'universal churches' as mere incidents, though very important ones, in the history of civilizations—it is the civilizations that he is studying. But round about the 2,500th page comes a hint of something different, and after another thousand pages or so it is clearly stated that the churches are not mere incidents in the life of the civilizations, but the civilizations are only incidents in the life of the churches —at one point he says that the civilizations bear the same relation to the churches as the 'parochial' national states bear to the civilizations (I do not understand just what this means, nor does it seem to fit Dr. Toynbee's own facts very well). But if the civilizations are only means to the churches, then a great deal of what Dr. Toynbee has previously said about the history of the civilizations must be reversed. For example, he began by treating their 'growth' periods as their acme, but if the civilizations exist for the sake of the churches, then it is the final stages of their disintegration (within which alone the churches emerge) that must be considered the best. Secondly, it now appears that those civilizations which have given birth to the 'higher religions' are better than the others, which was not made clear before. It is hard to see how Dr. Toynbee can have changed his mind on this cardinal theme in a work which, as he tells us, was carefully planned in 1929; but if he kept this ace up his sleeve for 2,500 pages, that is more extraordinary still.

Perhaps Dr. Toynbee's commonest, though not his most important, inconsistency is one of tone. He normally treats human history in terms of life-cycles, of nemesis, of collective sub-conscious psychology; but every now and then (especially at the beginning of vols. iv and viii, still more at the end of vol. ix) he approaches his subject in what most historians would consider to be much more realistic terms. Nemesis is replaced by errors of statesmanship, analogy and classification by a straightforward account of some particular historical theme, often (and this must surely be contrary to Dr. Toynbee's principles) in the life of a 'parochial' national state. Nowhere is Dr. Toynbee more realistic than in the very place where the average historian would be most likely to dogmatize and to talk nonsense—in his meditations on the present, and his speculations on the future, of modern Western society in the second half of vol. ix. Here he is unencumbered by categories or preconceptions, and few parts of the book are more to my liking. Perhaps it is no accident that Dr. Toynbee earns his daily bread by writing this kind of history, and his occupational habits have asserted themselves at the expense of his theories.

In few respects does Dr. Toynbee differ more from the ordinary historian than in his concept of what constitutes evidence. This seems to result mainly from his reading of Jung's psychology.

The myths deposited in the Sub-conscious Psyche have more value for him—they evince deeper truths, and more directly—than any record of fact. Thus, for Dr. Toynbee, the *ben trovato* is always at least as good as the *vero*, or better. He carries this to the highest level: he much prefers the Mahayana form of Buddhism, which embodies very little historical fact, to the Hinayana form, which probably embodies more; and, in the strange annex to vol. vi (which reads like a parody of the Higher Criticism, so slight and so forced are the resemblances upon which it relies) there is more than a hint that Dr. Toynbee would make no difference between a God who, for the purposes of salvation, had lived and died as a man, and a God who, for the same purposes, put it about, or allowed it to be put about, by means of folk-lore, that he had done so.

Dr. Toynbee goes further than accepting myth as evidence; he is equally ready to rely on metaphor which is by no means sub-conscious, but his own highly artificial construction. For this he quotes the authority of Plato; but most of the great Platonic myths which I can remember were not a substitute for explanation, but merely rendered visible something already explained. Dr. Toynbee, when he wishes to define his thought, too often resorts to metaphor and simile, and to them alone. (At one point he actually speaks of himself as having carried a simile 'far enough to ascertain' what he wanted to know; but when did a simile ever ascertain anything?) No doubt there are some things which can only be described by a metaphor; but the fewer, the better; to define by a metaphor is dangerous, to prove by a metaphor impossible. Nor do the similes always succeed even in conveying a visual image—for example, what clarity can we gain from the strange simile in vol. ix, pp. 333-4, in which a pig is attached by umbilical cords to a number of people who are all beating it, trying to ride it, and in danger of being led by the nose by it?

In another way, too, Jung's theories have affected Dr. Toynbee's practice. He is much given to judging and placing men and things by an aesthetic test; that is to say, he not merely distributes marks for 'creativeness' or 'originality', with the same light-hearted and mysterious confidence with which one marks the papers of scholarship candidates for these qualities, but he uses the judgements so arrived at in order to prove an argument. For example, he tries, in vol. ix, to prove something by establishing (or rather, by asserting) that the architecture of the European Renaissance and Baroque was 'a dismal failure'. Anybody who thinks that Wren, Gibbs, and Fischer von Erlach were great architects will presumably remain quite unce͏̈....ed by an argument which rests on this supposed fact. Dr. Toynbee, however, is confident in his power to argue thus, not merely because he considers that critical judgement in matters of taste has a validity independent of time and place (which surely is not confirmed by human experience?) but also because he believes that, according to Jung's psychology, the sub-conscious life-cycle of a civilization expresses itself above all in artistic style, and that the exact position of a person or thing in that life-cycle can be identified by placing it in the history of stylistic development.

Another of Dr. Toynbee's heritages from Jung is his practice of treating history in terms of psychological types. Some of these types certainly are illuminating, though only to a limited degree. Dr. Toynbee makes much play with the distinction between 'futurism' and 'archaism' as two almost equally futile methods of solving the problems of the present. (They surely cannot be *equally* futile, for, since the future must one day become the present, futurism cannot be very clearly distinguished from foresight.) But, although particular cases may be illuminated by this classification, Dr. Toynbee seems to go too far when he runs through a number of barbarians who were trying to defend their tribes against the encroachment of universal states, classifying each one of them either as a futurist or as an archaist. A similar psychological distinction is that of the 'zealots' and the 'Herodians', who solved in their different ways the question whether, and how, and how much, a weaker civilization was to allow itself to fall under the influence of a strong one. Here too there is a real problem, and this classification may sometimes help the historian to deal with it. But Dr. Toynbee's list of zealots and Herodians shows the weakness of excessive reliance on classification. Very nearly half the examples have to be written down as 'ambivalent'. A category which only succeeds in placing just over half the phenomena is not much of a category. Most historians would have preferred to think of these matters in a quite different way, and to say that there was a number of comparable situations, in which people had to behave in one of two ways. But Dr. Toynbee does not like thinking in terms of situations and of people trying to cope with them, for this would be, in his eyes, attaching too much importance to human wills and human intellect (which, as he says, only skate over the surface) and too little to the Sub-conscious Psyche, which expresses itself more readily and, in his opinion, more convincingly, in terms of psychological types.

The same excessive reliance on a psychology of the day accounts for Dr. Toynbee's reluctance to account for the course of history in terms of non-psychological causes. When he discusses the stimulus which a 'challenge' makes to the members of a given society, he often speaks as though everything were to be explained by it; for example, the course of the British Industrial Revolution is considered almost entirely in terms of the contrast between the 'stimulating' geographical and social circumstances of the north of England and the unstimulating south—and this, although Dr. Toynbee elsewhere shows himself to be quite aware of the fact that there were hardly any coal-measures or water power in the south. Still more obvious is his belief that all failure is psychological—at least half a dozen times he quotes George Meredith's line, 'we are betrayed by what is false within'. This conclusion is not always supported by Dr. Toynbee's own facts. For example, he ascribes the decay of Sparta and of the Ottoman empire to the principles of their systems of government; but he has himself shown that it was due rather to the perversion of those principles by the encroachments of hereditary privilege. The same tendency is shown by his frequently repeated explanation of the relative humanity of war in eighteenth-century Europe: the fanaticism of the wars of religion was a thing of the past, and the fanaticism of the national wars was a thing of the future. This is quite true, indeed Dr. Toynbee was not the first person to observe it; but it is not the whole truth, for it leaves out of account such things as the development of the military art, which had reached a stage when the defensive had, for the time being, the upper hand over the offensive. A particular example of this one-sided way of stating the matter is Dr. Toynbee's treatment of the Peace of Versailles in 1783: he ascribes the moderation of the French terms solely to this general psychological tendency, and does not observe that, in the first place, the war was (so far as the French were concerned) a draw, so that they could not insist on any terms they liked and, in the second place, they really did not want Canada, so of course they made hardly any attempt to get it back.

According to this reading of history, no society was ever killed by violence from outside; all were dead already, and most of them were suicides. This, too, is a thing which Dr. Toynbee does not entirely believe, for, although all is psychology in the main body of the text, there is more than one admission in the annexes that the course of human history was changed, not merely by a battle (which might perhaps be interpreted as an exclusively psychological affair), but even by a military invention, such as a chariot, which cannot so easily be explained on the same lines.

Dr. Toynbee goes further: his book abounds in overtones of theodicy. We read of rewards, birthrights, destinies, and, above all, of nemesis. We hear a great deal about missed chances and very little about having no chance, a great deal about doing too much and very little about having too much to do.

Three particular kinds of nemesis are thrust upon us again and again. Dr. Toynbee (with some insight) classifies certain peoples as 'marchmen'—that is to say, peoples who lived upon the frontier of a civilization or society, and defended it against other civilizations or against the outer barbarians. Good examples are the Habsburg empire, and the Persians at several stages of their history (with reference to defence against the Eurasian nomads). Dr. Toynbee is quite right to identify the marchmen as having performed this role, but he is less clearly right in asserting that it was the only role they could legitimately perform, and that, if they performed any other, or even performed that one too aggressively, they must necessarily be visited by nemesis. A war between peoples comprehended within the same society is not merely diagnosed as 'fratricide', but is said to have brought upon the perpetrators a special doom. Any kind of strain may be too much for the society which undergoes it, but what warrant is there for thinking that only those strains are fatal which result from 'fratricidal warfare', and that warfare undertaken in the fulfilment of the marchmen's true role has only a tonic effect? How, for example, can one blame Maria Theresa for trying to get back Silesia from Frederick II instead of pressing on against the Ottoman Turks? Just because she was a marchwoman, was she to submit tamely to depredations and aggressions by Prussia or France? Likewise was it really inconsequent of Alexander the Great to go for the Persian empire instead of polishing off the barbarians who might one day endanger the kingdom of Macedon? Sometimes

Dr. Toynbee is so exacting that the reader is driven to cry out in despair, 'But what was poor old Charlemagne (or Alexander, or Maria Theresa, or Hammurabi) to do? If he attacked another member of his own society, it was fratricide; if he attacked the barbarians, it was militarism; and yet Dr. Toynbee could have told him that if he left the frontier of civilization stationary it must ultimately recoil upon him.'

An even more conspicuous example of false nemesis is Dr. Toynbee's treatment of the invasion of civilized societies by barbarians. 'Every society', he says, 'gets the barbarians it deserves.' (A hard saying since, in a later volume, all barbarians are represented as equally disgusting.) But is it really true that civilizations always brought these incursions upon themselves? When Dr. Toynbee represents the barbarian invaders as instruments of divine wrath against the Egyptiac, the Syriac, or the Hellenic society, he forgets that he has already accounted for these incursions in quite another way, by ascribing them to the periodic desiccations of the Steppes. In particular, can this be true in the cases which Dr. Toynbee mentions, of the invasion of a society by barbarians who properly belonged to some other society but were 'passed on' by it? (The best examples which Dr. Toynbee gives are those of the Seljuk Turks and, earlier, of the Hyksos who invaded ancient Egypt.[3])

A third kind of nemesis upon which Dr. Toynbee loves to insist is the nemesis upon the use of force. He appears to think that only a peaceful radiation of culture can produce permanent results in the relations of civilizations, and that no institution set up by force can have any importance except in so far as it ministers unintentionally to a higher religion. But is this universally true? Can one really believe, for example, that Hellenic civilization could ever have made the impression that it did make upon the Syriac and even the Indic societies, if Alexander had never crossed the Hellespont and destroyed the Persian empire? Dr. Toynbee might reply that after 900 years these societies managed to slough off Hellenism, but are 900 years nothing? Dr. Toynbee himself

[3] In vol. x Dr. Toynbee points out that recent researches cast doubt upon the theory that the Hyksos were 'passed on' from afar by the Sumerian to the Egyptiac society. If so, it partly invalidates my argument, but it invalidates still more of his, for he repeatedly ascribes the peculiar development of the Egyptiac society to a convulsion of resentment against these invaders who were not mere barbarians but smelt of another culture.

inadvertently gives, in the example of the Highland Scots, a proof that, on occasion, forcible civilization may yield lasting results, and even beneficial results. One may well agree with Dr. Toynbee in admiring philosophers, missionaries, and artists more than conquerors, statesmen, and prelates, but is it altogether ingenuous to pretend that nothing that the latter classes did ever had any profound or lasting importance?

In all these things which I have criticized, Dr. Toynbee is only doing something very like what other historians do. Almost every historian, in the course of his business, daily says to himself, 'This reminds me of that', or 'If a was followed by b, then one would expect x to be followed by y'. Analogy is essential to history; but not all historians judge by the analogy alone: they expect some other evidence than the mere congruity to the analogy for proving, explaining, or judging a historical event. Again, historians often speak of a person (less often of a society) as fulfilling a certain role, and they may even, on occasion, venture to suggest that somebody mistook his true role; but they do not think it necessary to believe that such a mistake was always punished by nemesis. Again, some historians—art historians in particular—place a thing in its historic content by an 'aesthetic test'; but they are never happy when they have to rely on this alone, and they should be aware of the danger of arguing in a circle: of saying in the same breath, 'this is good because it is of a classical period' and 'this must be of a classical period because it is good'. Again, nobody can be a historian without using some sort of psychology, and perhaps those historians who are their own psychologists are in more danger of talking nonsense than those who, like Dr. Toynbee, go to the professional psychologists for their system (though, even so, they have to face a decision, which school of psychology to follow, which Dr. Toynbee has avoided for himself by writing as if only one school of psychology existed). But when historians write as if everything were a matter of psychological types and the situations, which human wills have created for each other to work in, counted for nothing, then they are leaving out more than half of history. Lastly, all historians except pure narrators are imposing, all the time, a pattern of their own discovery upon their material. But they must do this modestly, soberly, and honestly or else their work will become a monument of uncontrolled ingenuity.

Readers of this *Review* will probably be most curious to know what Dr. Toynbee says about professional historians as a class. Not only has he entered into the labours of hundreds of professional historians, but he has himself, perhaps, written more professional history than any other man living (although, in writing about the year, he has always had to be content with what could be known in the year or soon after it, so that his experience has not been such as to inspire him with much sympathy for those who, freed from this limitation, are tempted to dig deeper into archives before they write).

He thinks ill of historians as a class. They are guilty of two great crimes: maldistributing their effort and misconceiving their task.

Professional historians, according to Dr. Toynbee, have maldistributed their effort because they have had their eyes fixed upon their own 'parochial' national state or, at most, upon the Western civilization which they miscall 'Europe'. Whenever Dr. Toynbee mentions the concept of 'Europe', the shrillness and illogicality of his accusations betray the warmth of his emotion. For example, he argues that H. A. L. Fisher, by the mere act of writing a history of Europe, committed himself to nine propositions, some of which Fisher would almost certainly have denied and hardly any of which seems to be inherent in the concept of a 'history of Europe' (would Dr. Toynbee have thought that the same or similar propositions were involved in writing, for example, a history of Africa?). Gladstone's campaign against the Bulgarian atrocities is likewise denounced as involving a mistaken conception of 'Europe'—but surely Gladstone was thinking much about humanity, something about Christianity, but very little about Europe? Still more heinous is the historians' crime of confining themselves within the boundaries of their national state. Dr. Toynbee attributes this largely to a false parochial patriotism which he regards as inherently modern and Western (in spite of the fact that he has himself called attention to nationalism in the Balkans during the Dark Ages, and in Persia, and the fact that some of the 'universal states', about which he writes with such care, such as Russia and Egypt, could also be regarded as national states). We may fairly admit that Western historians have concentrated too much upon the history of their own countries and civilization, though Dr. Toynbee probably gives the wrong reason for it: it is not mere patriotism, still less a mistaken analogy from the Industrial Revolution, but is rather due to the anchoring of professional historians, as a class, to university teaching and still more to the existence of national public record offices. But surely it is going too far to suggest that only orientalists and archaeologists, in recent times, have discovered data of a 'sufficiently high order of magnitude'? A lucky archaeologist may certainly, by a stroke of the spade in the right place, open to our knowledge a whole new civilization, which is more than any historian, even of superior genius, could hope to do. But most archaeologists, like most historians, contribute little more than local history; and as for orientalists, the magnitude of their contributions varies enormously. In his vast appendix to vol. vii on the administrative geography of the Achaemenian empire, Dr. Toynbee is only doing what another historian might do for the Carolingians, though with a rather more daring use of etymology than would generally be thought allowable. Moreover, if there are historical laws to be discovered, can they only be discovered by comparing an Englishman with a Persian or an Indian, and never with a Frenchman or with another Englishman? Dr. Toynbee apparently believes that this is so, for he has adopted from F. J. Teggart the maxim that the whole science of man consists of accounting for the differences between the condition of humanity in different parts of the world. Perhaps it is inevitable that Dr. Toynbee should believe this: for, since he treats each civilization as a personality, based on a Collective Sub-conscious Psyche, he must necessarily believe that historical truth is better discovered by comparing them with each other than by attending to the relations of individuals within the society.

Historians not only, in Dr. Toynbee's opinion, maldistribute their effort, but they misconceive their task. The true task of history, in his opinion, is to ascertain historical laws, and to present a picture of world history as a whole, not to exploit the material in detail. Let us admit that there are historians who have chosen Martha's part rather than Mary's, who do no more than exploit material. Even they have their use and their excuse; although Dr. Toynbee rightly adopts Collingwood's maxim, 'No questions, no history', yet the mere fact that they approached the material without having decided beforehand what questions to ask of it is some guarantee (though not a sufficient one) of their transparency and of the honesty of their answers. Let us admit that some of them are too apt 'to know their wants, and go full-pelt for Norman fonts' (though not all Dr. Toynbee's jeers at the subjects of doctoral theses are well deserved, since such theses are not meant to be life-works but only training in research). Let us admit that some historians do not try to establish any universal laws. But even so, many of the historians whom Dr. Toynbee most admires have, by his own account, contented themselves with answering the modest question, 'How did this come out of that?' Were they not justified in so restricting themselves?

Dr. Toynbee accuses professional historians, as a class, of 'antinomianism'; and his accusations are not always fair. For example, he fastens more than once on H. A. L. Fisher's celebrated words (in the preface to his *History of Europe*) about the difficulty of discerning a pattern in history. Fisher never said that history was governed by blind chance, only that the historian must allow for 'the play of the contingent and the unforeseen'—a somewhat different thing; he never said that history did not repeat itself, only that it did not do so rhythmically. Dr. Toynbee is likewise somewhat nettled by Collingwood's attack upon him as a positivist historian, and here too he misrepresents his antagonist. Collingwood admitted that there were uniformities and recurrences; he only argued that positivist historians could not lay down universally valid laws about human history as a whole because human nature in one period was not exactly the same as human nature in another period. (One would have expected Dr. Toynbee to like this, not only because it resembles Wesley C. Mitchell's argument —which he much appreciates—that no trade cycle was exactly like any other trade cycle and that trade cycles might, in the course of time, change as a species, but still more because the idea of a human nature changing in time appears to be congruous with Dr. Toynbee's own idea of a Collective Sub-conscious Psyche changing in time.)

Dr. Toynbee's reasons for adhering to a positivist view of history are not convincing. Once more he is dominated by the idea of the Collective Sub-conscious Psyche, which obeys uniform laws (he does not tell us what they are). When he tries to explain the recalcitrance of the human race to these laws, he dismisses in one short paragraph the conflicts between individual human wills which are, for most historians, the whole of history and the true explanation of this recalcitrance.

Dr. Toynbee is himself a positivist with a difference. He eschews the example of the method of mechanical sciences, for he is indifferent to everything in human history which is not cyclical. He rejects geographical determinism, though he necessarily (and rightly) brings it back in a negative form when he discusses the geographical or climatic challenges which prove excessive. He is likewise indifferent to such things as the development of scientific technology or of the military art; these things do not, indeed, proceed continuously in a uniform direction, but they are certainly not cyclical. Most of all does Dr. Toynbee reject economic determinism. If he neglects economic history, it is not because he does not know any (though he appears to have concentrated largely on the theory of trade cycles, which have an obvious fascination for him just because of their cyclical character), but rather because he thinks economic life merely superficial: for example, except in the instances of ancient Greece and modern India, he is quite indifferent to the size of population or to the means for supporting it. His treatment of Marx is extremely cavalier: he dismisses him with a gibe about economic monomania, a few commonplaces about the 'religious' character of modern Marxism, and a reminder that the primitive Christian church was, in a sense, socialist. Whatever the merits of Marxist doctrine may be, this is to trifle with a serious subject.

If Dr. Toynbee rejects mechanical analogies, he falls victim to the far more dangerous biological analogies. He identifies and compares some twenty-odd entities, each with a uniform life-cycle (though the spacing of the intervals between the events in this cycle may be more flexible). Quite early in his book, the progress of civilization is compared to a one-way street, in which no vehicle can reverse. At the very beginning of the civilizations of the first generation, there may be some variety in the nature of the challenges, but, after that, they are treated as uniform and inevitable. Everything must bloom once, and nothing can bloom twice. Readers must decide for themselves whether this is superstition or science; I can only avow my conviction that an attempt to establish laws, or statistical generalizations, about so small a number as twenty-odd imaginary entities, each endowed with a very complicated life-cycle, was foredoomed to failure; that all attempts to make sense of history in this way have proved unsatisfactory, and that, in all probability, they always will prove unsatisfactory.

Does the baseless fabric of this vision leave not a rack behind? Like other grandiose failures, Dr. Toynbee's work contains many excellent ideas which other historians can use as clues in the construction of that intermediate kind of sense which is the most that they can safely try to make of history. Perhaps Dr. Toynbee's most popular contribution is the conception of 'challenge and response', which has already (thanks to Mr. Somervell's abridgement) made its way among the scholarship candidates and will soon be reaching the journalists. What Dr. Toynbee says about the 'marchmen' is highly illuminating, provided that one can divorce it from the idea of a nemesis upon marchmen who disregard their true role. The pages on 'new ground and old' and on 'garrisons' and 'colonies' are well worth reading. Some of Dr. Toynbee's ideas about the 'diffraction of culture' are worth considering, though they are partly expressed by means of deplorable metaphors about rays, nor are they always consistent in themselves. The idea of institutions transformed by the adventitious 'drive' of external forces into 'enormities', as war has been transformed by industrialism, is interesting and useful. One or two of Dr. Toynbee's psychological types are here to stay.

Dr. Toynbee writes in his first volume with pity, almost with disparagement, of the great Mommsen's error of judgement in abandoning his *History of Rome*, and renouncing all attempts at a still more universal history, in order to devote himself to the preparation of the *Staatsrecht* and the *Corpus Inscriptionum Latinarum*. But perhaps, if Mommsen might be allowed to prefer the duration of his fame and his usefulness to their diffusion, he did not judge so wrong after all. If he had written a history of the world, nobody would now be reading it, whereas the professional historians, at least, still bless him for the *C.I.L.* I think it is a safe prophecy that when *A Study of History* lies neglected, readers will still be thankfully consulting the *Survey of International Affairs*.

III

HUMAN NATURE IN POLITICS

[*The Listener*, 17 December 1953]

FOR the purpose of discussing human nature in politics, I shall concentrate upon the human nature of politicians, of the possessors of political power; since very few forces which have changed the course of history greatly have done so without obtaining any recognition or sanction in politics.

It seems to me that their intentions are, in the main, reasonable and consequent, and often disinterested too; but that the results are not often what reason would dictate or predict. There is a discrepancy between intention and result. Its cause is not, I think, what it is commonly supposed to be. Some people attribute it to unconscious forces, collective or individual, which dominate the action even of those who believe that they are behaving reasonably. I think the collective unconscious is somewhat overrated. Those who have any share of political power (which comparatively few people have) usually obtain it because they are exceptionally able to emancipate their purposes from the control of their unformulated wishes and impressions. They may occasionally be swept away by a tide of other people's unconscious emotions; but this is only likely to happen when disasters or great and sudden changes cause a whole people to lose sight of its habitual thoughts or to be unable to apply them.

Again, other historians have attributed this discrepancy between policies and results to what used to be called, in the last century, 'sinister interests'—private ambitions, family connexions, even sheer venality. Nobody can deny that such things have existed and still exist in politics. But I doubt if they have distorted policies quite so powerfully as one might suppose. No doubt there have been politicians who took pay to do what they knew to be wrong. But politicians have more often taken rewards for doing what they had no objection to doing, or even what they intended to do in any event. Possessors of political power are often so situated that they can get somebody or other to reward them for

whatever they may choose to do: in such circumstances they are
just as likely to choose their paymasters according to their policies
as to choose their policies according to their paymasters. If 'sinister interests' have distorted the operation of policies, it is not so
much by corrupting the policies themselves, as by entrusting their
execution to unfit agents chosen for reasons of private favour or
advantage.

There is another and a more plausible explanation of this discrepancy between intentions and results. Most politicians aim,
indeed, at some general good and are governed by some general
idea of what the world ought to be like; but the good at which
even the best of us aim is never, in reality, more than a partial
good, and our ideas of what the world ought to be like are only
ideas of what certain parts of the world, parts to which we specially
belong, parts of which we are specially conscious, ought to be like.
Sometimes these parts of the world are very small ones: the politics
of the United States of America have often been confused, in the
past, by senators and congressmen who were not thinking primarily in terms of the interests of the United States, but of the
north or the south or the west, or of Louisiana or Maine, or even
of the sugar-growers of Louisiana or the lumbermen of Maine.

Very few politicians have ever aimed at any good more general
than that of their own state or nation; and nearly all historians
have applauded them for this: how often do English historians
justify Queen Elizabeth I, or French historians justify Richelieu,
for having had the sense to sacrifice all other considerations for
the good of the English people or of the French state! Alternatively, this partiality attaches itself to a class; some people have
acted or spoken, consciously or unconsciously, as if the object of
politics were to make the world safe for business men, or even for
men of letters and science, or for the working class, or for the
adherents of a certain religion. Sometimes this is only a half-
conscious attitude; at other times it amounts to a world-embracing
philosophy, like Marxism, or like the *laissez-faire* dogmatism so
popular in the last century. But, even so, it is none the less a partiality.

I do not mention these things in order to condemn them. Very
few people are quick to see a point before they have to see it,
especially if it is something not easily reconciled with their own
interests and the interests of those near to them. For example,

very few members of the British labour movement had much notion, fifty or even twenty years ago, that they owed any duty to the peasants of Asia and Africa: if they concerned themselves at all with the Asiatic and African proletariat, it was rather to ensure that factory wages should be high enough in India and Japan to prevent Indian and Japanese goods from undercutting British goods and throwing British workers out of employment and reducing them to lower wages. Now, however, the working classes of western Europe and America are beginning to see a duty which they could not see before. They see it because, for compelling political or economic reasons, they have to see it; they would never have seen it before they had to see it.

One might expect that the politicians would keep a better lookout for these things than the man in the street. Indeed, they do so; but even they are not quick to look ahead and criticize the limitations of their sympathies or of their plans. This is not because they are more stupid and cowardly than the rest of us; very likely they are less so. They are slow to see a problem before they have to see it because there are so many other problems which they must see here and now. The limitations of human attention and of human effort explain, in my opinion, more failures than anything else in history—even more than the limitations of human sympathy or of human reason. The late J. L. Hammond showed, in his book on *Gladstone and the Irish Nation*,[1] that Gladstone, in his second ministry, failed to deal thoroughly with the Irish problem because he had to spend part of his time on the problems of England and Scotland, and failed, at the same time, to keep abreast of the problems of England and Scotland because he had to spend too much of his time on Ireland. Yet we never had a prime minister with more power of work than Gladstone. Even he could not keep up with the ceaseless flood of problems calling for solution, of situations calling for immediate action.

We are inclined to think of this as something which has only arisen in modern times; and, indeed, it does get worse every year. But nearly eight hundred years ago the chroniclers reported that King Henry II of England became bow-legged because he stood so long at his work of judging and deciding (he did it standing, for fear of putting on weight); perhaps, therefore, the flood of business was just as great even then, in proportion to the means of dis-

[1] [London, 1938.]

patching it. It is this, above all, that constricts the sympathies and limits the foresight of those who possess political power: in pursuit of some partial good they may compromise with those who pursue some other partial good, in order to obtain both, perhaps at the expense of some third partial good; but that is as far as they usually go. The goods they pursue remain partial and, for that reason, differ from each other.

I have dwelt upon this because it explains, to my mind, why conduct which is, in the main, reasonable so often brings about results which are not reasonable. History is the product of thousands (perhaps, nowadays, millions) of different wills, none wholly dependent upon any other; of thousands or millions of different reasons, none wholly amenable to any other; and these many wills and reasons bear, not on the same point, but on hundreds or thousands of different points. It is not a debate in which the best reason ultimately wins, nor even a knock-out tournament in which the strongest or luckiest will ultimately subdues all the others. It is something subtler than that, for it takes place in time.

Each will creates or changes the conditions in which all the other wills have to act and, by so doing, modifies their action or, at least, the results of their action. A, B, and C may be acting in a confined space, each with his own plans and desires, and A, by taking the initiative, may do something which either causes B and C to change their minds or, if they carry out their original plans, causes those plans to turn out as they had not intended; and D, whom none of them had considered, does it to all three, for reasons which have, perhaps, nothing to do with any of them; for what they thought to be a confined space was not one after all —there are very few confined spaces in history. The conduct which these mutual interferences produce will not cease to be reasonable; but it will be a variable sort of reason, for at least the same ends will be pursued by unexpected means, and perhaps unexpected ends will be pursued; for the average politician or administrator will have in his mind, as it were, a whole list of the things he would like to obtain, of which some must be pursued with the help of one lot of people at the expense of a second, and others, perhaps, with the help of the second at the expense of the first. When circumstances make some ambitions attainable and others unattainable, he will follow the dictation of circumstances.

All this is truer of some kinds of activity than of others. Above all, it is true of international relations, which are, by definition, the relations of independent wills, each one regarded by its subjects as embodying the highest and most general good which is practically conceivable; a good which is so general as to be self-subsistent. This is why diplomatic history, more than any other kind of history, is 'one damned thing after another', from which one can deduce no laws or principles, but only generally applicable techniques. But if international relations have to be considered as partially withdrawn from the empire of reason, it is no insignificant deduction from the sum total of politics. Furthermore, international pressures provide more than half the external interference which disconcerts schemes of progress and improvement in domestic politics. How often in history have social, political, or administrative reforms been laid aside or distorted in order to parry a real or supposed danger from some other state! (It is true that the contrary may sometimes happen—that improvements may be made or promised in order to keep up a nation's spirit and solidarity, as they were in Great Britain during the last war; but the casualties and waste arising from this cause far, far exceed the advantages.) If international relations could be abolished by the establishment of a world state, the greatest single impediment to the exercise of reason and foresight in domestic politics would be removed.

But even in domestic politics there are hindrances of the same kind. Nowadays we have got the idea that a government is there to deal with what has already been discussed and foreseen. But is that right? It could happen to Neville Chamberlain in 1939 no less than to Sir Robert Walpole in 1739, that a prime minister who had endeavoured and promised to keep out of war had to turn round and stake his reputation on waging war successfully. I could give examples more directly related to home affairs. In 1881 Gladstone introduced a scheme of Irish land reform which would probably have succeeded in ordinary times; but just then a long and severe agricultural depression set in all over western Europe, and made nonsense of the whole thing: the rents which were fair one year were unfair the next, and the British parliament was quite unable to run a race against this disaster. In 1929 a labour government came in, pledged to redistribute the national wealth; but, for causes quite outside their control, there was no wealth to distribute, and they had to deal with totally different problems.

In 1945 there was another labour government, admirably equipped for dealing with the economic problems of the 1930's (for the general staff of a party is just as good at curing the last slump as that of an army at winning the last war). But the problems of the thirties were not those of the forties, though they may be those of the fifties.

Our means of technical control and foresight are increasing. Probably we could prevent another Black Death from knocking society sideways for a generation. Perhaps we know how to cure slumps, though I shall believe that when I see it. But as long as there are independent wills and limited sympathies, as long as there is hurry in politics, the most pressing problems will be those of the unforeseen. Human reason will make a gallant attempt at these, too: Heaven forbid that I should disparage it, or deny that most human conduct is reasonable. But when we only partly know what we are reasoning about today and can never be sure what we shall be reasoning about tomorrow; when we do not fully know whom we are reasoning against, and are not aware that we are reasoning against anybody even when in fact we are doing so —human reason cannot answer for the results. They must be left, I will not say to the chapter of accidents, for very little of it is an accident; but they must be left to what I might call Providence or, if you do not like that term, to history.

IV

BERNARD PARES: A MEMOIR

[Introduction to Sir Bernard Pares, *A History of Russia* (3rd ed., revised and enlarged, London, Jonathan Cape, 1955)]

My father, who wrote this book, was quite unlike any other academic person I ever knew. Gifted as he was, it was not scholarship, nor insight, nor even style that distinguished him from other historians, but his unusually dynamic will. He gave the impression, not merely of a man of action strayed into academic life—there are many of them, they sit on committees and, if they are wise, become principals of universities—but something more: a man with a mission. This mission was to interpret Russia to the English-speaking world, and even to bring the two worlds into political partnership with each other.

He was born, at Albury in the county of Surrey, on 1 March 1867, into the midst of a happy, religious, and somewhat Philistine family of five brothers and five sisters. My grandfather came of a midland family of country bankers; he had an unearned income, and no occupations but such as he chose for himself. He was a high church Anglican, in politics a liberal—a combination by no means uncommon, best exemplified in Gladstone, whom he admired with a devotion which must have been slightly absurd. My father reacted against this liberalism, but only on the surface. As a pert little boy, he used to make disrespectful verses about Gladstone and, upon remonstrance, only turned them into Latin, in which form they were still more disrespectful. As a man, he prided himself on belonging to no party. But fundamentally all his ideas and sympathies were liberal, and he seems to have allied himself somewhat more definitely with liberal parties in Russian politics than in British, though many of his best friends, such as Guchkov and Homyakov, were moderate Octobrists.

The chief preoccupations of the five brothers and five sisters, besides churchmanship, appear to have been practical jokes, light verse, cricket, and football. Of the practical jokes, the less said the better; they do not stand the test of time. The light verse was not all very subtle, but my father developed an astonishing verbal dexterity: when he had nothing better to do, he amused himself by composing rhymes upon the names of the railway stations on his journeys, and I have always thought that a man who could find a plausible rhyme to 'Worplesdon' could have rhymed anything. This gift served him particularly well in translation. He rendered German student songs into very singable English verse (many of them were published in the *Liverpool Students' Song-Book*). His masterpiece was the translation of Krylov's fables, in which he contrived to reproduce exactly the complicated metrical structure of the original, without undue contortion or loss of idiom—it was, perhaps, a somewhat wry idiom, but an idiom nevertheless. Nor was this dexterity confined to verse. When I was a boy, I used to spend hours playing with him what was called the 'Sir George Back game': I was to make any remark I liked, and he was to introduce, with some appearance of relevance, the name of his great-uncle Sir George Back, an Arctic explorer, into the first or at least the second sentence of his reply. He always won.

The cricket and football were a more serious matter. Three of my uncles were rather distinguished players at a time when amateur and professional sport were less sharply separated than they are today; and my father, who was far the most talented member of the family in other respects, was long content, even proud, to be known as its fourth-best footballer. He kept up an interest in these games to the end of his days, and continued, in his seventies, to visit his old school, largely for the purpose of inspecting its performance at cricket. There was a reason for all this. In that age and class, the manly character was thought to be formed, tested, and exhibited in outdoor games. My father held this belief; and I think he may have been partly right, for, certainly, by his account of it, he had often discerned nobility, resourcefulness, or egoism in an innings at cricket or a run up the football field. For those who have the patience to watch character unfolding at the leisurely pace of a three-volume novel, a cricket match is still a good school of life. For my father, character was everything, intellect of no more than secondary importance. I do not think I ever heard him express admiration for cleverness unaccompanied by moral excellence—awe, yes, but never admiration. It was perhaps for this reason that he had a penchant for over-rating the intellect of men of character. His favourite term of praise was 'simple'; but he liked to think that in the simple there was more than met the eye. Thus he admired most of all men like Sir Edward Grey and Sir George Buchanan, who were really, I suspect, more commonplace than he believed. Perhaps, at the bottom of his heart, he liked them because they reminded him of my grandfather, who was stable, generous, and moderately wise, but obviously not at all clever.

He was a promising boy, and his career started well. He was a scholar at Harrow, then at its greatest, the nurse of great politicians and great teachers. He shared a room with a future prime minister, Stanley Baldwin, but found difficulty in remembering anything about his character forty years later. He went on to Cambridge with a scholarship at Trinity College. There he came to grief. Probably he had had too much of the classics; he would have liked to specialize in history, but there was no escape from the classics in those days. He made matters worse by confusing himself in an attempt upon ancient philosophy; his cast of mind was essentially historical, undistinguished in abstract thought. Yet he seems to have worked out for himself, from the study of Plato, some elementary principles which made part of his religion ever afterwards; and this is more than many people retain who get much higher marks for ancient philosophy than he did. At the time, however, the result was disaster: he did badly in his degree examinations, and an academic career seemed to be out of the question. He was destined to spend his next few years teaching at a second-rate school. I think he felt this very much: when I won a college fellowship, his pleasure seemed to be much heightened by the feeling that he would have liked to hold one himself.

It is important to remember that he was, at this stage of his career, a failure: if he had succeeded more easily at the first, he would probably have been a less remarkable man later, for his strength of will and sense of mission were nourished in the bitterness of frustration and in the determination to make his mark on the world in spite of all disadvantages. Also, perhaps, the paltriness of the daily task left his mind more open to new impressions than the preoccupations of a successful professional career would have done.

It is not easy to say when he discovered his passion for Russia. In his *Memoirs* he suggests that Russia had drawn him unconsciously, like a magnet, from the first. But I think his memory may have deceived him. He may, indeed, have felt keenly the impression of the great war scare of 1877–8, when every English schoolboy of 10 was either a 'Russian' or a 'Turk', and he, as the son of a Gladstonian liberal, must undoubtedly have been a 'Russian'. Perhaps it was at this early age that he formed the opinion (which he still expressed in the last year of his life) that the British had no right to keep the Russians out of Constantinople. But there is not much other sign of an early interest in Russia. After he left Cambridge he visited, as a student or as a sightseer, almost every European country before Russia; and he learnt French, German, and Italian thoroughly before he knew a word of Russian. At one time he was particularly interested in Italy—not only in Dante, Ariosto, and Tasso but also in the *Risorgimento*—and it was he who first interested his friend G. M. Trevelyan in Garibaldi by giving him a copy of the *Autobiography* as a wedding present: surely one of the most momentous wedding presents in literary history. Russia came last in time. I may mis-remember, but I certainly got the impression that he first went there in order to visit the Napoleonic battlefields. He had a passion for battlefields, especially those of Napoleon, and would speak of them in the same tones in which other connoisseurs might have spoken of a vintage claret. He had seen all the others, and none now remained to visit but the Russian.

Whatever the reason for his going, his first two visits to Russia changed the whole course of his life. The charm of the Russian peasantry captivated him. Those who have experienced this charm at first hand are better able than I am to explain why this son of an English rentier, whose experience of peasantry had been confined to the depressed yokels of Surrey and Cambridgeshire, should have been so completely overpowered by it as to make Russia his second homeland, one might almost say his first. His emotions seem to have been comparable to those of the *Narodniki*, who felt that they had not begun to live until they had got into immediate and unsophisticated contact with the people. It was much easier, at that time, for an Englishman of the middle class to indulge these feelings in Russia than in England, where rustic society was especially vitiated by snobbery and subservience. Add to this, that Russian politics had reached a stage peculiarly interesting to an English liberal, when it seemed likely that all the institutions and ideas which were taken for granted as the foundations of English political development would be domiciled and established in Russia under the observer's eyes. Here was history, which my father had always wanted to study, and, what was better, history in the making.

These are the best reasons I can give for the new orientation of my father's life, which came to appear to him so natural and necessary that he hardly ever explained it; and if he did try, it is likely that the explanations were quite trifling in comparison with the thoughts and feelings which moved him.

The mission which he now took up brought him, in time, a position almost unique in British life. There were other passionate experts, who interpreted to the British public the feelings and the needs of Yugoslavs, Arabs, Albanians, Persians; but none of them, except Colonel T. E. Lawrence, made such an impression as my father. This was chiefly because none of them specialized in a country half so important as Russia. By luck or by skill, he had backed the best horse in the stable. But he had to pay for his eminence. The mission almost became an obsession. It ate up nearly all his other interests. Some of his friends thought him a club bore, because he would talk about nothing else. He could read about nothing else: the former student of Michelet and Ariosto could hardly be tempted to open a book even about cricket, and, when he was not reading, writing, or talking about Russia, he would spend hours playing patience with *élan*, puffing furiously at a rather dirty pipe and, no doubt, thinking about Russia. Also, he planned his journeys to Russia without much consideration for his family, who were often left for long periods, sometimes in difficult circumstances.

This concentration of his interests did not come about all at once. In the meantime his knowledge of Russia had led him back to academic life. He had already made half the journey from schoolmastering when he became a lecturer under the Cambridge University Extension Scheme. (It is difficult now to realize the importance of the University Extension Schemes, both as education and entertainment, before the days of cinema and radio; the Workers' Educational Association did not exist, and even some of the newer universities themselves were only half-fledged.) Probably it was in the service of this movement that he perfected his skill as a lecturer, equally effective with the deadly serious miners of County Durham or the genteelly curious middle classes of the

Home Counties. He was by far the best lecturer I ever heard: he had a peculiar gift for characterization and for dramatic narrative, but everything he said was exciting, for his mind was full of it. He used a few scribbled notes, but they can hardly have been necessary to the performance, for he could not always have found them in the appalling chaos which he stuffed into his pockets, nor can they have been easy to decipher when found. He could never see why certain elderly ladies used to come, year after year, to the course of public lectures which he gave in the University of London; but I have no doubt that they went as one goes a second or third time to an exceedingly well performed play. It was as good as a play even to listen through the door. If he had gone into politics or had taken Holy Orders (which he once thought of doing), he might have had an electrifying effect in the pulpit or on the platform.

His first real university post was at Liverpool. That was the heroic age of the English provincial universities: they had only just been founded, and were pervaded by a mood of generous enterprise and unbounded optimism; for the limits to the potential number and quality of the students, which have since become apparent, could not then be perceived. Not only the early professors, but the city fathers too had the *goût de la fondation*. My father's Chair was itself an example of this civic and mercantile enterprise; for there was then no other professor of Russian in the country. Even the academic controversies were heroic: there were two factions, known as the 'Old Testament' and the 'New Testament', and their campaigns in the Senate, as recounted by my father, sounded to my youthful ears like the War of Troy. My father belonged to the New, so I have never discovered what the Old stood for; by his account, they were a set of mere *routiniers* without an idea in their heads—I have sometimes wondered if they were as bad as that. The New Testament won, but itself dissolved, soon after, in intricate personal feuds; and the great days were over before the war of 1914.

My father described his war experiences so fully (in a book published at the time, *Day by Day with the Russian Army*, and later in his *Russian Memoirs*) that I need not describe them again. He spent nearly the whole of the first three years in Russia. His status was undefined, and changed from time to time; but that made no difference, for he never cared about his status any more than he cared about his appearance. His mission was really personal, and it seems to have been on his own initiative that he did the most important things, as when he brought home the list of the shortages in munitions and other supplies to the British government. Most of the time he was at the front or near it (he was nearly 50, but very tough and quite indifferent to hardship). Finally, when society and the army began to dissolve behind the lines, he ceased to have any British status at all, and virtually became a Russian: as such he found himself joined with four Mensheviks—two civilians, an army lieutenant, and a sailor—in a curious body called 'The League of Personal Example', which toured the country making speeches in order to revive morale and keep Russia in the war. Luckily for him, he was in England when the October Revolution came, and was stopped in Stockholm on his way back to Russia. Then followed the queerest journey of all —the British government sent him out to Siberia, with a roving commission to keep up the spirits of the farmers behind Kolchak's lines and give them the (largely illusory) impression that Great Britain meant to see the intervention through. From this nightmare he was lucky to escape in a fur-trading vessel down thousands of miles of Siberian river and through the Arctic Circle.

Thus he had been repelled from the front door of Russia and from the back door. It was sixteen years before he saw the country again. They were very unhappy years for him. At first he believed, like many other people, that the working-class unrest of 1919-21 might lead to some kind of revolution in Great Britain itself; he therefore engaged in a tournament of public debates, up and down the country, with British communists and sympathizers with the Soviet government. These debates, conducted with 'sportsmanlike' fairness on both sides, first made him a public figure in his own country. Even after the danger of a British revolution had obviously receded, he was not happy. He was, in a certain sense, an exile; cut off from the country whose current history was his chief interest and his business, and necessarily influenced by other exiles who (as always) underrated the stability and overrated the difficulties of the régime they hated, he found it difficult to maintain in London an advanced post of observation from which developments in Russia could be reported or judged with scholarly detachment. He tried to condemn the Soviet authorities out of their own mouths, using only facts and figures provided by their own newspapers. But even thus he was misled, for he continued to believe, down to the advent of Hitler, that the end or at least the total transformation of the Soviet régime was just round the corner. His only opportunity for constructive work was the establishment of the School of Slavonic Studies in the University of London. Here his astuteness and determination in committee work and his standing with the general public enabled him to free the school from influences that might have cramped it and to obtain for it an independent status and an international reputation. He enjoyed this work: it had not quite the same excitement as the wars of the Old and New Testaments, but he met foemen worthy of his steel.

The rise of Hitler, which caused the Soviet government to reorient its foreign policy, also made a great change in my father's life. He revised his attitude to the Soviet government, and it revised its attitude to him. He had, for many years, been a Russian liberal rather than a British liberal, and perhaps a Russian patriot rather than a British patriot. For Russian liberalism, in the narrower sense, there was no more hope: my father's friends had had their hour in 1917, and lost it. Even so, he could take comfort in the apparent liberalization of Russian institutions and in the triumph of Stalin's common sense over doctrinaire Marxism in certain fields of art, literature, and education. Moreover, when Russia was once more in danger, his feeling of Russian patriotism returned in full force. Already he had welcomed the victory of Stalin, the Russian national leader, over Trotsky, the international revolutionary. Now he was well on the way to becoming once more the partisan of an Anglo-Russian alliance. The Soviet government, on its side, had a use for such partisans, in the days of national and international 'Popular Fronts'. The *rapprochement* took some time to bring about: there were even more than the usual delays about visas and so forth. At last, towards the end of 1935, my father set foot in Russia once more, and any remaining doubts vanished at once. He had not left the Moscow railway station before his mind was flooded with the realization that the Bolsheviks were, after all, Russians. The second conversion was even more instantaneous than the first.

He was an old man, but the best part of his life was still to come: he had his best books to write, and he was, for the first time, the oracle of a cause in which nearly everybody wanted to believe.

For a few months in 1939–40 the Russo-German pact and the Finnish war put him out of his stride: he was hardly popular with the general public, and still less so with the Foreign Office, which was understandably irritated by his pursuing a private foreign policy of his own in interviews with the Russian ambassador, although he was in its employment. But Hitler's invasion of Russia proved him right, in his own mind and in that of the public. He now became more active, and had more influence, than ever before. He lectured up and down the country, regardless of blackout and even air-raids. He wrote a little book in paper covers —perhaps the best of all his books—which sold more than half a million copies. Finally, at the age of nearly 76, he crossed the winter seas infested by submarines to start the same career on an even larger scale in America.

He ought to have died about that time, at his finest hour. It is a pity that he lived to undergo a second disillusionment and some confusion of mind. He stayed on in America after the war, and found useful work to do in advising American universities on the creation of schools of Slavonic studies such as that which he had built up in London. But the break-up of the war-time alliance which he had preached made him very unhappy. He did not pretend that the faults were all on one side, but the faults he minded most were on the British and American side. I think he would have accepted almost any extension of Russian power, if only the Soviet government had not shown that it meant to return to rigid communism at home. Thus, suspected of un-American activities on the one hand and scurrilously abused by communists on the other, he hardly knew what to think or what to hope. He died in New York on 17 April 1949.

He was not one of the great scholars, in the sense in which the word is commonly used; but he was a creator, which is, perhaps, something more, even in academic life; a great orator, a vivid and magnetic personality, and a man of indomitable will.

V

THE ECONOMIC FACTORS IN THE HISTORY OF THE EMPIRE

[*Economic History Review*, vii (1937), pp. 119–44]

SOME vague and misleading things have been said about economic imperialism in late years; but there is no reason for doubting that there is such a thing, or rather that there are such things. Colonization and empire-building are above all economic acts, undertaken for economic reasons and very seldom for any others. At some times in the history of England and France, as in that of the Greek cities, emigration has appeared to proceed from στάσις—political or religious discord. But such exceptions as the Pilgrim Fathers are not so complete as they look. Even the conscious founder of a new City of God, like John Winthrop, thought it a material consideration that 'My means here are so shortened (now my 3 eldest sons are come to age) as I shall not be able to continue in this place and employment where I now am . . . and with what comfort can I live with 7 or 8 servants in that place and condition where for many years I have spent 3 or 400*li*. per ann. and maintain as great a charge?'[1] No doubt there were in the English and French civil wars some people who emigrated for religious or political reasons though they had enough economic inducement to stay at home. But such exiles probably did not make up a majority, though they may have been the dominant political caste, even in their own colonies, while in other colonies they were hardly to be found at all.

It is therefore necessary to look first of all for the economic motives of imperial expansion and exploitation. Since these motives probably have not remained the same throughout the history of empires, no theory will suit every age and type of empire. Certainly the modern Marxist theories are subject to this limitation, as their wiser authors admit.

[1] *Winthrop Papers*, vol. ii (Massachusetts Historical Society, 1931), p. 126. It may be objected that this is not a perfect instance because Winthrop had just been deprived of a small office on account of his politics; but it is not the reason he gives, and his latest editor even doubts the fact (ibid., p. 100).

E

The best method of discussing the matter will be, I think, to describe the successive theories of empire, and the practice with which they corresponded—or did not correspond. This method has one advantage: it helps us to remember, or does not prevent us from remembering, that the most important thing in the history of an empire is the history of its mother-country. Colonial history is made at home: given a free hand, the mother-country will make the kind of empire it needs. This is particularly true of the British empire, because England, more than any other colonial power, has had such a free hand. Others may have had to content themselves, up to now, with the kind of empire they could get; we have been able—after many struggles, indeed—to make the kind of empire we wanted. It is important, therefore, to know what kinds of empire have we wanted, and why? For this reason and because it is the empire about which I can generalize with most confidence, I shall confine myself to discussing the British empire.

I

The great object of the mercantilist was to create employment.[2] So long as he did so he was curiously indifferent to the productivity of the labour employed. Hence, for example, Cary congratulated himself on the fact that in the colonial trade 'the commodities exported and imported being generally bulky do thereby employ more ships, and consequently more sailors, which leaves more room for other labouring people to be kept at work in husbandry and manufactures, whilst they consume the product of the one, and the effects of the other in an employment of a distinct nature from either.'[3]

It is not necessary here to explain this preoccupation with em-

---

[2] It has been justly doubted whether the economic historian ought to speak of 'the mercantilists'. When I use the phrase, I mean the mercantilist 'man in the street', of whom, I think, a fairly consistent picture can be drawn.

[3] J. Cary, *An Essay on the State of England in Relation to its Trade* (Bristol, 1695), p. 68. Perhaps most people would have given a military reason for encouraging sailors; Cary prefers to argue that sailors are kept from competing for other people's jobs. He is not quite consistent, for he praises labour-saving devices and denounces unproductive employments such as alehouse-keeping. This is a point on which even the best mercantilist writers were far from clear; they thought of national wealth so much in terms of international trade that they did not attend enough to the distribution of industry and rewards within the nation. (See Mun's curious reflections on lawyers, and his ambiguous handling of the question of luxury.)

ployment, or the pessimistic attitude which Professor Heckscher has labelled 'Fear of Goods'.[4] As a result of this attitude, the average mercantilist was almost equally preoccupied with foreign trade.[5] The first enthusiasts judged a colonial adventure as they would have judged an extremely 'favourable' branch of foreign trade. A colony was to yield raw materials and dispose of English manufactures, in order, as the younger Hakluyt said, that 'what in the number of things to go out wrought, and to come in unwrought, there need not one poor creature to steal, to starve, or to beg as they do'.[6] How this was to come about, and in particular how an effective demand for English manufactures was to be discovered or created, the prophets did not always stop to answer. In their ignorance they could not yet distinguish colonies of settlement and of exploitation from trading-stations, and they seem to have imagined that the demand for woollens among, for example, the Red Indians of North America would be immense. Few of them asked themselves how the Red Indians would pay for their purchases; and of those who did, like the elder Hakluyt, still fewer could give anything like a satisfactory answer.[7] Only time was to show which of the countries open to imperialist exploitation were to be valued for the markets and the products of their native inhabitants, and which were not. The former, such as the East Indies, were destined to furnish the basis of a trading empire; the latter had to be used another way, if they were to be used at all.

When they talked of raw materials and markets, of course, the mercantilists meant, above all, the raw materials of industry and markets for industrial products. In fact, most of them seem to have assumed without question that the national interest of England in economic affairs was the interest of a trading, or rather an industrial nation. This is curious, because her main source of wealth was still agriculture, and the fact was recognized in a great deal of her policy. The mercantilists usually assumed that the duty or the destiny of colonies was to confine themselves to agri-

---

[4] [Eli F. Heckscher, *Mercantilism* (2 vols., London, 1935), ii. 57, 117, 148.]

[5] Mr. Keynes has explained this connexion of thought very ingeniously in terms of his own theory (*General Theory of Employment, Interest, and Money*, London, 1936, pp. 334–8).

[6] 'Discourse of Western Planting', printed in *Original Writings and Correspondence of the Two Richard Hakluyts* (Hakluyt Society, 1935), p. 238.

[7] 'Inducements to the liking of the voyage intended towards Virginia' (ibid., pp. 332–3).

culture and leave industry to the mother-country. This was even true of Ireland, which was treated as a colony and sometimes even called one. Cary set out to prove to the Irish that their true interest was in agriculture. He did not produce any economic arguments, nor could he have done so, for he obviously thought that industry was in itself more eligible than agriculture: it was so much less 'laborious' and provided so much more 'easy' a subsistence that nobody, according to Cary, would remain on the land if he saw a chance of employment in a town. Finally, Cary gave away his case by conceding that if Ireland could find an industry—the linen industry—which did not compete with our own, Englishmen would be very glad.[8]

There were certain difficulties about this division of labour between England and Ireland. Cary recognized that if England was to have a monopoly of industry, Ireland must be free to make a living by engaging in every form of agriculture. But he knew it would be hard to persuade the English land-owning class that this was not contrary to its interest. Ireland competed with England in cattle-raising. The English parliament, dominated by land-owners, and ready to protect agriculture quite as much as industry, therefore passed the famous Act of Limitation, which forbade the importation of Irish cattle—the counterpart in agriculture to the various measures for putting down manufactures in the colonies. Cary thought this act ought to be repealed. How did he set about persuading the English agriculturalists that they would suffer no injury? By arguing that the prohibition had driven the Irish into pasturing sheep, and selling their wool abroad or manufacturing it for themselves; this diminished the export from England—not, indeed, of wool, for that might not be exported, but of woollen manufactures; this in turn lessened the profits of our woollen industry, and lowered the rents of English lands. 'Nothing', said Cary, 'will advance their lands like trade and manufactures, therefore whatever turns the stream of these elsewhere lessens the number of inhabitants who should consume their provisions, and when these increase, so do the others.'[9] In other words, the destiny of English agriculture was to supply the home market of an industrial nation, in free competition with colonial agriculture; all were to receive their reward from the high prices or large exports of the workshop of the world. The English landed interest, however, was

---

[8] Cary, op. cit., pp. 91–94.   [9] Ibid., pp. 100–7.

not convinced by this kind of imperialism (no more it is now), and preferred to deal with the matter by a further increase of the restrictions upon Irish enterprise: it kept up the prohibition against Irish cattle, and tried to avoid the predicted results by preventing the growth of the woollen industry in Ireland and the export of Irish wool to foreign parts.[10]

In the American colonies and colonial trades, the merchants and industrialists were better able to impose their idea of an imperial division of labour without the same opposition from the landed interest. Although writers like Child growled occasionally at New England for producing foodstuffs which might compete with the products of our own agriculture in our West India markets, this was not a serious grievance.[11] The English farmer more or less willingly resigned the markets of the sugar islands to the North American farmer. Those islands received very little of their food from England in the eighteenth century, before the American Revolution. Conversely, the North American wheat-grower had hardly begun to compete with the English exporter in the markets of Europe. Difficulties of transportation were the reason for this. Had New England and the bread colonies been as near as Ireland, no doubt the English landlord would have obtained protection against their wheat as he obtained it against Irish cattle.[12] But he had good markets nearer at hand which they could not share, and the only articles in which the farmers of the old and the new world competed were beef and dairy produce; since it was Irish, not English, beef and butter that competed against the American, the English parliament saw no reason for favouring either side against the other.

Competition between the agriculture of the mother-country and that of the colonists was the last thing the mercantilists intended.

[10] As Professor G. N. Clark points out, the only effect of the Act of Limitation was to turn the thwarted Irish exporter of cattle into a very successful producer of beef and butter. He also doubts whether the Irish woollen industry would have grown very much if the English parliament had let it alone (*The Later Stuarts*, Oxford, 1934, pp. 289, 303–7). He is right; but this legislation, though ineffectual and unnecessary, shows how an imperial parliament thought fit to treat a colonial dependency.

[11] *A Discourse about Trade* (1690 ed.), p. 204.

[12] When the agricultural interests of an imperial nation are strong enough politically, they may put an end to the imperial connexion altogether, as the very powerful sugar interest in the United States helped to bring about the disannexation of the Philippines.

Unlike the nineteenth-century theorists, they never meant to send colonists abroad to produce in the new world what they had produced in the old. The object of colonization was to obtain goods which were complementary to the products of the mother-country—raw materials of industry such as silk, cotton, and dye-woods, and articles of consumption which could not be grown at home. True, unexpected and unwelcome articles of consumption, such as Virginia tobacco, were sometimes thus brought into common use. But other commodities were more respectable; and one of the oftenest-repeated arguments for colonization was the phenomenal fall in the price of sugar which we believed—perhaps wrongly—to have been caused by the production of our sugar islands after 1640.

This was the more important because we considered that we had thereby emancipated ourselves from the national monopoly of the Portuguese. It was a commonplace of many mercantilist writers that a nation which had a monopoly of an article could and would squeeze the consumers of the world. It could be done by crop restriction (as the Dutch burnt half their spices to sell the rest at a better price).[13] But the mere existence of a 'staple' might be enough in itself.[14] In fact, no sooner were we free from the Portuguese monopoly of sugar than we tried to come to terms with the Portuguese government in order to set up an English one.[15] The mercantilists did not explain what was the point of these national monopolies; they did not think it needed explaining. Presumably, given an inelastic demand (which the mercantilists, with their 'fear of goods', mostly assumed), the monopoly would increase the 'favourable' trade balance.

The schemes for world monopolies of colonial products broke down through the competition of empires. The English and French rivalled each other in many branches of American production, the English and Dutch in many branches of Eastern trade; tobacco was the only colonial industry in which we obtained a

[13] Cary proposed that we should get the 'staple' of wool and destroy what we could not sell at a good profit.

[14] Some of the wilder journalists proposed that we should contrive to charge higher prices to foreigners than to the home consumer (very unlike the modern cartel or state monopoly which dumps abroad to sell high at home). It is hard to see how the merchant could do this without the help of the government; and the government was generally too much afraid of losing the trade to squeeze the foreigner—hence the large and frequent drawbacks of duty on exportation.

[15] *Hist. MSS. Comm., Heathcote MSS.*, pp. 19, 23.

dominating position, and even there we had competitors. But even without the monopolies, the colonies were well worth while. The emphasis which pamphleteers laid upon rich tropical commodities was justified by the great fortunes which the sugar-planters made in the seventeenth century. Here was an article for which the demand was great and increased all the time. Although the British sugar islands went through a period of depression after 1720, when their produce was beaten out of the world market by the French, the home demand grew so consistently that it had certainly caught up with the supply by 1740, and in the fifties the refiners were beginning to ask for free trade in raw sugars. Here was a new kind of monopoly which the founders of colonies had hardly contemplated: geographical limitations and (according to some conjectures) a deliberate policy of restriction had put a certain class of colonists in a position to lay a monopoly tax on the English consumer. The obvious remedy was expansion of sugar cultivation in the empire. But that required conquests, which the planters did their best to prevent for many years, until experience convinced them that they would gain more in safety from certain strategic annexations than they would lose by increasing the competition within the empire.[16] Even after the Peace of Paris had added to our sugar acreage, the home market could take all that the planters could grow; this probably accounts for the disproportionate development of the sugar industry in the ceded islands, at the expense of the other forms of production.[17]

Those who, like the sugar planters, applied themselves to raising the tropical goods for which western Europe was crying out, became rich enough to buy the English manufactures which they could never have bought if they had stayed in England. This, according to the mercantilists, was the second great justification of colonies. America, unlike Asia, had disappointed us by the insufficiency of her native markets, but she compensated us by making rich customers out of Englishmen. Child estimated that 'every Englishman in Barbadoes or Jamaica creates employment for four men at home'.[18] As Child could see, the Englishmen in

[16] I have discussed this subject at length in my book, *War and Trade in the West Indies* (Oxford, 1936), chaps. iii and v.

[17] L. J. Ragatz, *The Fall of the Planter Class in the British Caribbean, 1763–1833* (New York, 1928), pp. 38–39, 119–20.

[18] *A Discourse about Trade*, pp. 176, 208.

those colonies were somewhat exceptional, for each of them represented, besides himself, eight or ten negroes whose labour he exploited. For this reason their value as consumers threw into the shade the humbler colonists north of Maryland. The West India colonists were, in the mass, England's best customers per head of white population, and for a long time they were her best customers absolutely. The immense increase of the North American population changed the situation about the middle of the eighteenth century. But if we distinguish the colonies of exploitation from the colonies of settlement within the mercantilist empire—a much more real distinction, economically, than the more popular one between North America and the West Indies—it can easily be seen that the colonies of exploitation, which alone possessed staple export crops, remained until the American Revolution the most important part of the empire in every respect; they employed more shipping, produced more valuable goods, consumed more English manufactures.[19]

With few exceptions, theorists and governments disliked the other colonies or ignored them. They did not fit into the picture. They consumed, it is true, a great deal of English manufactures; but they paid for them by somewhat dubious means, such as competing with English fishermen or with English ships in the West India trade, or—worse still—trading to the enemy in war-time. The government tried to make honest men of them by introducing them to a staple crop which should really supplement the resources of the empire; but it did not succeed. The extension of this kind of colony was a very doubtful benefit. Some politicians like Bedford and the elder Pitt were willing to gain popularity by taking up the cause of these people against the French; but at other times the government questioned the wisdom or necessity of letting them penetrate the hinterland too freely.[20] Above all, it was economically a matter of comparative indifference, because it did not much affect any class of people in England. General farming was about as much use to the community whether it was conducted in Suffolk, Ulster, or Massachusetts; in fact, as it was

[19] The line would be drawn between the colonies north of Maryland with the hinterland of the southern mainland colonies, on the one hand, and the sugar islands with the coastal districts of the southern colonies on the other.

[20] As in the celebrated Board of Trade Report of 7 March 1768. [Printed by C. W. Alvord and C. E. Carter in *Trade and Politics, 1767–1769* (Illinois Historical Collections, xvi, Springfield, 1931), pp. 183–204.]

more likely to be pure subsistence farming on the frontier than in the settled parts of the empire, the move from Suffolk to Massachusetts was a retrograde step. The colonist without a staple crop, and therefore without an easy method of paying for English goods, was almost worse than useless to a mercantilist empire. Small wonder, then, that a mercantilist government usually regarded him with indifference or vexation. And not only a mercantilist government; for the *trekboers* of the nineteenth century were even more of a political liability to the empire than the American backwoodsmen of the eighteenth, and no more of an economic asset. This kind of imperialism, which consists in the advance of the subsistence-farmer into lands claimed by native tribes, has very often been partly or entirely involuntary, so far as the home government is concerned.

Another disadvantage was thought likely to result from the frontiersman's lack of resources: already, since he found such difficulty in selling and therefore in buying, he was in the habit of making his own clothes, no matter how cheap they might be had from England. It was feared that he would soon manufacture for a market. This was not likely to happen in a hurry, as Adam Smith argued and later American history showed; but the imperial government left nothing to chance, for colonial manufactures were the great bugbear of economists. Hence the several acts of parliament which struck at the development of manufactures in the colonies. Some of them, like the Hatters' Act, were procured by blindly selfish interests. Others, like the Iron Act of 1750, implied a coherent, though perhaps equally selfish, conception of the imperial division of labour.

Something of the same kind might be said of the Calico Acts, which tried to restrain the use of certain East India textiles in the interest of the English woollen industry. After some false starts, the trade between England and India had become an unusual and perhaps an objectionable one for a mercantilist country: since the vogue of chintzes and calicoes, more manufactures were imported than exported, and those of a kind to interfere with our chief industry at home. Naturally the woollen interests demanded protection and got it. It did not succeed in protecting them, nor did it destroy the Indian textile industries directly; but it unintentionally established the English cotton industry which destroyed them a hundred years later. The Calico Acts were certainly framed without any regard to the interests of India; but it would be a mistake to represent this as a breach of England's imperial obligations to a dependency, for India was not yet part of our empire, and there was little reason for thinking she ever would be. We behaved to India as we would have behaved to any other foreign country—in fact, very much as we did behave to France.

The part played by capital in imperial expansion was seldom discussed. This is not surprising. The mercantilists were only beginning to see what capital was, and what part it played in production. Moreover, there is little evidence that England was, or wanted to be, a capital-exporting country. True, there were many complaints of unemployment and decay of trade, which might be interpreted in a modern capitalist society as symptoms of the capitalists' uneasiness and desire for expansion; but it is doubtful if mercantilist England was such a society as to make this argument admissible. It is true, again, that the very miscellaneous activities of such early colonial and foreign trade magnates as Sir Thomas Smythe and Sir Martin Noell are a little reminiscent of the modern finance-capitalist in search of new worlds to conquer. But such men were few and their resources cannot have gone far, even with the joint-stock companies which some of them controlled. Again, it is true that colonization and overseas trade call for exceptional concentrations of capital. Indeed, the greatest trouble of colonies was getting enough capital;[21] the undertakers had no idea of the amount that would be wanted, and many a colony starved or came near starving because the 'adventurers'[22] at home had run out of money or patience, and could not finance the undertaking any further without impossibly large return cargoes.[23] That, to be sure, does not prove that these inadequate capitalists were not impelled by capitalistic motives. But the best proof that mercantilist England had no surfeit of capital waiting to be released abroad is that she was a capital-importing country. There was a great deal of foreign, especially Dutch,

---

[21] [See the author's *Merchants and Planters* (Cambridge, 1960), pp. 6–13.]

[22] It is significant that the name 'adventurer' was used for the capitalist who stayed at home and ventured his money, not the planter who ventured his person.

[23] August Sartorius von Waltershausen attributed the financial difficulties of modern German colonial enterprises to the impatience of small investors for dividends (*Das Volkswirtschaftliche System der Kapitalanlage im Auslande*, Berlin, 1907, p. 136).

capital in England. In the eighteenth century the Dutch capitalists specialized in government loans, but in the seventeenth they seem to have taken a part in commerce and industry. Their participation was sometimes strangely resented in England.[24] In the colonies it was more welcome to the settlers, but the government tried hard to reject it. There were later occasions when the exclusive attitude had to be relaxed; the planters were glad to borrow Dutch money after a financial crisis in 1773, and parliament was glad to let them do it.[25]

Although it is unlikely that English capitalists badly needed an outlet in the mercantilist age, a great deal of capital was exported to the colonies, for colonization is impossible without it. Of course the advance of capital need not imply the export of capital goods. That might be usual in such heavily capitalized forms of tropical agriculture as sugar-planting, where a capital investment might take the form of machinery and slaves; but it was inappropriate to such enterprises as the first planting of Virginia and New England. There it was more necessary to advance food and consumers' goods to the colonists while they devoted themselves to building up their own capital equipment. The chief effort, therefore, of such capitalists as the Virginia Company was to send out successive 'supplies'. Unfortunately they could not see that they were contributing to the formation of capital in the colonies, and too often rebelled against what they regarded as a waste of money without any commercial returns. Perhaps, though it may seem strange, the best capitalized ventures were those which were least inspired by capitalist motives. When a man like Winthrop resolved to remove for New England, he sold out, if he could, in the old country and took with him, or ordered after him, enough articles of consumption and some necessary tools to start a career as a farmer in the new world.[26]

[24] See the documents in the Timmerman case, 1616 (Public Record Office, State Papers, 14/87, no. 74). Timmerman's desire to set up a sugar refinery was opposed because he had 'combined with divers strangers beyond seas, and hath there so great a stock of money, as if he should be suffered to use this art, it would suck out the heart and power of this business from the English'. In 1635 some applicants for leave to refine sugar promised not to 'employ strangers' estates', but only their own (S.P. 16/279, no. 79).

[25] 13 Geo. III, c. 14.

[26] A comparison of Plymouth and Massachusetts Bay shows, to some degree, that the colonists were best off where they had least to do with English merchants.

But Winthrop and his like were well-to-do men. Few emigrants could afford such a degree of independence; the others were beholden to capitalists for the effort of transplanting them and starting them in their new careers. Those who could not even pay their passage had to sell themselves to the shipowners, to be resold in the colonies as indentured servants for a term of years. Many young merchants were set up in business in the colonies with stock advanced them from England; and they dispensed part of the credit they received to the consumer in the backwoods, who might not pay for years, so that the merchants of England, and the bankers and manufacturers who credited them, must at all times have had a large floating capital outstanding in the colonies. Even the rich planter of sugar and tobacco was deeply in debt to his factor, and indirectly to his factor's banker. The factors had to keep by them a great capital for paying duties, answering bills of exchange, and executing orders for goods; besides this, they must advance large sums upon bond and mortgage if they were to have any business at all, for many planters expected to have the benefit of their consignments requited by loans.[27]

Since the capital invested permanently or currently in the colonies must have been very large, it is surprising that the writers upon colonization did not say more about it. Perhaps this is because they did not consider it an advantage. It was not thought advantageous to the nation because nobody believed that the nation needed to get rid of capital. It was not much advantage to the individual, who gave a great deal of this credit involuntarily or very reluctantly. A few families like the Beckfords and the Lascelleses lived by lending money to planters rather than by planting; they might even consider it an injury to be repaid by a safe debtor.[28] But they were exceptional. Most of the people concerned in the colonies were only anxious to see their money again; and well they might be, for what with paper currency in North America and serious restrictions upon alienation or division of estates in the West Indies, the colonies did all that debtor communities can do to frustrate their creditors.[29] No public loans were

[27] [See the author's description of the system of West India finance in his *A West-India Fortune* (London, 1950), chap. xi. See also below, pp. 218 seqq., and *Merchants and Planters*, pp. 48–50.]

[28] Henry Lascelles occasionally tried to avoid receiving payment of a good debt, but he pressed for repayment far oftener.

[29] [Cf. *Merchants and Planters*, pp. 43–47.]

floated for the colonies in England, so the capital invested there was all private; but perhaps, *mutatis mutandis*, the government's suppression of colonial paper money in 1751 and 1764, and the disallowance of countless laws for the purpose of protecting debtors, may be compared with such later measures as the Colonial Stocks Acts and some of the Indian financial safeguards.

Since the colonies absorbed as much capital as they could get, they cannot have done much to build up capital in England and thereby to promote the Industrial Revolution. It has been suggested that the profits made by merchants in the colonial trade had this effect; but since the most lucrative and important branches of colonial trade were those in which the English merchants acted as factors for the planters, and since, whatever the size of their commissions, these men had to employ all their capital and all they could get from their bankers in financing the trade itself, they can hardly have had much to spare for the Industrial Revolution. Indeed, the manufacturers were lucky if they did not have to give them credit. The planters themselves seem to have been recipients of capital rather than sources of it. True, if a Beckford could build Fonthill or buy a borough seat, he could have set up a factory; but from what can be learnt of the way the West India millionaires spent their money there seem to have been more Fonthills than factories among them, and more overdrafts and protested bills than either. Some of the Bristol and Liverpool banks arose from the wealth accumulated in the colonies or colonial trades, but few or none of the great London houses; and it is beginning to be clear that it was the agricultural rather than the colonial wealth of England that was tapped for industrial development in the later eighteenth century.

II

As England became industrialized, a very different way of thinking about empires began to prevail. Historians have generally concerned themselves with its negative side—the rejection of mercantilism. It undoubtedly had such a negative side, ranging from the qualified negation of Adam Smith to the more complete negation of Bentham and Cobden. But it had also a positive side, which is sometimes forgotten; and this positive theory of empire is the better worth discussing because the free trade era was the great age of colonization and colonial trade.

The positive theory of empire dealt chiefly with the emigration of capital and labour. The chief writers on the subject—especially Wakefield, Merivale, and J. S. Mill—were dominated by Ricardo's law of rent. They believed that increases of population and manufacturing technique were of little use to capital and labour if the only result was to put money in the landlord's pocket by causing more food to be produced from inferior English soils. So far, they kept company with the adversaries of the Corn Laws. But they did not stop short at admitting foreign food free of duty. Wakefield, at least, believed that the whole world supplied too little available corn for industrial England, and that if we merely obtained more 'use of land'—that is, food—from foreigners, we should have to wait upon their very slow agricultural improvements. It was not more 'use of land', but more land, and above all more first-class land, that was wanted.[30] J. S. Mill wrote, in sentences which the others quoted with approval, 'Much has been said of the good economy of importing commodities from the places where they can be bought cheapest; while the good economy of producing them where they can be produced cheapest is comparatively little thought of. If to carry consumable goods from the places where they are superabundant to those where they are scarce is a good pecuniary speculation, is it not an equally good speculation to do the same thing with regard to labour and instruments?'[31]

Judged historically, this was very good sense. England, and indeed all western Europe, needed cheap food and raw materials in order to pursue its career of industrialization. Not all the increase has come from new lands; a great deal of it has proceeded from agricultural improvements in Europe itself. But that would not have been enough, as Wakefield saw. Again, it may be objected, and was objected at the time, that many of the emigrants from the British Isles went to the half-urban United States rather than the purely agricultural colonies. That is true; but the United States were less than half-urban before 1860, and moreover the immigration into the settled districts was still being

[30] *The Art of Colonization*, letter xvi (1849). There are similar passages in *England and America* (1833).
[31] *Principles of Political Economy*, book v, c. xi, § 14.

balanced by some emigration from the settled districts to the frontier.

The same theory of colonization had certain important corollaries. Capital and labour were said to be too thick on the ground at home. Mill and Merivale believed that the competition of capitals with each other might lower the rate of profit to such a point that accumulation would cease. Wakefield thought capital was redundant with respect to the 'field of employment'. It was not merely that capital was tempted abroad by a higher rate of profit; capital must get away from home at any cost. The theorists did not quite agree on the question whether it was necessary to export more capital than labour. Merivale gave two different answers; Mill was sure that it did not matter. Wakefield was preoccupied with another side of the question—the proportion of capital to labour arriving in the colony. He was one of the first to see how much the new Englands overseas differed from the old. He wanted to reproduce in Australasia and North America the old England with something like its class-stratification; he was therefore shocked by the half-barbarous equality of the one-class society in the backwoods. He could only realize his ideal by making the colonies safe for capitalists and wage-earners, which he hoped to do by his celebrated land system. It was not so important to him that England should be relieved of her plethora of capital, as that the colonists should not be starved of it. Merivale criticized his theory as too sweeping. Capitalization of colonies could not be an end in itself; there must be some inducement, and that must come from the profitable nature of the product. He thought Wakefield's system would only work in a colony with a staple export. That, again, was roughly true. Capitalism itself causes, to some extent, the production of commercial crops, because it demands a payment in some currency that can be realized at home; but it is equally true, or more so, to say that commercial crops invite capitalism.

Of course the capital and labour that went overseas had, and were meant to have, an effect upon the capital and labour that stayed behind. It was not only by the relief of simple evacuation, but by the new markets which the colonies afforded. The increased productivity of the labour of transplanted Englishmen has, in fact, given more employment to Englishmen at home than any extension of markets in other parts of the empire. That is how, in spite of their small populations, the development of their own industries, and the increasing proportion of their trade which has fallen to foreigners, the self-governing dominions have taken off a great and increasing proportion of English exports.[32]

This is only one side of the story. Another great development was taking place in the empire at the same time. The transformation of the economic relations between England and India in the nineteenth century throws a strong light on the nature of free-trade imperialism.

Towards the end of the eighteenth century England's trade with the East was very largely a reciprocal exchange of manufactures —woollens and hardware for cottons and silks; the East India Company was exporting a smaller proportion of bullion than it had done fifty years earlier. In the first half of the nineteenth century this state of affairs was much changed: England exported more manufactures than ever, though of a different kind, and her imports from India consisted more and more of raw materials. Some Indians have concluded from this that England systematically destroyed the industries of India and reduced her from a manufacturing to an agricultural country. Their complaint is the more bitter because the English cotton industry, which so reversed the fortunes of India, had grown up under a protective system aimed at the cotton industry of India.

There is no doubt that the change took place: it is less certain that it was deliberate. Certainly the abolition of the East India Company's trade monopoly in 1813 was in some ways unfortunate for the Indian cotton-weavers. The company had aimed at exporting as much English woollen manufactures as possible (for which reason the older-established woollen interests supported it, almost alone, against the private traders), and importing as much Indian textiles as the European market would take. (This, perhaps, was because its greatest commercial strength in India was its command over the cotton-weaving industry, which it maintained by almost

---

[32] Professor Flux called attention to this in 1899 (*Journal of the Royal Statistical Society*, lxii. 496–8). Mr. J. A. Hobson controverted him (*Imperialism*, London, 1902, p. 39). It was a matter of classification: Mr. Hobson classed the South African colonies with the tropical dependencies, Professor Flux with the self-governing dominions. It is a nice question which of them is right; for my own part I prefer Professor Flux's view. The economic and social affinities of South Africa with the tropical colonies are strong, but not, in my opinion, decisive. Compare both these sets of figures with Table xxxix in Grover Clark's *Balance Sheets of Imperialism* (New York, 1936).

feudal means.) The directors were monopolists of the old school. Like all monopolists, they were pessimistic about the chances of increasing the volume of the trade; they could handle a luxury article for which the possible demand was limited, but they could not, and perhaps would not, drive a new kind of trade which might upset the social and economic conditions in a sub-continent. The company's tenacious conservatism, therefore, gave the Indian weavers some sort of protection; and when the private traders, heavily backed by the cotton towns and other comparatively new export industries, succeeded in getting the trade opened, the immediate result was a rush of English cotton goods to India, the cessation of India's cotton textile exports to England, and a gradual increase of her exports of raw materials, especially raw cotton. The Lancashire cotton interests made it clear that, when their goods were excluded from the European markets by the continental system and their supplies of raw material interfered with by the war of 1812 with the United States, they looked to India to make good both deficiencies. A few people on both sides of the controversy saw that the final result might be the transformation of India from a manufacturing to a raw material producing country. Most Englishmen saw nothing to regret in this; but a few conservative eccentrics regretted it, like Tierney and, some years later, the colonial historian Montgomery Martin.[33]

But it would be temerarious to pronounce that agriculture was substituted for industry in India by the policy of the English government or the enterprise of the English merchant. In the first place India was not an industrial country to begin with, and Indian weaving was not wholly destroyed. The finest and best manufacturers, such as those of Dacca, appear indeed to have been ruined; and such dislocation as was caused in this way must have been unusually cruel and disastrous among Hindus because their caste-system prohibited industrial transference. But the coarser kinds of weaving survived, and suffered comparatively little from English competition. A division of labour was maintained during the rest of the century: India imported her finer goods from Lancashire and made her coarser goods at home.

[33] For Tierney's speech, see *Hansard*, 1st series, xxvi. 525; Montgomery Martin's evidence before the Select Committee of 1840, *Parl. Papers*, 1840, viii, especially question 3920.

Moreover, so far as the fine Indian craftsmen were ruined, it was chiefly by English competition in neutral markets. Indian weavers did not depend wholly or even principally upon the English market. Bengal, at least, exported more cotton goods to the United States, Portugal, and the Far East, and it was the failure of these markets too, about 1818, that so much damaged the industry.[34] True, it was English competition that had this result; but it can hardly be thought a Satanic policy for a manufacturing nation to undersell its dependencies in neutral markets. Nevertheless, the Indians had some cause to complain of the heavy internal transit-duties which crippled the development of manufactures until they were removed in 1836, and the protective duties levied in England not only on Indian silks, which competed with English industry, but on cottons which could no longer hope to undersell the English weavers in any circumstances. These duties were materially lowered by Peel's reformed tariff, but only after the employers and still more the workers in the silk manufacture had showed how far a backward industry was from appreciating the beauties of free trade in the year of grace 1840.[35]

As for the swollen imports of raw cotton from India, the English merchants do not seem to have stimulated its production in the early part of the century so much as to have diverted India's exports of this article from other markets to England. In the American cotton famine of the sixties the Lancashire cotton interest was indeed very much to blame for encouraging an injudicious extension of cotton-growing in India and then returning to American cotton as soon as it could, leaving India with a serious over-production. But that was partly because, in spite of the Cotton Supply Association's measures for improving the quality of Indian cotton, India could not, in the time, produce material good enough for the Lancashire machines—which is shown by the fact that a great deal of Indian cotton was re-exported at the height of the famine. Still, though it may have been nobody's fault, it was a disaster for India.[36] The only compensation was

[34] See the table in *Parl. Papers*, 1832, x, part ii, pp. 883–7; also the interesting letter quoted by Larpent in answer to question 2776, *Parl. Papers*, 1840, viii.

[35] A great deal of the evidence before the Committees of 1840 is very interesting; that of Thomas Cooper, silk-weaver of Macclesfield, before the Commons Committee is particularly so (*Parl. Papers*, 1840, viii).

[36] Isaac Watts, *The Cotton Supply Association; its Origin and Progress* (Manchester, 1871), passim.

that the glut of cotton probably helped the Bombay spinners to develop their industry.

The influence of Lancashire was soon afterwards exercised again in a manner which was uncongenial if not positively injurious to Indian industrialists. This was in the celebrated controversy of the seventies over the Indian cotton duties. Lancashire was beginning for the first time to foresee the exclusion of its cottons from some of the protected markets of Europe, and claimed the right, once more, to fall back on India as a market as well as a source of raw materials. At the same time a large-scale cotton industry was just beginning to develop in India itself. The Indian government let itself in for a pretty quarrel by refusing to abolish the cotton import duties before it had lowered the general import duties or removed certain more burdensome forms of taxation. The matter was really one of revenue, and as such it was finally treated; but since the cotton duties were in fact, though not in intention, protective, the Lancashire members of parliament, regardless of party, pressed continually to have them removed before any other kind of tax was remitted in India. The discussion was interesting, if only because it was one of the few occasions when Gladstone spoke almost disrespectfully of free trade: he contrasted the merciless vigour with which we applied free trade principles 'against the feeling of the Indian people' with our acquiescence in the protective policy of the self-governing colonies.[37] The contrast, which Lansdowne later described as 'swallowing the colonial camel and straining at the Indian gnat', was indeed invidious. But the complete free trader replied that though we could not prevent the Australians from making fools of themselves, we might and should restrain India. At the same time it was argued (for instance, in a strong minute of Sir Henry Maine) that we had a right to expect from India an open market for our goods as a compensation for the very serious liabilities which her possession and defence had laid upon our foreign policy.[38] (This was just after the Eastern crisis of 1875–8, in which our connexion with India was felt to have been an important element.)

---

[37] *Hansard*, 3rd series, ccxlvi. 1746.
[38] *Parl. Papers*, no. 392 of 1879, pp. 9–10. Sir John Strachey made some rather similar remarks in his Financial Statement of 1877 (*Parl. Papers*, no. 241 of 1879, p. 3).

The duties do not seem to have been serious economically; they were more important as a symbol of India's dependence upon the commercial policy of Great Britain and the interests which could so easily dominate that policy. For it was apparent before the world that the government had capitulated to Lancashire, and had imposed its will on the very reluctant authorities in India. Again, in 1894–5, when the Liberal secretaries of state forced the Indian government to impose a countervailing excise duty on Indian yarn in order to mollify Lancashire's aversion to the re-imposition of the cotton duties, it was plain that the opinions of India's responsible authorities could easily be overridden by interested parties in England. This incident, even more than the other, was a very important one in the development of Indian nationalism.

It cannot exactly be said that in these tariff controversies Lancashire tried consciously to force India out of industry into agriculture, but it is true that Lancashire only began rather late in the day to insist upon a fair field for competition between England and India. The case of India is a rather exceptional one, because an industrial power does not often conquer another power with a very similar export industry. The history of Lancashire and India shows, to some degree, what is likely to happen when it does so.

III

The exchange of commodities, however, is not the whole story. Recent theorists of various schools have insisted on the capitalist nature of modern imperialism.

Most of them connect it with capital export in particular; but not all do so. Rosa Luxemburg explains why imperialism is immanent in capitalism without laying much stress on the necessity of exporting capital. She tries to show, by a very elaborate analysis of the schemata at the end of volume ii of Marx's *Capital*, that capitalist accumulation cannot take place unless the capitalist can sell to somebody outside the capitalist system that part of the surplus value which he means to capitalize as an addition to what he has already accumulated. This is one way of saying that capitalism needs markets and finds them, for preference, in those classes at home, and those foreign nations, which are not yet producing on a capitalist basis. That is a truism. Imperialism, both capitalist and pre-capitalist, has always tried to exploit, to control, and even to create such markets.

Another similar explanation comes from other Marxist sources. One effect of capitalist competition, to which Marx often drew attention, was the necessity of cutting costs of production by producing on an ever larger and more efficient scale. In fact, schemata or no schemata, the capitalist would have to accumulate, and to multiply his products and his markets for this reason alone.[39] This argument, however, does not offer so much reason as the other for the necessity of selling the product to 'non-capitalists'. Professor Flux suggested a somewhat similar explanation of economic imperialism, when he wrote that industrialists might prefer 'markets for standard lines of products', which should bring about a profitable 'expansion of production on lines similar to those which long experience has smoothed', to speculating upon the latent demands of their own countrymen for new lines of goods.

The other Marxists do not altogether deny Rosa Luxemburg's thesis; indeed, they adopt it, in part, for their own. Bukharin says that one kind of imperialism (one kind only) may be compared to a vertical trust, where 'the state capitalist trust includes an economically supplementary unit, an agrarian country for instance'. Lenin did not disdain the comparison; but when Kautsky defined imperialism as 'the striving of every industrial capitalist nation to bring under its control and to annex increasingly big *agrarian* regions', he had his nose bitten off by Lenin for saying so. Lenin replied that 'The characteristic feature of imperialism is *not* industrial capital *but* finance capital. . . . The characteristic feature of imperialism is precisely the fact that it strives to annex *not only* agrarian regions, but even the most industrialized regions. . . .'[40] His proof of the last proposition was weak, for he was

---

[39] Adam Smith saw the connexion between industrial development and the size of the market, but applied it somewhat perversely to the case of colonies, for he attacked our concentration on the colonial trade as making us depend too much on a single market. His arguments were political. In so far as the American colonies were a single market, they must have contributed to the growth of large-scale industry; but the very great social diversity of colonial life—planters, slaves, and backwoodsmen—made it impossible to describe them as a single market for this purpose.

[40] N. Bukharin, *Imperialism and World Economy* (London, 1930), p. 120; Lenin, *Imperialism, the Highest Stage of Capitalism* (London, 1933), chaps. vi and vii.

thinking of purely strategic conquests; but the distinction of finance capital and industrial capital is a more serious one.

While Rosa Luxemburg argues that capitalism requires an ever-increasing export of goods, other Marxists say rather that it demands an export of capital. Not necessarily capital goods; they do not agree to lay stress on that. Rosa Luxemburg seems to have thought that consumers' goods would be exported, rather than producers' goods; indeed it must be so, if Marx's schema was to be taken literally, but she did not insist on it—in fact she thought that now more goods of the one kind would be sent abroad, now more of the other. This is true. It is not necessary to export capital goods in order to export capital, and capital export has often taken the form of advances of consumers' goods; on the other hand, at certain important epochs when capital has been exported at a great rate, capital goods, especially railways, have been the principal exports. Bukharin and Lenin, however, laid more stress on the export of capital goods. Lenin had a particular reason for doing so. Whereas Rosa Luxemburg saw imperialism as the necessary result of capitalist competition, Lenin saw it rather as the necessary consequence of capitalist monopoly. He connected it with cartels and tariffs, which were particularly prominent in the capital-goods industries: when once a cartel has obtained a monopoly of the home market, its need and its power to export some of its produce will increase, and by limiting the amount of capital which can be profitably employed within the monopoly area it will force capital—that of its possible competitors, or its own surplus—to leave the country in search of occupation elsewhere. The argument is put rather more explicitly by Bukharin than by Lenin.[41]

It is an interesting point of view. No doubt trusts and cartels may make it more worth while to dispose of surplus products abroad than to raise the standard of life at home. They may also make it more profitable to invest surplus capital in developing foreign industries than to work up for the home market the products of cartels upon which an excessively high price has been fixed. But this theory does not explain the largest empire which exists at present. The development of the British empire and the movements of capital within it cannot be ascribed to cartels, tariffs, or monopolies. In spite of the efforts of Chamberlain (whose

[41] Bukharin, op. cit., p. 97.

imperial preference schemes were represented by Lenin as a retort to the cartellized national monopolies of other industrial countries), the British empire cannot really be said to have entered the monopoly stage before 1932.

Lenin and Bukharin insist upon the exportation not only of capital goods but also of capital. Why does capital emigrate? Partly in order to smooth the path for the emigration of goods: this is particularly true of the capital-goods industries, for there have been many occasions when the flotation of foreign loans, especially for armaments and railways, has gone hand in hand with large orders for capital goods. In these cases capital may be identified with capital goods; capital emigrates chiefly in order that capital goods may do so.[42] Apart from this special case, the export of capital is explained from two ends: either capital has got to emigrate because it cannot stay at home, or it is tempted abroad because it finds better employment there. Neither the second nor even the first of these explanations is the peculiar property of the Marxists. J. S. Mill and Wakefield thought that capital could be absolutely redundant at home, so that it must either go abroad or cease to be capital, i.e. must be consumed instead of being accumulated.

I am not qualified to discuss, as an economist, the analysis of the formation of capital upon which these explanations of imperialism depend. It is certain that in the last hundred years a great deal of capital has been exported from England. The amount and pace of the flow are difficult to determine. L. H. Jenks and C. K. Hobson agree in naming 1875 as the epoch when the 'primary' export of capital ceased and only secondary export remained: that is, when we ceased to build up our foreign investments by a surplus of exported over imported goods and services, and only added to them by reinvesting part of our income from earlier investments.[43] According to Hobson there was no 'primary' export of capital in any year between 1875 and 1907; Hobson's

[42] Sartorius von Waltershausen thought it was the national economist's duty to see that the export of capital was used as a means of pushing the foreign sales of capital goods. Not every flotation of a foreign railway or mining loan results in a corresponding export of material; most of the early ones did, but according to C. K. Hobson (*The Export of Capital*, London, 1914, p. 8) the English railway loans to Argentina did not in 1910–11; moreover, few of the later United States railway loans floated in the London market can have done so.

[43] [L. H. Jenks, *The Migration of British Capital to 1875* (New York, 1927), p. 333. Cf. Hobson, op. cit., p. 197.]

table depends indeed on a reduction of Giffen's allowance for shipping earnings, but even if Giffen's original figures are accepted the year 1875 still appears to have been something of a turning point. The greatest era of English railway-building abroad was past, though there was still plenty to do, especially in South Africa; the greatest exports of railway materials were therefore over too. This is important, because railways seem to have been the great basis of England's foreign investments; there are still[44] countries, such as India and Argentina, where the railways account for more than half the English capital invested, and the United States was such a country before the repatriation of English capital in the war [of 1914–18]. Therefore the passing of the age of overseas railway-building is one of the significant dates of English history.

Another important development in the tendency of English foreign investment is noticed after 1875: before that date it was cosmopolitan, but afterwards it appears to have been concentrated to a greater degree within the boundaries of the empire. Foreign railway and government securities must have been sold and the proceeds reinvested in similar securities within the empire. This process is hard to trace or to explain, but it is there. C. K. Hobson suggested that the British capitalist was the frontiersman or pioneer who opened up a new and difficult field of enterprise, developed it to some degree, then sold out to foreigners who liked a steady investment in an established concern, and himself moved on to new adventures. This has an element of truth in it; certainly the pioneer British enterprises in France and America were generally bought out by the natives as going concerns. Whatever the causes, the relative concentration of capital—it has never been more than that—is yet a third example of the usefulness of a political empire as a standby: the investor, like the seeker for a market or the consumer of raw materials, is glad to turn to the empire when, for one reason or another, the more fully developed independent countries begin to be less attractive than they were.

Capitalist imperialism has certain important secondary consequences. It tends to replace the self-sufficient economy and subsistence agriculture of the colonial lands by production for the world market. Colonies of exploitation and, indeed, colonies of settlement, so far as they are obliged to make a return upon in-

[44] [i.e. in 1937.]

vested capital, must produce for a market. Hence, perhaps, the persistent monoculture of the most highly capitalized tropical countries—and before the abolition of slavery all tropical agriculture in the British colonies and the United States was highly capitalized. Where the loan is granted on condition that the borrower shall give the lender the benefit of his consignments or his orders—which was common in the eighteenth-century sugar business—this effect is even more obvious. The railway is another important agent of capitalism which tends to produce similar results. Sometimes, as in the American prairies, railways cause or promote production for a market; at other times, however, production for a market has caused railways. The efforts of the Cotton Supply Association to goad the India Office into sanctioning or undertaking railways are interesting in this respect. Of course the Association was concerned only with the promotion of cotton-growing, so that some critics were unkind enough to suggest that its efforts had caused, or were likely to cause, a shortage of food in certain districts; presumably this accusation was founded on the fact that the Madras Irrigation and Canal Company, which was much patronized by the Association, was at work in some of the districts where the dreadful Orissa famine broke out in 1866. The Association defended itself, and claimed to have proposed nothing but what would promote the general development of India. There was not much in its earlier memorials to the India Office to substantiate the claim; and it is obvious that a capitalist industry in search of raw material might easily, in a poor country with patchy communications, cause subsistence farming to be replaced by commercial crops to an unhealthy extent. The government of India had been aware of the danger, and sometimes vetoed provincial measures for the undue encouragement of cotton-growing by remission of taxes. At the same time it is fair to say that the railways which were designed to carry cotton to the ports could also, in an emergency, bring food supplies to the cotton districts.

The Cotton Supply Association contemplated, at one time, an attack on the whole system of landholding in India; but on second thoughts it decided that the existing systems would enable cotton to be grown without much change. Capitalist imperialism is often charged with destroying communal land tenure for its own purposes; and there is no doubt that in many parts of Asia and Africa it has resulted in, or been accompanied by, a revolution in the native land-holding system. Capitalistic motives have not always been responsible for this; for example, they do not account for the injudicious rigour with which the *ryotwari* system was pressed upon some communal economies in Madras, or the policy of Sir George Grey which turned British Kaffraria into a slum. White imperialism has had more effect on the native's way of life, especially in Africa, by limiting the quantity of his land than by altering the tenures. This has not always been the doing of capitalism. It was the white farmer who first deprived the African native of his land, partly that he might own it himself, partly that he might dispose of the labour of the landless man. This limitation of native resources and an often deliberate policy of high taxation have undoubtedly played into the hands of industrial capitalism as well—Kimberley and Johannesburg are largely founded upon such policies. But the policies were not invented, in the first place, for the sake of Kimberley and Johannesburg; they were not even invented by the type of capitalist agriculture which uses them, to some extent, in Kenya today. They were invented by the Boer—a curious kind of capitalist, for most of his capital consisted in cows, whose accumulation became almost an end in itself.

This brings us to the last of the criticisms directed against capitalist imperialism. Capital is said to leave the country of its origin, where high wages, Factory Acts, and limitation of hours reduce its profits, and fly to new countries, where it carries on the same industries that it carried on at home, with the advantage of cheaper labour and fewer restrictions. This certainly happens, sometimes even within the limits of a single country like the United States. The spectre of 'raising up foreign competitors' has been conjured up very freely; and just as mercantilists tried to prevent wool, skilled labour, or machinery from being exported to a possible competitor, special taxes upon foreign investments were discussed before the war [of 1914–18]. But it is difficult to be sure how much English capital has been applied to the development abroad of England's own staple industries. Some part of this foreign investment takes the form of banking capital, or loans to foreign governments for general industrial development; the further application of this capital is not easily traced, statistically. Moreover there have lately[45] been many instances, even within

[45] [as of 1937.]

the empire, of capital establishing itself where it may take the benefit of protective duties instead of paying them. Apart from these, capital does not appear to prefer investment in the staple industries which compete with those of its mother country. The typical British investments in the United States were once railways; in India, railways again, and tea plantations—certainly not cotton mills, which British capital has avoided in a remarkable way. In China? Again, not cotton mills, for the British-owned mills are a small proportion of the foreign mills, while British capital is a much higher proportion of foreign capital as a whole. In South Africa, gold mines; in Argentina, railways again.[46] Ordinarily, therefore, foreign investment more often contributes to the general development of colonial lands than to 'raising up foreign competitors'. This consideration is strengthened by the fact that the industrial and capital-exporting lands (which are, in spite of certain variations, roughly the same) lend little to each other but a great deal to the agrarian countries. The United States are no exception to this rule, for in the days when they were great borrowers they were an agricultural nation.

The secondary effects of imperialism upon the mother country are also important, but cannot be discussed here at length. Obviously they tend to create a 'labour aristocracy' and a rentier nation. The great improvement of the English workman's standard of life after 1850 was helped, though not solely caused, by the development of the industries which flourished on capital export. This in its turn did something to create a rentier class by

[46] In Argentina the British investment in railways is currently estimated at £277 million, the total British investment at £441 million [1937 figures]; in the United States before the [1914–18] war, £616 million in railways, total British long-term publicly issued investment, £754 million (Herbert Feis, *Europe, the World's Banker, 1870–1914*, New Haven, 1930, pp. 23, 27). In India the estimates vary. Feis gives, for 1914, £140 million in railways, total British investment £378 million; but this is very misleading, as most of the government loans were contracted for railway building; D. H. Buchanan (*The Development of Capitalist Enterprise in India*, New York, 1934, p. 154) puts the capital outlay on railways, 1914–15, at 65·6 per cent. of the total investment in India. This includes Indian as well as British capital; for British capital alone, probably the figure would be higher. According to figures quoted by Buchanan (p. 206), only 9 cotton mills out of 345 were entirely owned by Europeans in 1921, against 322 entirely owned by Indians. In China, according to figures quoted by G. E. Hubbard (*Eastern Industrialization and its Effect on the West*, London, 1935, p. 223), British investments in 1931 stood in the ratio of 54 : 40 to Japanese investments (the next largest), but British investments in cotton mills stood as 4 : 39 to Japanese in spindles, as 8 : 44 in looms.

the expansion of industrial towns and increase of ground-rents. But the returns upon capital invested abroad have done far more in that respect; ever since the days of the Nabob and the sugar millionaire, the luxury trades at home have received a stimulus from the imperial rentier. This parasitical imperialism was transforming the economy of London and the home counties even before the war [of 1914–18].[47] England's 'tribute' is not exactly similar in its origin to that of Imperial Rome,[48] but its internal economic effect is not unlike, and, if there are no shocks from outside, the finance empire shows signs of outliving the industrial and the political empire. As the colonial lands become industrialized and independent, it is the only kind of imperial relation that remains appropriate.

To sum up, it is pretty clear that imperialism is above all a process—and, to some degree, a policy—which aims at developing complementary relations between high industrial technique in one land and fertile soils in another. These relations are pre-capitalist relations; they are also capitalist relations. Not all the Marxist teachings apply to all the facts, but many of them open the eyes of colonial historians to things which they ought to have seen before.

[47] See the eloquent description in J. A. Hobson's *Imperialism*.

[48] I have not been able to discuss at length the so-called 'tribute' of India. The earliest fortunes brought back from India were not returns to capital in India, but were gained in India itself by privileged, though illicit, trade, and often by sheer oppression. It was remitted home, not, I think, as dividends, but as repatriated capital. When the East India Company's servants ceased to make money in this way, there were still considerable remittances of savings from the very generous salaries (Macaulay saved a competence for life out of four years' salary as Law Member), the still more generous pensions, and the heavy military charges payable by India to England. Later again, this 'tribute' was increased by the normal payment of interest on British capital invested in India. That does not call for special comment, but I think the 'tribute' does, because it is almost the only instance I know which supports the Marxist view that pre-capitalist imperialism was designed, like the Roman and other ancient empires, to extract tribute from the subject peoples. (Incidentally, the Romans were not above investing in their empire—there was Seneca with his *usura per totam Britanniam exercita*.)

VI

THE REVOLT AGAINST COLONIALISM

[*The Listener*, 1 August 1957]

'COLONIALISM' is the commonest term of abuse nowadays throughout more than half the world. The Russians use it with deadly skill for their own purposes; it troubles the consciences of the most anglophile Americans; and even the Germans, of all people, look virtuously down their noses when colonies are mentioned and thank God they are not as other men are. More serious still, this word represents and inflames the feelings of millions of Africans and Asians—feelings which may have originated as outbursts of generous elation but are in danger of becoming plain race hatred. This hostility is not always proportionate to our deserts: for example, we appear to be more popular among the West Indians, against whose ancestors we committed the unforgivable sin of buying and holding them as slaves, than among the East Indians, whose ancestors we may more plausibly claim to have rescued from national disintegration. Nevertheless, with different degrees, the feeling is widespread indeed.

The chief forum where accusations of colonialism are bandied to and fro is the Trusteeship Council of the United Nations. For many years our representative on that council was Sir Alan Burns, who has been moved to write a book *In Defence of Colonies*.[1] I have no doubt that, like many other imperial civil servants, Sir Alan Burns can justly claim to have done his best for the peoples whom he has governed, and even to have loved them in his way. Such a man must itch to answer accusations which are too often ignorant or malicious. But I doubt whether his answer is the most effective which could be made. He has allowed himself to be nettled. Small blame to him: I should have been nettled in his place. But a *tu quoque* hardly ever persuades anybody. It may be true that there is more illiteracy in Central America than in the British West Indies, fewer roads proportionately in Liberia than in Ghana or Nigeria; that many of the independent countries who

---

[1] [London, 1957.]

criticize us are governed by oligarchies or even tyrannies; and that they criticize because they have their eye on territories which we possess and they want. But, even when we have shot off these often devastating retorts, whom have we persuaded in Africa or Asia?

We cannot claim a mandate to govern all the countries where the politicians, if left to themselves, take bribes, or let the economies run down, or even erect tyrannies where there ought to be democracies. The people of such countries would say to us, as the Jew said to Moses in the second chapter of Exodus, 'Who made thee a prince and a judge over us?' We must even be prepared for finding that they do not recognize the standards by which we judge ourselves and them—standards which we believe to be absolute: we are already being told that our virtues are out of date, or irrelevant, or not virtues at all—which is much worse than having to part with privileges, or to listen to wild accusations of which we can acquit ourselves. Already there are African writers like Mr. Richard Wright who imply that fascism is more up to date and more suitable to African conditions than liberal democracy, that there is no great harm in fascism so long as it is African fascism; one might say that President Nasser and President Sukarno are acting on this doctrine.

This ought not to surprise us: backward and despised peoples have often been tempted before to take short cuts to grandeur and esteem. It is not an accident that very few of the former Spanish colonies in America, with their large illiterate populations, have maintained for long a system which we should recognize as democracy. Even the leaders of the American Revolution, whom we now consider to have been admirable men engaged in an admirable cause, supported their power, or allowed it to be supported, by the odious tyranny of tar and feathers. These things are more than the accidents of nationalism, and it has yet to be proved that nationalism will, in the long run, do the world less harm than imperialism. But, though historians five hundred years hence (if there are any such people) may be able to look back with indulgent contempt upon the antics of that comic but dangerous little creature the nation-state, yet we cannot pretend that imperialism, holding on to colonies, is any remedy for nationalism here and now. On the contrary, it creates more nationalism than it destroys.

What answer are we to make to the revolt of three-quarters of the world against colonialism? Obviously we shall not say to the liberated peoples: 'Come and stamp on us for a hundred and fifty years; then we shall be all square, and you will feel better.' Very likely they would feel better, but we should feel worse; we are not called upon to cure other people's neuroses by contracting similar neuroses of our own; no people ever willingly did such a thing, and none ever will. Nor ought we to ignore the whole matter, saying to the rest of the world: 'Very well: if you don't wish to thank us for what we have done, we wash our hands of you.' It would be easy to shrink within the boundaries of western civilization, practising our own virtues, tracing our own history, reading our own masterpieces—teachers who have ceased to teach but are not willing to learn. I think I see, for example, among historians, the beginnings of such a movement of withdrawal. But those who choose to go about blindfold like this are likely to trip over something before long.

It would be better to face and consider the charges against our forefathers as a dispassionate historian might hope to consider them in the distant future. Many of these charges are absurd or fantastic, but they bear a disquieting likeness to reality, which can be dispelled only when they are faced. Some critics write as though Christopher Columbus and Vasco da Gama were the villains of the piece, as if nobody had a right to leave the shores of Europe until Lenin gave the word. Criticism of this sort is meaningless. But if we strike the balance between the good and the evil that Europeans have inflicted upon the rest of the world since 1492, we must acknowledge that there is a huge heap of evil in the scale— think of the slave trade in the past and the colour bar in the present—though we may hope that it is outweighed by an even larger heap of good, which was not always intentionally done for its own sake, but good nevertheless. Sometimes only an economist could strike this balance.

For example, we are charged with 'plundering' the other continents of their metals and their oils; but not every extraction of metals and oils from the soil of another country is harmful to the people of that country—it depends upon what they get out of it. We are charged with building up our own high standards of life at the expense of Asians and Africans whom we robbed and enslaved. Sometimes in the distant past our ancestors did rob and enslave them and some part of our capital did come from this source; but no economic historian would seriously argue that even the greater part of it did so: many countries with no colonies and no colonial trade have built up their capital by exploiting their own resources, and even the colonial powers have probably derived only a very small part of their capital from their dealings with their colonies. In fact they were building up the capital of their colonies even faster than their own.

We are also accused of interfering too much and at the same time of interfering too little with native institutions. Both these charges may be true. We may have interfered too much because, in the days when missionaries were the only anthropologists, nobody understood that to interfere with one institution—even a harmful institution—was to destroy the balance and the morale of the whole society; incidentally, the interference might have been very much the same if we had never exercised political domination over colonial peoples at all, but merely sold them goods or built them railways which they desired. At a later date we may have interfered too little because we were too frightened of the anthropologists, or because we could not spare enough expensive man-power to change things as much as we ought, or because certain established classes and institutions were likely to favour our rule, so that it suited us to preserve them. Some of these motives are better than others, but this does not answer the extremists who claim that we never had any right to interfere at all. But do they really believe that the rights of a people are so absolute, even to the detriment of the individuals who belong to it, that no other people ought to interfere in order to put down cannibalism, human sacrifice, and slavery? On the other hand, it would be hypocrisy for us to pretend that we conquered so many African and Asian peoples simply for the purpose of improving their morals. But we do not have to pretend this in order to argue that, on the whole, as things are, our interference brought about more good than evil.

Again (and this is to some degree the same accusation in another form) it is said that we did less for the social welfare of the subject peoples than they would have done for themselves in the same time. The answer to this accusation varies according to the times and places. It is true that we did little until lately for the social welfare of these peoples, partly because we were not doing much more even for the social welfare of our own people. But would they have done more for themselves at that time? Probably, in most of the countries which we ruled, there was a long period at the beginning when European paternalism did more than could have been done by the efforts of the people themselves, followed by a short period at the end when the people would have gone faster than their European rulers. In India since 1947 (and perhaps we are seeing the beginning of the same process in Ghana) political independence seems to have released a vast flood of beneficent energy which is developing the resources of the country and improving the standard of living much faster than we ever improved it. As Gerald of Wales said nearly eight hundred years ago: 'the hilarity of liberty makes men capable of honourable actions'. But if this is true in India and Ghana now, it probably would not have been true fifty years ago.

Lastly, we are charged with training the peoples of our empire too slowly for the business of governing themselves. It would be hypocrisy to pretend that we always wished or hoped that they could govern themselves at all. We may point to a few enlightened men like Sir Thomas Munro, who believed that India would one day govern herself; but he was an exception. Most members of the former Indian civil service sincerely believed that India would never be fit for this—and the sincerity of their belief was, from the Indian point of view, the greatest insult of all. Others disbelieved it because they did not wish it. Disraeli, for example, who is often quoted as a great tory imperialist, seems rather to have disliked the white dominions just because we did not rule them, they were beginning to rule themselves; India fascinated him because we really ruled it and, so far as he could see, always would rule it.

Yet the British government and the British public have acquired, by this time, a capacity, unusual among governments and governing classes, for taking a hint. They may have been slow to acquire it: we must not forget the long agony which Ireland had to go through before we could agree to let her go. But no other imperial power has any capacity at all for taking such hints. Many times in history one empire has yielded its dependencies to another empire, but I know of no earlier example in human history of an empire willingly or even half-willingly setting them free to govern themselves. The Habsburgs toyed with this problem in the nineteenth century, but they never dealt with it seriously. The Russians have hardly given up anything of their own free will to this day. We alone can claim to have taken the hint at all, however slowly and reluctantly.

All this, you may say, is a mere historian's exercise. I would agree that our relations with the liberated peoples are going to depend far more on what we can do for them in the future than on an impartial view of what we have done to them in the past. They need capital and experts much more than they need good textbooks of history. They may, of course, be unwilling to accept capital from any foreign source. If they insist on building up their own capital the hard way, like the Russians, then they will certainly have to resort to dictatorships—perhaps communist dictatorships—since no other form of government can so easily oblige the peasant and the worker to tighten his belt for the sake of the future. It is worth an effort to save them from this. But even if they ask for foreign capital, we shall only be able to help them if we have it to provide, if we are still capable of forming capital for export. They will also (and this is more certain) need foreign experts, above all technicians. Here, too, we can only hope to help and influence them if we can provide what they want, and provide it cheaply. Soviet Russia is probably going to have a great advantage over us, in that she will have more technicians to export, and can, if she pleases, force them to serve abroad for the same wages as native technicians, or compensate them from her own public money for the risks and the hardships of exile. We shall be able to compete only if we, too, train thousands of additional technicians, and even so I do not see how we are going to make them serve in Africa and Asia for African and Asian salaries.

It is certainly on these things that our friendship with the African and Asian peoples will principally depend in the future. But, though less important than future supplies of capital and experts, it is also worth while to try to come to an agreement with the African and Asian peoples on the rights and wrongs of our relations with them in the past. Good history cannot do so much service as money or science; but bad history can do almost as much harm as the most disastrous scientific discovery in the world. It will be the historians of Asia and Africa who will have the power to prejudice the next generations for or against us. If our claims are unrealistic, their claims are certain to be unrealistic too. If we can admit mistakes and even crimes where mistakes and crimes have been committed, there is some chance that they will admit, and will teach their posterity, that our connexion with their countries has not been an unmitigated misfortune. They may even be willing to accept as disinterested the advice we can offer them about the immense political difficulties which remain for them to face.

VII

A QUARTER OF A MILLENNIUM OF
ANGLO-SCOTTISH UNION

[The major part of an address delivered at the Franco-British Conference of Historians, Edinburgh, 20 July 1954. *History*, N.S. xxxix (1954), pp. 233–48]

Is Edinburgh a capital city? That is a difficult question; the answer is 'Yes and No'. What have been the relations of Scotland and England in the quarter of a millennium which has nearly passed since the Union of 1707—have they led separate lives, or a common life? What, even, is denoted by the name 'Great Britain'? This name has not been without overtones. When George III proclaimed in his accession speech that he 'gloried in the name of Briton (or Britain)' no doubt he did so with the generous intention of signifying that he made no difference in his mind between his English and his Scottish subjects. But I am sorry to say that most of his English subjects thought he would have expressed himself in better taste if he had said that he gloried in the name of Englishman (or England). The national song 'Rule, Britannia!' was written by a Scot; had he been an Englishman, it is not certain that he would have used the name 'Britannia' at all. Even to these conferences, which are so often loosely denominated as Anglo-French south of the border, we are careful in Scotland to give their proper title of Franco-British.

This question of the Union is a controversial one, particularly for an Englishman speaking in Scotland. But if an Englishman who has lived in Scotland for nearly a decade and enjoyed every minute of it cannot approach this question without bias, then I do not know who can.

The motives for the Union are immaterial to my present purpose: put very briefly—so briefly as to be almost misleading—the chief thing that the English obtained from it was the power to preclude, at the height of their struggle with France, the danger of a separate Scottish foreign policy, and the chief thing which the Scots obtained was access to the English colonies. (Why that was so necessary to them, I shall show later.) The Union of 1707 was essentially a union of parliaments. Forty-five Scottish members were added to the House of Commons, sixteen Scottish peers to the House of Lords. These numbers are small in proportion to those of the Englishmen who already sat in parliament; for example, there were already 513 English members of the House of Commons.

Neither the Scottish M.P.s nor the Scottish peers were thought entirely respectable in the eighteenth century. The peers were elected under the thumb of the British government; it promulgated a list of its candidates, and most of the members of this list were duly elected. Perhaps for this reason, the Scottish peers in the House of Lords were nearly as subservient to the British government as the English bishops—and one cannot say much more than that. The Sottish M.P.s were no better. They commanded little respect by reason of their method of election: there were few really popular constituencies in England, but none at all in Scotland before 1832. Their behaviour after election was no more edifying. They were a byword for jobbery and bargaining: when that great inventor the Earl of Dundonald wanted to get parliament to prolong a patent in 1786, he chiefly feared that the proposal would be laughed out of court as a 'Scottish job'. The Scottish M.P.s traded their votes in return for advantages for Scotland, for their particular constituencies, and for themselves. For Scotland they demanded tax exemptions; for their constituencies the encouragement of local industries; for themselves, their friends, and their constituents, posts in the customs, posts in the colonies, above all posts in the East India Company's service. These bargains might be made with other sectional interests.[1] Usually, however, they were made with the government, which had most to offer. In return for concessions of these kinds the Scottish M.P.s voted obediently under the discipline of the lord advocate, a Scottish law officer whose business generally included the management of the Scottish element in the House of Commons. There is a story, which may not be true but is a good story to tell, about the Scottish M.P. who complained that the government ought to have appointed a tall man as lord advocate; when the Scottish M.P.s did not know how they were expected to vote, they looked to see how the lord advocate voted, and if he was so

---

[1] For an example of such a bargain see my book, *War and Trade in the West Indies, 1739–1763* (Oxford, 1936), p. 510.

short that they could not watch him, they were bewildered. By methods such as these Scotland was managed as a constituency for the government by one politician after another—by the third Duke of Argyll, by Lord Bute and his brother, above all by Henry Dundas. In the middle of St. Andrew's Square, Edinburgh, stands a column rather like the Nelson column in Trafalgar Square, London. On the top of it stands Dundas; he had certainly deserved well of the British government; whether he had deserved so well of Scotland is another matter.

This kind of thing was not thought respectable. But why should not the Scots behave in this way? What did they care about the politics of the English political clans in which they were immersed? The original difference between whigs and tories had certainly meant as much to the Scots as it did to the English; but that cannot be said of the difference between one whig clan and another—between, for example, the Duke of Newcastle and the Duke of Bedford. Why should not the Scots sell their votes to these bosses in return for advantages of a more tangible and intelligible kind?

In time, the Scottish members of parliament became both less venal and less separate. They became less venal, as everybody else became less venal, in the middle and late nineteenth century when real constituencies and a real party system were created. They became less separate, for reasons which I shall give later. But until these processes were complete, or at least begun, Scottish politicians did not rank very high. Sir Gilbert Elliot, a Scot prominent in British politics, wrote in 1763 to his friend David Hume that although the post he held (the treasurership of the chamber) was a lucrative one, he might have hoped for a more active position but for the prejudice against Scots.[2] A few years earlier than this, George III had made the experiment of appointing a Scottish prime minister. Nearly all his English subjects cried out at once that this was quite intolerable, and nothing more of the kind was attempted for many years. In the nineteenth and twentieth centuries there have been Scottish prime ministers— the Earls of Aberdeen and Rosebery, Arthur Balfour, Sir Henry Campbell-Bannerman, Ramsay MacDonald—none of them great statesmen, but at least they proved the point that a Scot could

[2] G. F. S. Elliot, *The Border Elliots and the Family of Minto* (Edinburgh, 1897), p. 387.

reach the highest post of all. The Scots not only ascended the seat of power, but penetrated those English institutions which they must have considered the most irrational—the law and the church. Scotland has given to Great Britain a whole series of lord chancellors and lord chief justices, some of them great ones, and to the Church of England, in the last century, two archbishops of Canterbury, Archbishop Tait and Archbishop Lang.

But all this was at Westminster; in Edinburgh there was a political vacuum. Scotland had no parliament, no independent executive. The want of these things was not felt quite so keenly as one might have expected. The historians tell us that though the Scottish parliament was an old institution, it had never played, in the life of the nation, a part comparable to that of the English parliament in the life of England. Only in 1688 did it begin to acquire real authority and prestige; twenty years afterwards it was swept away, before it had had time to take root in the affections of the people. There was another legislature which, before and still more after 1707, occupied the limelight—this was the general assembly of the Kirk of Scotland. For all these reasons, the Scottish parliament was not much missed. As for the Scottish executive, it had already been, in a great degree, a mere agent of the English government, or at least of the king of Great Britain living in England, since the union of the crowns in 1603. It had not always been an obedient or an effective agent; often it had flinched before Scottish public opinion. But an agent it had been and little more. The disappearance of such an executive was not felt much more keenly than that of such a parliament.

Many Scots and some Englishmen consider that there should today be a Scottish parliament or at least a quasi-parliament after the model of Northern Ireland. This is a controversial question, into which I shall not enter. But I should point out that the Scottish executive has been, in many ways, partially restored to Scotland already. For example, the royal family: no king of Great Britain came near Scotland for more than a century after the Union. The first to do so was that exhibitionist George IV, who paid a wildly popular visit to Edinburgh in 1822. His niece, Queen Victoria, went further: she set the fashion, now so widespread among her English subjects, of taking her holidays in Scotland. She built herself a hideous palace at Balmoral in the Highlands, and spent the best part of every summer there, to the great annoyance of her British ministers, who often wished she had been at hand near London to transact business. The identification of the royal family with Scotland has never been so strong as it is in the present generation. Her present Majesty is half a Scot—her mother is a lady of a noble Scottish family. This is probably why the Scots now feel a proprietary interest in the royal family, such as they have not felt since the reign of Charles I. In another sense too the Scottish executive has been partly restored to Scotland. In the development of the 'Welfare State', it was found necessary to set up separate departments for the administration of British policies in Scotland—departments of health, education, agriculture, and so forth. From 1885 these departments were combined into a Scottish Office, under a secretary of state for Scotland. A few hundreds yards east of the centre of Edinburgh there stands a large building which is, in effect, the Scottish Whitehall.

Nevertheless, the political vacuum which was created in 1707 has only been partly filled up; and if a nation which has such a political vacuum cannot be in the full sense of the term a nation, nor its capital in the full sense a capital, then one must hold that Scotland is not a nation nor Edinburgh a capital. But when Scotland parted with her parliament and her separate executive, she kept other institutions which were meant to maintain, and have maintained, her nationality—the law, the church, the universities, and the whole educational system. If we consider the part played by churchmen, lawyers, professors and teachers, in the history of modern national movements, we must allow that a nation which succeeded in preserving the independence of these institutions has always been a nation in the most important senses of the word.

The Scots tried hard to preserve their independent legal system at the Union, and in the main they succeeded—not completely, for the English overreached them on certain important matters such as the appeal to the House of Lords, but these exceptions are not all-important. In substance, the law is administered from Edinburgh, not from London, and it is Scottish law. The original law of Scotland, widely different from that of England, has been only partly modified by later British decisions, or even by British acts of parliament, for it is the custom, when creating or changing British policies, to pass separate acts of parliament for Scotland which take account of the Scottish legal proprieties. An independent legal system means an independent legal profession. If you take your stand on the hill which leads from the New Town of Edinburgh to the Old about 10 o'clock in the morning, you will see gentlemen ascending it in the black clothes and the prosperous-looking hats which lawyers wear: these are the judges and the Faculty of Advocates who are going up the hill to administer the law of Scotland. They and their predecessors have played an important part as bearers and defenders of nationality. It is not for nothing that the great Sir Walter Scott was something in the law line.

What is true of the law is still more true of the church. This too was preserved, in substance, at the Union. Here again the English overreached the Scots on some important points, such as the system of patronage in the church and the right to suppress Episcopalian worship. But no British government has ever tried to destroy the Presbyterian character of the Church of Scotland. Indeed, it has not the means of doing so. In England the crown, which means the government, appoints the bishops, deans, and so forth; the moderator of the Church of Scotland is elected by his fellows. In the eighteenth century the power of promotion was even more important than that of appointment in the Church of England: a few of the bishoprics and deaneries were 'plums', the rest afforded only an indifferent livelihood. It was the hope of translation from a poorer to a richer benefice which kept the English clergy under the thumb of the government. In Scotland, on the other hand, the inequalities of income were fewer and the subservience much less. The government is, indeed, represented to this day in the assembly of the Church of Scotland by a lord high commissioner. In the past, some of his predecessors have interfered in the doings of the church, but I do not believe that he ever does so now. In fact, he has hardly more control over the proceedings which take place under his eye than a policeman, stationed at the door of a theatre, has over the dramatic performance within. Perhaps the most curious example of the Church of Scotland's independence is the fact that the queen, as head of both churches, is officially Episcopalian in England, Presbyterian in Scotland. Her conscience south of the border is an Episcopalian conscience, north of it a Presbyterian one. One might almost say that the constitution has condemned the sovereign of Great Britain to a condition of religious schizophrenia.

Even more than the law and the church, Scotland's system of education preserved her nationality and determined her national character. From 1616, the authorities in church and state were trying to set up a school in every parish of Scotland. This effort must have been nearly unique. Recent research[3] has perhaps shown that this system was not quite so good in practice as it looked: in some parishes no school was permanently established for more than a century after 1616; other parishes were so large that one school was not nearly enough for them; even when and where the schools existed, the admission was neither compulsory nor gratuitous (though special arrangements were often made for educating very poor children gratis); the schools were not always well inspected; and at one time more than half the children were outside them, attending the (usually inferior) private 'adventure' schools. But with all these reservations, the system, judged by its results, must have had merits, and it is easy to see what they were. It was more nearly universal, especially in the country districts, than anything else in the British Isles, perhaps in western Europe. England had many fine endowed schools, mostly in the towns, but never even attempted at that time to give a school to every parish. Many of the Scottish village schools gave secondary as well as primary education; Latin was taught, sometimes even the beginnings of Greek, and few parts of the world could boast, as could the north-east of Scotland, about 1830, that the average age of children leaving the parish schools was as high as fifteen. Moreover, probably the schoolmasters were unusually efficient, if only for the reason that in Scotland, a country poor in commercial opportunities, there were few other careers for educated men. Lastly (although there were exceptions, which I shall discuss later), the social classes mingled in these schools to an unusual degree, at any rate before the industrialization of the Lowlands. Thus the schools created a strong tradition of social equality.

In the universities it was the same story. England had two, Scotland had five (for the city of Aberdeen alone had two universities in the eighteenth century). The two English universities were very inactive, the five Scottish universities very active. The eighteenth century was the worst age of academic torpor at Ox-

[3] E.g. J. C. Jessop, *Education in Angus; an Historical Survey of Education up to the Act of 1872* (London, 1931).

ford and Cambridge; in the Scottish universities, at least after 1750, the pace quickened. Here, too, we must be careful not to exaggerate: the Scottish universities were not quite so good as they looked. At least in the faculties of arts, they were glorified secondary schools: the boys came up from the villages at fifteen. The professor of Greek at Edinburgh University had to teach some members of his class the alphabet. If such were his duties, he cannot have had much time or incentive for the highest kind of scholarship. Learning in Scotland was widespread, but did not often reach great heights, at any rate in classical and theological studies. Bishop Burnet remarked that the Presbyterian ministers had a great command of theology but within a narrow range. A century later Dr. Johnson said the same thing in a more un-friendly fashion when he declared that the state of learning in Scotland was like that of bread in a besieged city: everybody had a little but no man had a full meal. This may have been true of the studies that interested him most, classics and theology, at the time when he said it; it certainly was not true later, for the Scot-tish universities made great efforts after eminence in these studies in the nineteenth century, and are holding on to them like grim death in the twentieth.

Even in Dr. Johnson's own time, his remark was quite untrue of the technical and social sciences in which Scotland so much ex-celled. In 1716 a chair of chemistry was established in the Univer-sity of Edinburgh. Oxford had to wait many years for such a chair; Cambridge had one, but the professor by no means always lectured, and one holder of the chair obtained it, as he avowed, without ever having studied any chemistry beforehand. (It is only fair to add that he got it up afterwards and published some lec-tures which were useful, though perhaps not original.) In 1790 Edinburgh obtained the first university chair of agriculture in the English-speaking world, for all I know the first anywhere. The professors were just as useful outside their classroom as within it. For example, the great Professor Black corresponded with inven-tors of chemical processes all over Scotland, and in some parts of England.[4] The influence of such professors must have contributed much to the speedy industrial development of Scotland, and to the equally speedy transformation of Scottish agriculture from

[4] See the remarkably interesting book of Archibald and Nan L. Clow, *The Chemical Revolution* (London, 1952).

the worst in western Europe to one of the best. In medicine it was the same story: medical students came to Edinburgh, in the second half of the eighteenth century, from England and all her colonies, and Scottish doctors were in demand everywhere. In 1771 when Sylas Neville, a Norfolk squire, decided to become a doctor, he was advised to go to Edinburgh for his training: a friend told him that the doctors educated at the English universities were so ignorant of chemistry that 'it is no uncommon thing for Oxford and Cambridge Physicians to prescribe what will not mix'.[5] That could not have happened in Scotland, where Professor Black taught the medical students chemistry. The same story again in engineering: about the same time, it was said that nearly all the higher officers in the engineering corps were Scots, since they alone possessed the necessary mathematics. I need not speak of the eminence of Scotland in all the social sciences.[6] They may almost be said to have invented political economy; this, at least, was the opinion of the novelist Peacock, whose political economists are almost all Scots (and figures of fun).

There were good reasons why the Scottish universities should flourish at this time. One was a mere technical matter of university organization. In the first half of the eighteenth century the Scottish universities changed from the 'Regent' system to the professorial system. A 'Regent' took charge of a whole age group—all the boys entering the university in a given year—through the whole curriculum from beginning to end; when his charges took their degrees, he went back to the beginning with a new generation.[7] A professor, necessarily, specialized in one subject and lectured to his class on it alone. Perhaps the systematic—at times, the rather drearily systematic—character of Scottish thought is explained by the fact that in Scotland education was purveyed by professors lecturing to classes, not by tutors listening to themes. Possibly, even, the learned Scots' slightly absurd habit, satirized by Peacock, of beginning their lucubrations on every subject with the words 'in the infancy of society' can be traced

---

[5] *The Diary of Sylas Neville, 1767–1788*, ed. B. Cozens-Hardy (Oxford, 1950), p. 127.

[6] See Gladys Bryson, *Man and Society: the Scottish Inquiry of the Eighteenth Century* (Princeton, 1945).

[7] For a description of this system see the delightful book by my colleague Professor W. Croft Dickinson, *Two Students at St. Andrews, 1711–1716* (Edinburgh, 1952).

to the same cause; naturally, the first lecture of the professorial course would begin with the infancy of society.

The English universities had professors too, but they were usually appointed for reasons of political patronage, and they often left their duties unperformed. King George III believed that Regius professors ought to be appointed for their learning alone, and actually to lecture; but this was one of his amiable eccentricities, and perhaps he derived it from his Scottish friend Lord Bute, who came from a country where the professors did lecture. At Oxford and Cambridge, as a general rule, those students who received any education at all did so by 'reading with their tutors', which is something like the 'Regent' system over again. It is hardly surprising that even Englishmen frequented the Scottish universities: not only the dissenters, who would not, in any case, have been admitted to the Anglican universities, but some eminent members of the English governing class—two future prime ministers, Lord Palmerston and Lord John Russell, received a part, perhaps the best part, of their education at the University of Edinburgh, and a third, Lord Melbourne, at the University of Glasgow.

But it was something more than a mere trick of organization which caused the Scottish universities to flourish. They flourished, above all, because they shared in the great development of Scottish national culture, in the golden age of Scotland. Where did this golden age come from? What stimulated it? One might naturally suggest that the Union itself was the cause: it preceded the beginning of the golden age by forty or fifty years—*post hoc ergo propter hoc*. Though natural, this explanation is probably superficial. No doubt contact with English culture had some effects, not all of them fortunate (for example, the deplorable vogue of Pope's style among certain Scottish poets). But some of the best things could not have come from England, and indeed we know where they did come from. For example, the flourishing state of the Edinburgh medical school could not have derived from any English stimulus, and we know that it did derive from the very close relations which the Scottish universities had long had with those of Holland, especially with the great University of Leyden. Likewise, the writers of the Scottish Enlightenment avowedly drew more of their ideas from the French *philosophes* than from any political thinkers in England. Perhaps, however, it is even a mistake to think at all in terms of stimulus from outside. Probably the golden age would have come of itself in Scotland, as theological Calvinism lost its hold on the Scottish people, and the great mental and moral energies which it generated were transferred to secular studies and secular interests.

Whatever the cause, it was a golden age. It has been said, and I think truly, that Adam Smith and Hume were the two most influential writers of their day in the English language. On opposite walls of the Senate Hall of the University of Edinburgh are two portraits: one of Principal Robertson, who was not the greatest British historian of his time, but only because he was a contemporary of Edward Gibbon; the other of Adam Ferguson, whom many modern sociologists revere as the founder of their science. (Incidentally, the painter of these portraits was incontestably the greatest British portrait-painter of his generation: they are early works of Sir Henry Raeburn, an Edinburgh Scot.)

In time, 1830 or thereabouts, the golden age faded. Just as some have been tempted to ascribe its beginning to the Union, others have been tempted to claim that the Union made possible its decline; for, it has been argued, the absence of political barriers made it possible for the man of letters and the publishers (London is full to this day of publishers with Scottish names) to leave Scotland in order to be nearer the market for literary talent. I think this argument is probably untrue: it was rather the absence of language barriers that allowed this drift to London to take place. There has been, I believe, a comparable drift of talent from Brussels and Geneva to Paris in the last two centuries, yet neither Brussels nor Geneva has been under French political rule for more than a few years at a time.

Even after the golden age of literature and science had faded, and politics and religion had resumed their sway in Scotland, the educational system left behind a yet more important achievement: the powerful, perhaps over-powerful, development of the Scottish middle class. We cannot understand modern Scottish history without remembering that Scotland has been a country, poor in natural resources, with an educational system several sizes too large for it. Intense competition resulted in all the black-coated professions, especially in the church. The Scots use the phrase 'a stickit minister', which means, among other things, a candidate for the ministry, fully qualified by his education, who cannot obtain a cure of souls. Since all the professions were over-crowded in Scotland, the middle-class Scots had to leave home. The Union did not create this emigration, but merely controlled its direction. If these Scots could not have been customs officers in Jamaica, or doctors in London, or district magistrates in British India, they would have become admirals in Russia. In fact, some of them did so. The most spectacular event of the years 1769–70 was the voyage of the Russian Baltic fleet through the Sound, the English Channel, and the Straits of Gibraltar all the way to the Levant, where it met and destroyed a Turkish fleet at the battle of Cheshmé.[8] Many observers believed that the Russians would never have got anywhere near Cheshmé but for Admiral Greig and Captain Elphinston, two Scots in the empress's service.

Above all, the Scots went to the English colonies. Many of them were there even before 1707, for servants were almost the only commodity that Scotland was allowed to export straight to America in the seventeenth century. After the Union they flooded in. The English colonists did not much like this invasion. They looked upon the Scots, like the Jews or the Quakers, as a kind of epidemic—if you had one Scot, the next time you looked there were forty Scots, and soon after that four hundred. One Scot drew many others after him. The English did not understand the profound sociological reason for this—namely, the importance of the family in Scotland. The Scots have always thought in terms of family, far more than the English. If you ask an Englishman about a stranger, 'Who is he?', the Englishman will think you mean, 'What post does he hold?' If you ask a Scot the same question, he will think you mean, 'Of what family is he—a McLeod of Dunvegan or a McLeod of Raasay?' The Scots very often emigrated by families, and where they did not, as soon as a young Scot was firmly established, or even sooner than that, he sent for his brothers, his cousins, his friends, and his fellow townsmen.

Even England itself is full of Scots. If the telephone directories are any guide, there are not many fewer people with the names of Macdonald and Mackenzie living in London than in Edinburgh. I have heard one Oxford don say to another, 'If you were a Scotsman you would have some chance of becoming a head of

[8] For this episode see M. S. Anderson, 'Great Britain and the Russian Fleet, 1769–1770', *The Slavonic and East European Review*, xxxi (1952–3), pp. 148–63.

a college'; and in my time there have been four successive vice-chancellors of Oxford bearing the names of Lindsay, Gordon, Ross, and Livingstone—all excellent Scottish names. There is some traffic the other way: the chair of history which I occupy in the University of Edinburgh has never yet been held by a Scot.[9] But the trickle of Englishmen to Scotland does not compare with the flood of Scots to England. Recently, however, the Scots may have been losing some of the educational advantage which has made this emigration possible. Their own educational system has not retrograded; but that of England, since the Education Act of 1902, has improved out of all recognition.

There has been another emigration, perhaps temporary or seasonal, but none the less important. Soon after the Union the Scottish aristocracy and some of the lairds began to send their sons to English schools and universities for their education: William Murray, the future Lord Chief Justice Mansfield, was brought up in England some time before 1730. In 1799 Lord Cornwallis proposed to the Duke of Portland, then home secretary, to establish a second university in Ireland; the duke rejected this advice,

more especially in the present circumstance of the impending Union, which no means perhaps are so well calculated to perfect and to render us indissolubly one nation, as inducements to the better orders of the people of that kingdom to receive a part of their education either at the Schools or Universities of this country.[10]

No doubt he was thinking of this custom which had long prevailed among the Scots.

There were many reasons for this practice. For one thing, many members of the Scottish aristocracy were Episcopalians, who would naturally wish to send their sons to a kingdom where the education was Episcopalian. Even the Presbyterian aristocrats probably did not much relish the middle-class theocracy of their own country. Above all, they wished to prepare their sons to play a part in the British governing class.

Here the question of accent was important. The Scottish accent may be more pleasing, but the English was more profitable.

---

[9] This statement is fortunately no longer true at the date of publication [1954].

[10] *Memoirs and Correspondence of Viscount Castlereagh*, ed. Charles Vane, Marquess of Londonderry (12 vols., London, 1848–53), ii. 382.

Those who wished to plead before London juries, or to harangue a House of Commons consisting mainly of English squires, would be well advised to do so in an English accent. Here the Scots were in a dilemma: Henry Dundas and his contemporary Alexander Wedderburn (the future Lord Chancellor Loughborough) chose different horns of it: Dundas, to the end of his days, spoke with a northern burr in order to prove that he was a plain blunt Scot, whereas Wedderburn transformed his accent into an English one. Neither of these things impressed the English, who continued to think Dundas a brutal, cynical boor and Wedderburn a rogue. Perhaps the great Lord Mansfield's otherwise inexplicable reputation for falsity can be accounted for by the fact that he had a synthetic voice. (We know that he had one: according to Lord Shelburne he 'always spoke in a feigned voice like Leoni the Jew singer'.[11]) Most Scots chose, like Mansfield and Wedderburn, to change their accents, and many came to England with no other purpose in view. Francis Horner wrote to his father, 'With respect to one great object for which you were at the expense and trouble of placing me here, I think I am beginning to *pronounce* some *words* as Englishmen do, and just to *feel* the difference between the *rhythm* of their conversation and mine.' Nearly a year later he wrote more optimistically, 'I am sensible that I have by no means made myself master of all the variety of the English accents: I am now and then detected in a Scottish inflexion, but hardly ever without previously detecting myself. This circumstance will inform you of the degree of advance I have made.'[12] But Horner, who had already attended the University of Edinburgh before he went to England, started too late, and probably this is the reason why he had such difficulty. The best way to get the accent was to go to school in England from ten years old, or thereabouts; and many people do it to this day. Nearly all the nobility and gentry of Scotland, most of the rich Edinburgh lawyers, and many Scottish businessmen send their sons to an English public school and then to Oxford or Cambridge. The Scottish universities are impoverished by this practice; in consequence of it, the University of Edinburgh is not a

[11] Lord E. Fitzmaurice, *Life of William, Earl of Shelburne* (2nd ed., 2 vols., London, 1912), i. 67.
[12] *Memoirs and Correspondence of Francis Horner*, ed. Leonard Horner (2 vols., London, 1843, i. 7, 17.

complete cross-section of Scottish society. But at least it promotes the fusion of the British governing class, and thereby holds Great Britain together.

Britain has not been held together by her governing class alone, but by the emigration at all levels, and, above all, by a real community of interests. It is instructive to contrast the behaviour of Scotland in the nineteenth century with that of Ireland. There was an Irish national revolt against Great Britain, but no Scottish national revolt against England. Why was this?

For one thing, the English never treated the Scots nearly so badly as they treated the Irish. They made little attempt to suppress Scottish nationality. They did, indeed, try, about 1750, to destroy the emblems and the sentiment of nationality in the Highlands; but in this they were fervently assisted by the Lowland Scots, who had even more than the British government to gain by taming the Highlands. The attempts to suppress the 'Irish' language, which have pushed back the linguistic frontier to the north and west, began in the seventeenth century if not sooner than that, and were the work of Scots rather than Englishmen. (Incidentally, Scottish nationalism is weakened to this day by the absence of a linguistic shibboleth: the linguistic frontier lies within Scotland, not between Scotland and England, and in this way Scotland bears the same kind of relation to England that Belgium does to France.)

Not only did the English make little attempt to keep Scotland under, but the two countries had a real community of interests, as Great Britain and Ireland had not. England and Scotland both became industrial countries; Ireland never did. Consequently, the Scots and the English shared political problems, especially the problem of parliamentary and local government reform, which was indeed more necessary in Scotland than in England. Scottish radicals allied with English to achieve these reforms together. This alliance was strengthened by an additional common grievance. Even before, and still more after, the great disruption of the Church of Scotland in 1843, many Scots were nonconformists in religion, and wished to attack the privileged position of the Establishment. Some millions of Englishmen were in exactly the same position, and it was nonconformity, as well as political radicalism, in the two countries, that created the motive power for the British liberal party down to 1918. Perhaps the social problems which they shared did even more to keep the two countries together than the political problems. The Emperor Francis Joseph of Austria, in one phase of his long career, tried to distract his subjects from their excessive preoccupation with nationality by offering them social questions upon which they could divide on different lines. Nobody ever tried to do that in Great Britain, but the result was exactly as if somebody had tried. When the whole town of Paisley was out of work and on the dole, it worried the British prime minister and the British public exactly as much as if the same thing had happened in Huddersfield or Blackburn. Scotland and England shared not merely social problems, but socialism: there were Scottish Chartists, and the labour party may be said to have been started in Scotland by Keir Hardie. In Scotland as in Wales, perhaps the most serious obstacle to separatism today is the feeling of the Scottish and Welsh trade unionists that they would be better advised to keep close to the English trade unions in order to advance their interests in common.

There is no logical reason why these things should be so. The fact that the social problems of Holland are very much the same as those of Belgium does not make strongly for a union of the two countries. In fact, however, the common problems which Scotland and England have shared have been a bond for the last century or more, and it is safe to prophesy that so long as common interests are thought to outweigh separate interests, the Union of 1707 will survive in something like its present form.

VIII

GEORGE III AND THE POLITICIANS[1]

[*Transactions* of the Royal Historical Society, 5th series, i (1951), pp. 127–51]

G EORGE III's opinions on politics and the constitution have usually been contrasted with those of some people called 'the whigs'. The contrast and even the terminology are no mere invention of historians. Quite early in the reign, politicians were already reviving the terms 'whig' and 'tory', and using them no longer, as in 1760, to denote certain groups of men who called themselves whigs and tories, but to indicate differences of opinion between people hitherto called whigs, about the constitutional rights of the crown and their proper exercise. Whigs called other whigs by the name of tories, and 'pure' whiggism was increasingly identified with a kind of anti-monarchism which may or may not have been a whig principle in earlier times but was not often expressed openly in 1760.[2] This identification had proceeded pretty far by 1780, the date of Dunning's famous resolution; and two years later, when George III made Shelburne his prime minister without consulting the cabinet, Fitzpatrick thought it natural to say, 'If it is suffered, there is certainly a total end of whig principles.'[3] It was Charles Fox, above all, who

---

[1] I should like to thank my friend and colleague, Dr. D. B. Horn, for his valuable advice on the preparation of this paper.

[2] It is not easy to ascertain the earliest occasion upon which a whig called another whig a tory for pursuing a tory policy; for the whig dukes—Newcastle and Devonshire—were also obsessed by the belief that George III and Bute were re-admitting to power the survivors of the old tory party, and the two accusations got mixed up. The earliest instance I can find in George III's reign is a remark made by Henry Fox to Horace Walpole in the spring of 1762: 'The Duke of Devonshire says it is a Tory measure to abandon the Continent. For my part', Fox added significantly, 'I do not know who are Whigs' (Horace Walpole, *Memoirs of the Reign of King George III*, ed. G. F. Russell Barker, 4 vols., London, 1894, i. 123). The elder Pitt was also among the earliest whig politicians to stigmatize a fellow whig as a tory. In August 1763, during one of his ostentatiously whig moods, he called the administration of his brother-in-law George Grenville a 'tory administration' (*Grenville Papers*, ed. W. J. Smith, 4 vols., London, 1852–3, ii. 199).

[3] Fitzpatrick to Ossory, 3 July 1782, printed by Lord John Russell in *Memorials and Correspondence of Charles James Fox* (4 vols., London, 1853–7), i. 459.

treated this anti-monarchism as the main principle of the British constitution, and even as a general maxim of politics by which the conduct, for example, of French revolutionary politicians might be tried.[4] Later developments of this classical whig theory, in which history and historians played such an important part (for the politicians themselves refreshed their zeal by historical researches into the anti-monarchist movements of the past), are so well known that there is no need to illustrate them here.

Yet it is misleading, in some respects, to speak of a conflict between George III and the 'whigs' as such. Although George III was a conservative, he was not a tory; his offence against the whigs was only that of thinking that there was no important difference between them and the tories—offence enough, in the eyes of Devonshire and Newcastle, who must have considered it almost as bad as thinking there was no important difference between virtue and vice. If George III's enemies were whigs, so were almost all his allies until 1807. Moreover, his allies gave him just as much trouble as his enemies, or more: the claims of the 'pure' whigs, like Rockingham, who developed a whig theory and tried to monopolize the title of whig, were no more inconvenient, in practice, than those of the 'impure' whigs like Grenville and Bedford. In view of all this, George III and Bute must be considered as striving against the practices of a political class rather than the doctrines of a political party; against the politicians, rather than the whigs.

But was there any conflict at all? It has lately been suggested that George III merely 'carried on, to the best of his more than limited ability, the system of government which he had inherited from his predecessors'.[5] This is quite true, in one sense: George III did not innovate. In another sense, I think it less true: George III did try to restore something which possibly ought to have existed, but did not exist, when he came to the throne. He did what George II ought to have done, rather than what George II had done.

If George III only did what George II had done, why did the politicians suddenly make a fuss about it? An answer has been

---

[4] Fox's letters of 3 Sept. and 12 Oct. 1792 to Holland (ibid. ii. 368–9, 373) show his naïve attempts to apply British constitutional principles to French politics.

[5] *Letters from George III to Lord Bute, 1756–1766*, ed. Romney Sedgwick (London, 1939), p. xlii.

offered to this question: it has been suggested that the normal resource of an eighteenth-century Opposition was to cultivate the heir-apparent; that, since there was no adult heir-apparent between 1760 and 1782, the Opposition, still determined to oppose, had to find some other justification and invented, by a 'literary afterthought', what came to be known as the whig theories of constitutional government. Now it is very true that Oppositions had, in the past, relied upon the heir-apparent, and that they continued, with astonishing inconsistency, to do so as late as 1812 or even later, at the same time that they were consciously trying to limit the king on the throne in the exercise of his powers. Yet I do not think this theory accounts for all the facts, or even for the most important ones.[6] Some of the stratagems of the 1760's had certainly been invented earlier. The claims and prejudices which opposed George III may have been irrational but were genuinely, even subconsciously, felt—they have not at all the air of 'literary afterthoughts'; and they were not confined to the Opposition, who might have relied on the reversionary resource. George II and George III suffered, as I have said, not only from their opponents, but even more from their own employees: from Grenville's idea of the rights of a prime minister as much as from Devonshire's idea of the rights of the nobility; in short, from nearly all politicians.[7]

Perhaps it would be unwise to lay too much stress upon the general denunciations of the political class, with which George III's early letters to Bute abound,[8] for neither of them knew anything of politics at first hand, and both of them were inclined to cant. In their innocence they believed that it was their task to reform the public and private morals of the politicians,[9] and to inaugurate a new world in which a just king and minister would reward merit alone—as Bute gave Dr. Johnson a pension without any political stipulations—instead of bribing the venal and the factious.[10] These day-dreams did not long survive the light of ex-

---

[6] [See the author's review of *Letters from George III to Lord Bute* in *English Historical Review*, lv (1940), pp. 475–9.]

[7] The elder Pitt, down to 1769, is the most conspicuous exception; and even he made difficulties, though of a different kind.

[8] For example, *Letters from George III to Lord Bute*, pp. 6, 19, 45–46.

[9] See George III's letter to Bute, Nov. 1762, ibid., p. 166.

[10] There is an amusing example of the difference between the king's and the politicians' ideas of the public service in George III's memorandum printed by

perience. Bute told his friend Baron Mure, 'within a twelve-month I have seen so much, that I blush at my former credulity, and now know that the school of politicks and the possession of power is neither the school of friendship nor the earnest of affection'.[11] George III found himself obliged 'to call in bad men to govern bad men'. From that day he was living in the real world, the world of second best. It was some time before he was willingly subdued to the material in which he worked;[12] and it is worth remembering that George III, whom the later whigs considered as the arch-corrupter, set out with a sincere distaste for the corruption which he believed to be the gravest fault of the politicians as a class.

Even in his later years he tried, perhaps harder than his adversaries, to limit the infection of public life by political patronage. As a sovereign, and as the product of a largely German upbringing, he valued professional ability, professional probity, and professional experience above the qualities which passed for political qualities in the England of his day. George II too had denounced the amateurishness of noblemen and demagogues, and tried to save the army, at least, from political jobs.[13] George III might dislike and despise his grandfather, but took after him in this respect. He too favoured the professional element in the public service and in politics. In the days of his personal rule he showed a marked preference for advancing ex-ambassadors to be secretaries of state.[14] He had a concern for the organization of the army as a

Sir John Fortescue as no. 139 in his edition of the *Correspondence of King George III* (6 vols., London, 1927–8). The king objected to making the disreputable Weymouth lord-lieutenant of Ireland—a post which particularly required private virtues in its holder, as he represented the king's person. Grenville replied, in effect, that he should support any nominee of his colleague Bedford's for this post, whatever his character might be. The king thought this a very strange idea; the minister, no doubt, was equally surprised at the king's.

[11] *Selections from the Family Papers preserved at Caldwell* (2 parts in 3 vols., Maitland Club, Glasgow, 1854), part ii, vol. i, p. 242.

[12] See his letter to Bute, c. Mar. 1763, *Letters from George III to Lord Bute*, p. 198.

[13] See, for example, his remarks to Fox about Pitt and Sir Thomas Robinson, reported by Horace Walpole in *Memoirs of the Reign of King George II* (3 vols., London, 1846), ii. 267.

[14] Rochford, Stormont, and Grantham had all been ambassadors, and George III often thought of making Sir Joseph Yorke a secretary of state. This was not altogether a new thing: Stanhope, Carteret, Harrington, and Chesterfield had all had diplomatic experience. Presumably this was due, in part, to the earlier Hanoverians' preference for professional efficiency and, still more, to the

professional service, with promotion according to seniority and merit undisturbed by political or family favouritism.[15] He would probably have liked to keep politics out of the army altogether, though he reconciled his conscience to a casuistry by which officers who voted against the ministry in the House of Commons could be punished without actually depriving them of their commissions.[16] He seems to have restricted the interference of politics with the higher appointments of the church[17] and the universities; he stipulated that Regius professors should be appointed for their learning alone, and that they should actually lecture.[18] Presumably, in the eyes of a Newcastle or a Grenville, political *naïveté* could go no further than this.

He even favoured the professional element in politics itself. The 'man of business'—the comparatively humble and assiduous politician who climbed the ladder of the 'efficient' offices, step by step, stood close to the crown in politics; so close, indeed, as to be called a 'King's Friend'. Here, too, George III sometimes tried to create something like an organized service with promotion by merit.[19] He once complained to North, in a fit of bad temper against the coalition ministry, of 'every man brought forward into offices of business being either declaimers or owing their situation to such persons, instead of being regularly bred as in

fact that a diplomatic career was the only place where aristocrats—especially members of the House of Lords—could and would serve a paid apprenticeship in public business.

[15] See, for example, his correspondence with North, Barrington, and Jenkinson (*Correspondence of George III*, nos. 1010, 1702, 1773, 2096, 2110, 2130, 2144, 2146, 2157, 2164, &c.).

[16] Many soldier-M.P.s had regiments and governorships of forts. George III told North, 16 Feb. 1773, 'the taking away regiments I can never think adviseable but Governments are a very fair prey' (ibid., no. 1201).

[17] Mansfield advised George III to take the counsel of a bishop on church preferments so as to keep his ministers out of the business (George III to Bute, 7 Apr. 1763, *Letters from George III to Lord Bute*, p. 212). George III did not altogether take this advice; but he did, in 1765, join the Archbishop of Canterbury with Newcastle in a mandate to recommend church preferments, instead of leaving it to Newcastle alone, like George II. More than once he announced his intentions to North, or told him to consult the archbishop, before North can have tendered any advice (*Correspondence of George III*, nos. 1550, 1923, 1981).

[18] Ibid., nos. 928, 1117.

[19] As when he declined to promote a silent relation of Weymouth's, probably to the Board of Trade, because 'his not taking an active part in debates would have hurt those that stand forward in the House of Commons' (*Correspondence of George III*, no. 678). Yet he had to acquiesce, a few years later, in the promotion of the even more silent Mr. Gibbon to that board, as part of a political job.

other countries in the offices where they became secre-taries'.[20]

He had also to deal with the members of certain other professions—sailors, soldiers, and, above all, lawyers—who often entered the House of Commons and even the ministry with a view to professional advancement. These men were not in politics for politics' sake, but for the highest rewards of their professions, which happened to be annexed to politics. They would, perhaps, have preferred to receive those rewards by merit or seniority, and to hold them during professional, not political, good behaviour.[21] But since that could not be, it was natural for them to attach themselves to the king, who entertained somewhat similar ideas, and represented, above all, the element of continuity in politics. They stood closer than their colleagues to the king; and it was no accident that Lord Chancellors Northington, Thurlow, and Eldon were all, in a peculiar sense, 'King's Friends'—that the lord chancellor was often employed to negotiate the formation of ministries—that he sometimes tried to emphasize the professional and non-political character of his office by dissociating himself from a tottering ministry.[22] In the eyes of the politicians, these men were rats; in those of George III, they were rather public servants who had the misfortune of being politicians. He does not seem to have shared the *n'importe-quisme* of the English, who saw nothing strange in calling a scatter-brained, horsy nobleman of tender years and untried capacity to the office of first lord of the Treasury or lord lieutenant of Ireland and replacing him, after a year or two, by another of the same kind.[23]

[20] Ibid., no. 4472.

[21] Charles Yorke seems to be a good example of this, among the lawyers; it is evident that, for him, his professional rivalry with Pratt was the one reality in politics. Perhaps Conway's unsatisfactoriness as a politician can be explained partly by saying that he was not interested in politics, but in military preferment. Charles Yorke's brother Joseph, though a member of parliament, was primarily interested in his diplomatic career; indeed, since diplomacy (except a few great posts like the Paris embassy) was beginning to be considered outside politics, a politician like Hans Stanley, who wanted a quiet life and continuous employment, would flee to it (*Grenville Papers*, iii. 284).

[22] Northington did this in 1765 and 1766, Thurlow in 1781–2. Probably Bathurst, who acted similarly in 1778, believed that the ministry was going to fall. Conway, in 1782–3, allowed himself to be carried over from ministry to ministry, and claimed to choose whether he should be treated as a military expert or a cabinet minister (Horace Walpole, *Last Journals*, ed. A. F. Steuart, 2 vols., London, 1910, ii. 451, 510).

[23] Even the noble amateurs themselves sometimes thought their appointments

He did not like the dissipation of experience which these constant changes involved.[24] I suspect that he would have been happier if politics had been an organized profession.

If George III had only complained of the politicians' amateurishness, self-seeking, and personal immorality, he would have been saying no more than many business and professional men have said from his time to ours. But there was a more precise cause of quarrel: a serious difference, of practice rather than opinion, about the exercise of the king's constitutional prerogative. It is easy to state this difference wrongly by stating it too distinctly; indeed, so indistinct is it, that some have doubted whether it existed at all. In my opinion it did exist, and I shall try to state it as carefully as I can.

The so-called 'Revolution Settlement', as is well known, contained no positive statement of the king's prerogative or functions. There was a negative statement—the Declaration of Rights, which proscribed the use of particular prerogatives. This had been preceded in Charles II's reign, and was followed in those of William III and Anne, by other invasions of the crown's freedom of action—some wholly successful, such as the Mutiny Act and the new financial procedures; others wholly or partly abortive, such as the impeachment of William III's advisers on foreign policy and certain parts of the Act of Settlement.

It was possible to believe that all these things added up to something still more significant—to the principle that in a serious conflict with the House of Commons, the king must ultimately give way. Charles Fox exaggerated this idea when he asked, 'Had not a majority of the House of Commons, almost from time immemorial, governed this country?'[25] The same opinion was held in a more moderate form by Lord North, who, though he was George III's minister, was above all a House of Commons man:[26]

rather strange: see the second Earl of Northington's letter to Fox, 17 Nov. 1783, in *Memorials and Correspondence of Charles James Fox*, ii. 183.

[24] See his letter to Northington, 9 Jan. 1766 (*Correspondence of George III*, no. 179), and his conversation with General Irwin, reported in *Grenville Papers*, iv. 184.

[25] *Parliamentary History*, xxiv. 597 (18 Feb. 1784).

[26] North came to believe that he had been in no sense the king's 'tool', but a House of Commons man who had entered into partnership or service with the king. 'I was not, when I was honoured with office a Minister of Chance, or a Creature of whom Parliament had not experience: I was found among you when I was so honoured; I had been long known to you. In consequence, I obtained

Your Majesty is well apprized that, in this country, the Prince on the Throne cannot, with prudence, oppose the deliberate resolution of the House of Commons: Your Royal Predecessors (particularly King William the Third and his late Majesty) were obliged to yield to it much against their wish in more instances than one. They consented to changes in their Ministry which they disapproved because they found it necessary to sacrifice their private wishes, and even their opinions to the preservation of public order, and the prevention of those terrible mischiefs which are the natural consequences of the clashing of two branches of the Sovereign Power in the State. The concessions they made were never deemed dishonourable, but were considered as marks of their wisdom, and of their parental affection for their people.[27]

George III neither expressly admitted nor rejected this doctrine. It was only an opinion, though perhaps a very widely held one. The visible frontier of the king's political powers was not defined by this vague opinion; it was constituted by the Declaration of Rights and the other concrete precedents. It had moved little since 1714. Within this visible frontier, the job of king was what the holder made it.

George III's three predecessors had made less of it than they could have done. Historians usually lay stress on the early Hanoverian kings' ignorance of England and the English tongue. I suspect that this is a mistake of emphasis; for George I, who suffered most from these disabilities, seems to have been the most powerful of the three because he had the strongest personality. It was Anne and, above all, George II who let the powers slip out of their hands into those of their politicians.

With Anne we are not concerned; but George II was the immediate predecessor of George III and represented everything that George III despised and eschewed.[28] If the Princess of Wales

---

your support; when that support was withdrawn, I ceased to be a Minister: I was the Creature of Parliament in my rise; when I fell, I was its victim' (North's speech on parliamentary reform, 7 May 1783, printed in C. Wyvill, *Political Papers*, 6 vols., York, 1794–1802, ii. 664). This was a gross oversimplification; but there was in it an element of truth, which explains why North was always so much more sensitive than George III to defeats in the House of Commons. See their correspondence, in *Correspondence of George III*, nos. 1405–6, 2181–2, 2292, 2295, 2322, 2535–6, 2986–7, 2991, 3568.

[27] North to George III, 18 Mar. 1782, ibid., no. 3566.

[28] There are some scornful references to him in *Letters from George III to Lord Bute* (especially pp. 26, 28, 37).

really told her son to 'be a king'—and there is no reason why she should not—it is easy to conceive her meaning: George II had not 'been a king', at any rate since the death of his strong-minded wife in 1737. He spoke English; and he had an insatiable appetite for business.[29] In Hervey's pages he is represented as stamping his foot, shouting 'Puppy' or 'Scoundrel', and even imagining that the decisions presented to him were really his own. That they were not; he had neither the wit to devise them nor the force of mind to insist upon them against opposition. After the death of Queen Caroline he fell into the hands of politicians—even quite minor ones, whom a strong and resourceful man could have routed. When he tried to take his decisions, the politicians combined to frustrate him and—to use the words of Carteret, one of the victims of his hesitation—the king 'had not courage or activity or sufficient knowledge of the country or perhaps of mankind' to get his own way.[30] His peevishness tried his ministers' temper; but even Newcastle, whose weak nerves could not endure the displeasure of Alderman Beckford or Mr. Hugh Valence Jones, should have known that there was no need to be afraid of his sovereign. As Hardwicke reminded him: 'Your Grace owns that he does what you wish and propose, both as to English affairs and foreign affairs. That takes in the whole circle of real business.' The king's reserve or ill humour therefore mattered little; and if he assumed the whole merit of measures which Newcastle had suggested to him, 'For God's sake, my dear Lord, let him do so, and flatter him in it.'[31]

---

[29] James, second Earl Waldegrave, *Memoirs from 1754 to 1758* (London, 1821), pp. 4–7.

[30] Conversation with Carteret, reported many years later by Shelburne (Lord E. Fitzmaurice, *Life of William, Earl of Shelburne*, 2nd ed., 2 vols., London, 1912, i. 37). Naturally there were some questions upon which it was impossible for anybody to dictate even to George II—for instance, the choice of his A.D.C.s or his Bedchamber (P. C. Yorke, *Life and Correspondence of Philip Yorke, Earl of Hardwicke*, 3 vols., Cambridge, 1913, ii. 172, 224–5). But Charles Fox himself never pretended that the king had no sphere within which his wishes must prevail: see his letter of 17 July 1783 to Northington, in which he appears to acquiesce in George III's refusal to oblige the ministers by making peers, and defends their decision not to make an issue of the question of the Prince of Wales's allowance. 'Everybody', he says, 'will not see the distinction between this and political points so strong as the Ministers have done' (*Memorials and Correspondence of Charles James Fox*, ii. 116–18).

[31] Yorke, op. cit. ii. 97. Ecclesiastical affairs illustrate well the respective strength of the king's and the minister's will-power. Here, as Professor N. Sykes has shown (in his article on 'The Duke of Newcastle as Ecclesiastical Minister',

The politicians were soon aware of their sovereign's insignificance, just as a class of schoolboys can discern, by some occult sense, when the form-master, however noisy, does not know how to keep order. Their correspondence, their diaries, and their memoirs show a certain insouciance about the monarch. Many of their anecdotes represented him as making a fuss; very few, as getting his own way. Of course, they could not ignore him. He occupied the central position in the constitution, even if he defended it very badly. The politicians did not so much take power from him, as use his power. When a politician wanted more power, he tried to obtain the use of it from the king. Hardwicke advised Newcastle that Pitt would be a safer partner than Fox, just because he had less influence with the king; and Pitt himself, conscious of his weakness in this respect, was reduced to 'practising Lady Yarmouth'—that is, to approaching the king through the *maîtresse en titre*.[32] But, as Carteret found to his cost in 1746 and Henry Fox in 1757, the king could not stand firm. He could say, 'I shall see which is King of this Country, the Duke of Newcastle or myself', and then agree to the very condition which was, according to him, to make the Duke of Newcastle king; and all the satisfaction he got for himself was the exclusion of one or two politicians from particular offices, and the pleasure of giving Lord Hardwicke a very uncomfortable three-quarters of an hour.[33] The ministers whom he had tried to appoint were forced to turn tail, and he had to submit to a coalition, got up by the Pelhams and their friends on the principle of buying up, at the cheapest rate obtainable, every politician who was worth buying at all. Newcastle was doubtless justified in maintaining that the unanimity thus purchased would promote the conduct of the king's business; but this excuse did not conceal from the king himself the fact that the arrangement had been made for him, not by him; that he was, as he said, 'a prisoner' in the hands of 'Newcastle's footmen'.[34] The politicians of the eighteenth century

English Historical Review, lvii, 1942, pp. 59–84), the king made a lot of fuss, but Newcastle nearly always got his way in the end.

[32] Yorke, op. cit. ii. 248; L. B. Namier, *England in the Age of the American Revolution* (London, 1930), p. 119.

[33] Yorke, op. cit. ii. 388, 401–5.

[34] Henry Fox to Strange, 10 June 1757, printed by Lord Ilchester, *Henry Fox, first Lord Holland* (2 vols., London, 1920), ii. 54; Horace Walpole, *Memoirs of the Reign of King George II* (1846 ed.), iii. 30. (This also rests on Fox's authority.)

were perhaps too ready to believe the king a 'prisoner' in the hands of the political combine who constituted the ministry of the day: volunteer rescue-parties were got up to extricate George III himself from the 'shackles' of almost every minister from George Grenville to his son; but I do not see how it can be disputed that the coalition of 1757 (and, indeed, that of 1744) was negotiated by the politicians among themselves with very little regard for the king's wishes.

George III knew and despised all this. For these encroachments of the politicians upon the king's freedom to choose his ministry might very well be held to be a usurpation. Parliament, no doubt, had the right to remove a minister, by impeachment or otherwise, for criminal acts or definite failures of policy. Even this right it was expected to use in good faith, without trying to convert it from a negative to a positive power—to designate *X* by excluding *Y*. (This is why George III and his supporters demanded in 1784 that the hostile House of Commons should give the younger Pitt a fair trial unless they could allege some definite political crime against him.)[35] Still less was parliament credited with the power of nominating the ministers.[36]

For all that, the positive influence of the House of Commons over the composition of ministries was already greater than it looked; for the events of 1754 to 1757 had shown that the head of a government who did not sit in the House of Commons— whether he were a king or a Duke of Newcastle—could hardly hope to carry through his business without obtaining the support of at least one front-bench House of Commons politician and giving him so much power and confidence as would make him a partner rather than a hired advocate. The events of George III's reign made this clearer than ever. Even the great Earl of Chatham got into trouble from this cause. George III's personal government in the 1770's was only possible because he found in North that rarity among politicians, a House of Commons minister who was content, on the whole, to manage the House without claiming to promote himself from agent to principal; and the king had at last to capitulate to his enemies in March 1783, after the failure

[35] *Parl. Hist.* xxiv. 717 (king's message), 616 (Dolben), 740–2 (Dundas).

[36] This was George II's opinion (Waldegrave, *Memoirs*, p. 132) and Henry Fox's (*Life and Letters of Lady Sarah Lennox, 1745–1826*, ed. Lady Ilchester and Lord Stavordale, 2 vols., London, 1901–3, i. 76).

of a desperate search for one sizeable House of Commons figure—
'Mr. Thomas Pitt or Mr. Thomas anybody'—able and willing to
defend him.[37]

This limitation, however, did not seem very formidable in 1760:
George III counted on getting House of Commons ability easily
enough, and it was from another quarter—from the leaders of
the factions—that he expected interference with his free choice of
ministers. This free choice was all-important to him; indeed,
from the first political act of his reign to the last, the choice of
ministers was, as it were, the vital position in the political battlefield.

At first sight this is a remarkable thing: why should so much
more attention be concentrated on the king's right to choose his
ministers than on his relations with them after he had chosen
them? In part, for the obvious reason that if he could choose
ministers whom he liked, there should be less need to define his
relations with them exactly. (Cabinet procedure was extremely
informal in the days of Lord North, but became ostentatiously
definite and correct in 1782 and 1783, when the king and the
ministers were at arm's length.)[38] Moreover, it is far from certain
that George III set out at all with the intention of interfering in
detail with the daily conduct of the government. At first, in his
diffidence, he merely wished to confer this power on Lord Bute,
and, though he spoke of his subsequent ministers as 'tools', he
was still very nervous, for a time, about taking decisions.[39] There
is little evidence that he interfered much in day-to-day business
until the inattention and indecisiveness of Grafton and North
almost forced him, about 1768, to inaugurate a system of personal
rule.[40] In default of such a system, he could only bring his

[37] Fitzmaurice, op. cit. ii. 256. The search can be followed at length in *Correspondence of George III*, nos. 4133 to 4268.
[38] One cannot, however, be sure that this was the king's doing. Rockingham
and Fox may have thought that enlarging and defining the powers of the
cabinet as an institution was the best way of tying the king down. For example,
Fox claimed that the cabinet should choose a successor to a dead prime minister
—a power which it had only once exercised (in 1754) at the king's request and
somewhat to the distaste of the lord chancellor.
[39] As late as May 1763 he felt very nervous without Bute to hold his hand
(*Letters from George III to Lord Bute*, p. 234).
[40] This, I think, is a fair deduction from the paucity of such interferences in
his published correspondence (of which, however, much has been destroyed)
before 1768. See also Horace Walpole, *Memoirs of the Reign of King George III*,
iii. 66.

influence to bear upon policy through the choice of ministers. This, therefore, was the freedom and prerogative which he found it supremely necessary to claim; this was the symbol of the conflict between king and politicians.

George III accentuated this controversy by the use which he originally proposed to make of his power. Among the members of the 'shadow-cabinet' which, like other heirs-apparent, he kept in readiness, were some men of a certain parliamentary eminence, such as Dodington and Lord George Sackville; but the chief of them, Lord Bute, had not been a member of either House since 1741. In a country governed by politicians for the last twenty years, the new king was trying to give supreme power to a man who was not a politician at all.[41] This, I think, explains why all the politicians made a dead set at Bute. They could not have explained just why they were affronted; but affronted they were, and they let him know it. Pitt and Bute, it is evident, had long differed on the respective importance of court favour and popular eminence as titles to power. Bute, like other courtiers, thought of the court as the centre of the world, imagined that he, as the heir-apparent's representative, had made Pitt a minister in 1757, and considered as treachery Pitt's tendency to behave as if he were *sui juris*. Pitt, on the other hand, clearly thought that, though the king had a right to choose his ministers freely, yet to treat court favour as the one thing needful was, in some way, a retrogression.[42] The Duke of Devonshire, that symbol of whig jealousy whom George III's mother not inappropriately called 'the Prince of the whigs', could not bear to see his friend Fox serve under Bute because, in effect, Bute was a nobody.

You may fancy what you please about the power of the Crown, but believe me you will find yourself mistaken. If a King of England employs those people for his ministers that the nation have a good opinion of, he will make a great figure; but if he chuses them merely through personal favour, it will never do, and he will be unhappy.[43]

[41] George II's abortive attempt to install Compton in the supreme power was far less objectionable: Compton may have been a windbag, but he was Speaker of the House of Commons, which was still reckoned a high political office.

[42] See Gilbert Elliot's memoranda and correspondence in G. F. S. Elliot, *The Border Elliots and the Family of Minto* (Edinburgh, 1897), pp. 362–5, supplemented by Namier, op. cit., pp. 119–21; also George III's outbursts against Pitt's 'ingratitude', *Letters from George III to Lord Bute*, pp. 17–19, 34, 45.

[43] Devonshire to Fox, 14 Oct. 1762, printed by Ilchester, op. cit., ii. 203.

From Devonshire this doctrine filtered down to Burke, in whose *Thoughts on the Causes of the Present Discontents* it appears in denunciations of an attempt to set aside 'men of talents to conciliate the people, and to engage their confidence' in favour of 'men of no sort of consideration or credit in the country', and in the maxim that 'Before men are put forward into the great trusts of the state, they ought by their conduct to have obtained such a degree of estimation in their country, as may be some sort of pledge and security to the public, that they will not abuse those trusts.'[44] Burke said of Bute himself that he was a respectable man, 'but who, to the moment of this vast and sudden elevation, was little known or considered in the kingdom'. It is a little hard to see why these doctrines should exclude an Earl of Bute but not a Marquis of Rockingham—for how well 'known or considered in the kingdom' was Rockingham when he became first lord of the Treasury in 1765, and what 'pledges and security' had he given to the public? But this is one of the great mysteries of whiggery, which cannot be explained. By trying to foist Bute into the inner political circle, which considered him as a nobody because he did not already belong to it, George III began to create the belief that he was in some way disregarding the rights of his people and therefore returning to the practices of the Stuarts.

George III and Bute were not ignorant of these feelings, but expressly denied their validity; and in doing so, they were committing a slight anachronism. After all the water that had run under the bridges since 1688, it was hardly common sense, when talking of a lord chamberlain or a first lord of the Treasury, to say that it was a question whether his Majesty was to exercise the 'liberty that his poorest subject enjoys, of choosing his own menial servants'.[45] George III and Bute, however, were not alone in committing this anachronism. It is pretty clear that Henry Fox agreed with them; and Henry Fox was a House of Commons man (though perhaps a disloyal one), a whig, and, in some ways, the true political heir of Sir Robert Walpole.[46]

---

[44] Burke's *Works* (1852 ed.), iii. 118–19, 134–5. Incidentally this resemblance seems to me to show that the doctrines of the *Thoughts on the Causes of the Present Discontents* were not merely, as Mr. Sedgwick calls them, 'literary afterthoughts'; they were rationalizations of the prejudices which people like Devonshire had long held. [45] *Hist. MSS. Comm., Lonsdale MSS.*, p. 131.

[46] No doubt it satisfied Fox, emotionally and financially, to support Bute and George III against Pitt and Newcastle; but I have little doubt of the sincerity of

The Bute episode was a short one, but its consequences were important. Bute lost his nerve and resigned office in 1763, but he continued to obsess the imaginations of politicians for nearly a decade longer, above all because they believed that, though retired from active power, he continued to advise the king 'behind the curtain'.[47] Their jealousy of this real or supposed secret influence aggravated the bad impression created by his original appointment, and strengthened the belief that George III claimed some right of ignoring the opinions of the parliamentary politicians. This red herring was particularly unfortunate, for George III, between 1763 and 1768, was at his most constitutional. Never again did he try to put a non-politician at the head of affairs.[48] He had at this time no personal axe to grind, if we except his vehement desire to keep George Grenville out of his closet. Yet some of his actions in the negotiation of ministerial arrangements gave new offence to the politicians and strengthened the new 'whig' theories about the way in which ministries should and should not be formed.

It is dangerous to codify too precisely George III's ideas about the formation of ministries; for, when he was fighting the politicians with their own weapons, he often had to shift his ground, and he was no more capable than his subjects—far less, for example, than George Grenville or Rockingham, and scarcely more than the elder Pitt—of seeing life steadily, in an age when politics were too much dominated by the most recent friendship and the most recent enmity. Yet his ideas, I think, can be summarized thus. The public service was, in a real sense, the king's service,

his agreement with them on this point (Ilchester, op. cit. ii. 196; *Life and Letters of Lady Sarah Lennox*, i. 76). Fox was believed, much earlier than this, to hold 'arbitrary principles' and to have derived them from the Duke of Cumberland. There is very little evidence that Fox desired to set up a 'military tyranny'. I think it more likely that he derived his ideas of rigid parliamentary discipline under the minister of the king's choice from his old master Sir Robert Walpole or from his friend Carteret, who appears to have had illusions, in the 1740's, about the value of the crown's support to a politician.

[47] This was probably his original intention, though I am less certain that it was the king's. This is not the place to discuss the duration of Bute's influence. It is clear that he was seeing the king almost daily in November 1764 (*Letters from George III to Lord Bute*, pp. 239–40), but it does not follow that he was exercising any political influence.

[48] Possibly Addington should be treated as a non-politician, though the Speakership had not yet ceased altogether to be considered as a high political office. In any case, the dead set of some politicians against Addington is comparable to the dead set against Bute.

and all the public servants equally and directly the king's servants. Politicians ought not to oppose that service, and even ought to enter it, when called upon to do so, without making stipulations as to policy or persons—certainly without refusing to serve with their enemies,[49] and even, up to a point, without insisting upon bringing in their friends to serve with them (though this last, as George III knew, was usually too much to hope for, and he only once, in 1766, tried to make a point of it).

All these principles presupposed that party—'that hydra, faction'—did not or should not exist. George III, indeed, shared this opinion with many of his most respectable subjects, and there is no need to suppose that he derived it from Bolingbroke's *Patriot King*.[50] It was natural for a young man brought up in the early 1750's to believe that there were no important differences between one clique of careerists and another, for indeed there were none. But after 1754 and, still more, after 1762, the cliques began to differentiate themselves more sharply, and even—at least in appearance—real differences of opinion began to revive within the ramshackle entity known as the whig party. The brief tenures of office in the troubled 1760's, sometimes terminated by a symbolical proscription which only an equally symbolical restitution could avenge, created swarms of claims for each available post, thus aggravating the difficulty of composing a ministry which might endure because it satisfied a commanding majority of active politicians.[51] Moreover the German war, the Peace of Paris, the persecution of Wilkes, the Stamp Act, and the Declara-

[49] 'Have we really Monarchy in this Kingdom', cried Bute, exasperated by Granby's refusal to serve under an administration which countenanced Lord George Sackville, 'or is there only a puppet dressed out with regal robes to serve the purposes of every interested man' (Fitzmaurice, op. cit. i. 168). Sackville in his turn refused to let his son-in-law serve under the younger Pitt, because the foreign secretary, Lord Carmarthen, had once insulted him by a motion in the House of Lords (*Hist. MSS. Comm., Stopford–Sackville MSS.*, i. 82).

[50] Mr. Romney Sedgwick, in his introduction to the *Letters from George III to Lord Bute*, pp. xix–xlii, has most ingeniously traced the growth of this legend; but that does not prove that George III did not read the book, which he might naturally do, as it dealt with the duties of his station and was dedicated to his father. He might, however, equally have derived his ideas, which were commonplaces at the time, from the Rev. J. Brown's celebrated *Estimate of the Manners and Principles of the Times* (London, 1758); see, especially, i. 108, ii. 202.

[51] The most serious attempt to compose such a ministry—that of Chatham in 1766—was accompanied by a phenomenal expenditure on pensions, since there were not enough offices to go round.

tory Act were different symbolical issues upon which the groups multiplied and hardened their divisions. Nearly every stiff-necked political leader differed from nearly every other stiff-necked political leader upon at least one of these issues, and could not forget it.[52]

In these circumstances, how could the king's service be carried on? Nobody, before Rockingham, objected on principle to an *omnium gatherum*, a 'coalition of the wise and good'. The Pelhams had made one in the 1740's (though this was rather a coalition of nuisance-values), and the war had brought about another in 1757. But it was becoming increasingly difficult for the wise and good to agree, at the same time that disagreement between ministers was ceasing to be thought respectable. The spectacle of Chatham's House of Commons ministers at sixes and sevens over the East India Company was thought discreditable in 1767,[53] and that of the feebly pro-American Grafton, outvoted in his own cabinet by the anti-American Bedfords, was rightly treated by Burke as an awful warning against trying to form a ministry of the wise and good without regard to their political opinions.[54] Even Oppositions found some difficulty, from the same causes, in opposing successfully. Differences about America did something, though differences about General Conway did much more, to prevent the formation of a Rockingham–Bedford–Grenville coalition in 1767; and one shibboleth after another kept Chatham's and Rockingham's followers apart till 1779. Above all, when a great question of policy, such as the American war or the French wars, reduced the opposites to two, the belief in an all-party coalition under the king wilted away altogether.

[52] Similar divisions produced similar political anarchy between 1801 and 1812.

[53] It is not certain what Chatham thought about it himself. At one stage he was nettled by Charles Townshend's indiscipline, but later he seems to have thought it right for the ministry to throw this question at the House of Commons without giving it a lead; see his letters in *Autobiography and Political Correspondence of Augustus Henry, third Duke of Grafton* (ed. W. R. Anson, London, 1898), pp. 111–12, 116–17, and his similar advice to Shelburne, on another subject, *Correspondence of William Pitt, Earl of Chatham*, ed. W. S. Taylor and J. H. Pringle (4 vols., London, 1838–40), iii. 215. But for the fact that Chatham soon afterwards went out of his mind, one would say that he had some archaic idea that there was no need for ministers to agree beforehand on questions that were to come before the House of Commons; this would accord with his practice in the 1750's.

[54] No doubt the passage in *Observations on a Late Publication intituled 'The Present State of the Nation'* (*Works*, 1852 ed., iii. 100–1) is meant for Grafton.

This, however, was a gradual process, and was not nearly completed during the crucial parliamentary sessions of 1762–6. Even in those years the behaviour of the cliques was not such as to raise George III's respect for them; for it was perfectly obvious that in 1762 Newcastle's supporters had decided to go into opposition before they knew what they were going to oppose, and denounced a peace treaty which—in most respects—they would have been only too glad to make themselves; equally obvious that both Grenville and Rockingham had taken up their attitudes on the American question almost by accident. Once, however, the attitude was taken up, it could not be abandoned. Fatigued by all their claims, George III in 1766 took part, with the elder Pitt, in an ambitious scheme for pulverizing each of these connexions. Gower was to be offered the Admiralty on condition that he came unaccompanied by his fellow-Bedfords; and when Rockingham's followers within the ministry demanded, as a body, that one of their number should retain a certain office, Chatham and the king refused all accommodation—even though it could easily have been made by a rearrangement among the Rockinghams themselves—in order to point the moral that the king and the minister would only deal with the individual, not with the group to which he belonged.[55] They failed in both endeavours: Gower would not come alone; the Rockinghams resigned *en bloc*, thereby repeating the traditional manœuvre of the whig malcontents, which had twice brought George II to heel and never failed to annoy George III.[56] They did not, on this occasion, succeed in overturning Chatham's ministry, but they did destroy the last hope of an all-party coalition, and reduced Chatham to a very precarious parliamentary position. George III

[55] The affair of Lord Edgcumbe's dismissal is discussed by D. A. Winstanley, *Lord Chatham and the Whig Opposition* (Cambridge, 1912), pp. 75–86.

[56] Collective resignation was the weapon by which the Pelham ministry had imposed its will on George II in 1746, and Newcastle had been on the brink of arranging another (which was, significantly, to have begun with Rockingham) in June 1757, when the king saved him the trouble by yielding. Some of Newcastle's followers (Rockingham, once again, to the fore) affronted George III by resigning in November 1762 as a protest against the peace and the dismissal of the Duke of Devonshire (which was, itself, probably meant to show that the king was not to be impressed by resignations). Curiously enough Chatham, who withstood the collective resignation of Rockingham's followers in November 1766, eagerly hastened the resignation of Granby, Camden, and others in January 1770, in order to bring down the tottering Grafton ministry (*Chatham Correspondence*, iii. 388–9, 392, 394, 398).

too suffered by his conflict with this group, whose political theory was largely founded upon its leader's long memory for injuries received and determination never to make the same mistake twice. The king got the reputation of trying 'to dissolve every honourable connexion' between his subjects.

This accusation was strengthened in the 1770's, for it was widely believed that the king could not even refrain from playing off his own chosen underlings against each other. It is true that George III, who talked and wrote incessantly, could not always refrain from little asides which gave one of his ministers a hint that he did not think very well of another; nor was the favoured confidant always the person who might be regarded as the prime minister.[57] In the decline and disintegration of North's ministry even the minister of the king's own choice found the king colloguing with very junior ministers behind his back. This was mainly the fault of North himself, who was almost a case for a psychiatrist; when the chief minister's will is paralysed, it is a virtue in the king and the junior ministers to keep the wheels of government turning round. Nevertheless, North disliked it, and his resentment probably accounts, in part, for his unexpected decision to join with Charles Fox in the anti-monarchical coalition of 1783. Moreover, if North's inability to fulfil his task of co-ordination was one cause of the spirit of intrigue and backbiting, diffused so widely through the services and the British and Irish governments at this time, that spirit could not fail to derive encouragement from the facility with which an ambitious sailor or a discontented politician could open a correspondence, directly or indirectly, with the king.

The relation between ministers and underlings had already, for other reasons, become a matter in dispute between the king

---

[57] There are traces of such asides to Grenville against Bedford, Feb. 1764 (*Grenville Papers*, ii. 489, 493); to Northington against Chatham (*Correspondence of George III*, no. 462); to Northington against Grafton and Conway (ibid., no. 176); to Grafton against the Bedfords (ibid., no. 674); to North against Germain (ibid., no. 2202); to North against Sandwich (ibid., no. 2548); and, finally, a whole stream of correspondence with Jenkinson and Robinson about North, which is discussed by Professor Butterfield in *George III, Lord North and the People, 1779–80* (London, 1949), pp. 31–47. Much of this is good-natured and even well-meant, but one can understand how a suspicious man like George Grenville would come to think that George III's maxim was *divide et impera* (G. Harris, *Life of Lord Chancellor Hardwicke*, 3 vols., London, 1847, iii. 454). In some instances (for example, George III's treatment of Rockingham and Shelburne in 1782), this suspicion was clearly justified.

and the politicians. George III (as has been said) considered the public service as his service, and all the public servants, after the fall of Bute, as equally his servants. The politicians, especially the Rockingham whigs, came to consider that some of the king's servants should be the masters of others—that a Rockingham or a Grenville was, as it were, a principal contractor for political power, at whose service the king should place the humbler official furniture, the 'men of business' or 'King's Friends'. Horace Walpole satirized this view by asking 'if they expected that every man should depend on King Rockingham and nobody on King George'.

This idea may have derived from Sir Robert Walpole's conception of 'the minister' with full power of discipline over subordinate colleagues: George III willingly gave such power to Bute and to Chatham; was it not right that he should equally give it to Rockingham? But Rockingham's insistence on the power to discipline the junior office-holders was also inspired by something more topical than that: by his fear (which Bedford shared) of that able band of humbler politicians, the Elliots, the Dysons, the Jenkinsons, whom he suspected at the same time of following Bute and keeping up a clandestine connexion with the king. Perhaps also (here again his long memory for grievances plays its part) by the misunderstandings of February 1766, when George III would not or could not force these men to obey the ministers' orders and vote for the repeal of the Stamp Act. Whatever the cause, Rockingham was already, before the end of his first ministry, demanding the dismissal of Dyson as an emblem of the identification of the king's will with that of his ministers.[58] For the rest of his life he expressed peculiar vindictiveness against 'men who are ready to support all Administrations',[59] and the main achievement of his second ministry was the abolition of some posts which such men might hold. His follower Charles Fox, in the same tradition, seems to have thought that one House of Commons politician had a right to coalesce with another of the same kind, as he coalesced with North, but that it was discreditable for Pitt to coalesce with the Jenkinsons and Robinsons.[60] Portland symbolized the same idea in another way, by refusing to show George III any names but those of the inner

[58] *Correspondence of George III*, nos. 333–5.
[59] *Grenville Papers*, iv. 66.   [60] *Parl. Hist.* xxiv. 222.

cabinet, demanding, in effect, that the king should appoint them at once, and then leave them, as ministers already in full possession of power, a free hand to fill up the subordinate offices.[61]

This fear of the 'string of Janissaries, who are always ready to strangle or dispatch' a minister 'on the least signal',[62] was not wholly irrational. Two classes of politicians—the extreme amateurs who always voted for the king's government because it was his, and the extreme professionals who always had to be on the winning side—both wanted to know if the king was really behind his ministers. George III was aware of this, and sometimes arranged with Grafton or North to show defaulters which side their bread was buttered, by calculated rudeness in the levee or the drawing-room.[63] This was all very well, when it was preconcerted with the ministers; but what if it took the form of a demonstration, intentional or not,[64] against them? It would encourage all the unattached politicians to oppose them. This is why Bedford, in June 1765, demanded that the king should 'smile upon' his ministers and publicly 'frown upon' their adversaries;[65] the request was not childish, but highly rational, for the king's smiles betokened corn and wine and oil to the unattached politician, his frowns a long privation of those goods. This, again, is why George III ostentatiously refused, in 1783, to create any peerages upon the recommendation of the coalition ministers, that the unattached politician might know that he wished to be rescued from them—a signal so dangerous to the coalition leaders, that they seem to have thought of bribing the detested Thurlow with the Great Seal to persuade the king to change his mind.[66]

---

[61] *Correspondence of George III*, nos. 4236, 4268. Lord Grenville acted likewise in 1806, but met with less objection (*Hist. MSS. Comm., Dropmore MSS.*, viii. 2).

[62] A supposed phrase of George Grenville, quoted by Charles Fox in the House of Commons, 17 Dec. 1783 (*Parl. Hist.* xxiv. 213).

[63] *Correspondence of George III*, nos. 703, 1036.

[64] George III often had great difficulty in mastering the expression of his emotions and often made great efforts to do so; for this laudable attempt to comport himself as a constitutional monarch should do, he was somewhat unreasonably blamed by the elder Pitt, who compared him to his disadvantage with 'the late good old King'. No doubt it was just because George II's sallies were so spontaneous that nobody except Newcastle took any notice of them.

[65] Bedford's memorandum in *Correspondence of John, fourth Duke of Bedford*, ed. Lord John Russell (3 vols., London, 1842–6), iii. 289; the picturesque language comes at third hand from the Duke of Newcastle's *Narrative of Changes in the Ministry*, ed. Mary Bateson (London, 1898), p. 22.

[66] George III's letter to Temple, 1 Apr. 1783, in *Correspondence of George III*,

Not only the composition of the ministry and the relations of its parts, but even the act by which it was negotiated, were the occasion of endless sparring between king and politicians. The king's first principle was, that no candidate for office was entitled to make conditions about the policy to be pursued; all that should be settled after he had accepted. The politicians themselves seem to have agreed that such conditions were indecent. The elder Pitt once admitted that it was improper to talk about *carte blanche*, 'as it sounds like capitulating'.[67] Yet he proposed, almost in the same breath, that the king should agree to a programme of domestic and foreign policy, and refused to come in until these terms were accepted.[68] George Grenville, returning triumphantly to office in May 1765 because George III could find no alternative to him, confronted his sovereign with four demands; when George III asked him, 'Are these conditions, Mr. Grenville?', he repudiated the suggestion, but he admitted, a few minutes later, that they were *sine qua non*.[69] Rockingham made no bones about his right to impose conditions: his four points, in 1782, were meant to reverse George III's American policy and reduce the royal influence in parliament.[70] Probably the country would not have supported, in normal times, the imposition of terms upon the king; but the war-weary parliament now demanded that the struggle against America should be abandoned, and Rockingham, the only accepted leader of this resistance to George's American policy, was able to tack his own constitutional programme to the demand. In 1806 the situation was reversed: it was George III who wanted to know beforehand the ministry's proposals about army reform, and Grenville who tried to put off discussing it until the ministry should be in office.[71] The change of position is significant: in 1783 it was likely that the king's will would prevail in a question not covered by any previous arrangement; in 1806, more likely the cabinet's.

no. 4272; Fox to Northington, 17 July, and Loughborough to Fox, Aug. 1783, in *Memorials and Correspondence of Charles James Fox*, ii. 118, 205.

[67] Charles Fitzroy to Grafton, 29 May 1765, in Grafton's *Autobiography*, p. 51.

[68] Albemarle to Grafton, 19 June 1765, ibid., p. 83.

[69] This story is recounted at third hand (from the king through the Duke of Cumberland) in Newcastle's *Narrative*, p. 18. But it is certain that Grenville presented the conditions; see the king's memoranda, printed as nos. 139 and 141 of the *Correspondence of George III*.

[70] Ibid., no. 3654.

[71] *Hist. MSS. Comm., Dropmore MSS.*, viii. 2, 7–8.

The politicians began to go a step further: not content with imposing, upon some occasions, a programme of policy before they would negotiate, they tried, upon other occasions, to obtain a blank commission. The king did not like to give *carte blanche* to a prime minister designate, or even to negotiate directly with him at all. He had a number of reasons for this—the fear of committing his dignity; the fear of losing control over the forces which still supported the existing ministry (for if the 'rats' flocked to the side of the new minister before the negotiation was complete, the king might lose the power to break it off)[72]; perhaps, even, the fear of having a prime minister at all in the modern sense. He therefore generally preferred to have the negotiation conducted, or at least begun, by a third party—by the outgoing prime minister in 1763, by his uncle in 1765, by the lord chancellor in 1766, 1778–9, and 1782.[73] The politicians, on the other hand, sparred for a direct negotiation. Pitt insisted upon it in 1765. Rockingham in 1767 (though not in 1765) demanded that the existing ministry should be considered at an end and that he should receive a direct mandate to make any proposals that might seem good to him.[74] He does not seem to have insisted on this in 1779,[75] and was persuaded to waive it in 1782. He had cause to repent of doing so, for George III took advantage of the negotiations having gone through Shelburne's hands, to treat Shelburne as joint prime minister.[76] Profiting by this lesson, Portland obdurately insisted on a direct and unqualified mandate in 1783 and 1784.[77] It began to be held by 'pure' whigs that the king's part in forming a ministry should consist only in sending for a party leader and leaving the rest to him; so much so that in 1802 the Marquis of Buckingham spoke of 'forming an administration in the usual way, that is, with *carte blanche* from the king'.[78]

[72] This is why the king was in the weakest position when the old ministry had already resigned before the negotiation, as in 1782, 1783, and 1806.

[73] George III's correspondence with North in 1778–9 shows how much importance he attached to having a lord chancellor in office to conduct such a negotiation (*Correspondence of George III*, nos. 2310, 2336, 2354).

[74] Pitt to Shelburne, Dec. 1765, *Chatham Correspondence*, ii. 359–60; Rockingham to Grafton, 16 July 1767, *Correspondence of George III*, no. 547, ii.

[75] Richmond to Fox, 7 Feb. 1779, in *Memorials and Correspondence of Charles James Fox*, i. 213–20.

[76] *Correspondence of George III*, nos. 3627, 3632, 3639.

[77] Ibid., nos. 4210, 4236; Portland to Sydney, 15 Feb. 1784, in *Memorials and Correspondence of Charles James Fox*, ii. 235; Portland to Fox, 24 Feb. 1784, ibid. ii. 238–40.   [78] *Hist. MSS. Comm., Dropmore MSS.*, vii. 118.

All this sparring symbolized what came to be known as the 'whig' doctrine of the relation of crown and politicians. Accustomed to the political inertia of the crown, as they were in the reign of George II, the politicians came to feel, though they could not well argue, that the crown ought to be politically inert and to farm out its power rather than exercise it; to register decisions made among themselves rather than take its own decisions; that the phrase 'the king's service' was little more than a figure of speech.

Although George III's most conscious opponents were still astonishingly ready to rely upon the direct interposition of the crown's prerogative when they thought it likely to be exercised for their advantage, yet it is hard to believe that all their stratagems for limiting George III's freedom of action were merely a device for filling in time until they could look once more for the favour of an adult heir-apparent. In part, they arose out of the political warfare of the groups in the 1760's with which the king was necessarily involved; for, in seeking tactical advantages against each other, the groups incidentally obtained tactical advantages against the king, so far as he supported one group against another. In part, they were due to the ingrained prejudices of a political class, which had obtained the supreme control by sufferance and meant to keep it by right. The peculiarity of the Rockingham whigs—if they had any—consisted in little more than in grafting upon these prejudices the doctrine that party was a respectable and necessary means of ensuring the coercion of the king. The coercion itself was a thing upon which, whatever their professions, very many politicians of the 1750's— Grenville, Temple, Bedford, Newcastle, Devonshire, even Hardwicke—were perhaps unconsciously resolved. The theory of the constitution might not explicitly justify it; but the practice was to develop its own theory before long.

IX

THE YOUNGER PITT

[*The Listener*, 13 May 1954]

WILLIAM PITT the Younger may seem a curious subject to choose for the purpose of illustrating the manner in which we can know the characters of the past. Probably many people think that he completely concealed his character from the world or even that he had no character at all. He is thought of as a statue rather than a man, a great statesman perhaps, certainly a great orator who uttered one rolling phrase after another with an ungainly delivery, 'sawing the air with his body', but not a man of strong or attractive personality.

The real Pitt was quite unlike this. As much, perhaps, as any other leader we have had, he was the creature of impulse and of inspiration. He was to the last degree mercurial: at one moment, overweeningly confident and ambitious, he would disregard all possible difficulties, indeed he could hardly see them at all; at the next moment he saw nothing but difficulties, could think of no way to overcome them, and was lucky to retire in good order, throwing his policies overboard. Parliamentary reform and Catholic emancipation are good examples—each of them he took up too lightly, and too lightly dropped. He ran away from opposition to his anti-Russian policy in 1791; in the early part of the next year he was snapping his fingers at the idea of any possible danger from the French Revolution, but before 1792 was out he was in a panic and preparing for war. His policy, especially in war-time, was one long improvisation. He could get up a subject in a few days: for example, he once shut himself up for ten days with Henry Dundas in order to master the complexities of the Bengal land revenue. People who get up subjects quickly do not always leave their mark upon them, but at least it enables them to improvise. Moreover, Pitt was not only industrious—his mind worked fast. Even his enemies, like Lord Holland, admired him for his miraculous quickness of perception; and the story is told how, when Charles Fox (Lord Holland's uncle) once made a bad mistake in tactics by using an argument that no whig should have used, Pitt saw it in a flash. He slapped his thigh and said, 'I will un-whig the gentleman for the rest of his life.'

But in spite of these wonderful talents, Pitt's mind and habits were disorderly. He stayed late in bed every morning, he lost all his correspondence in the frightful litter on his desk, and the great administrator of the national finances sank thousands of pounds in debt—nobody knew exactly how, but I think one can very well guess, for a man whose kitchen is so arranged that at any time of the day there is a roast chicken nearly ready to eat, in case he should call for dinner, could hardly hope to save money.

Why was a man of this chaotically spontaneous character so much misunderstood that some historians have represented him as something scarcely more animated than a statue? Many things explain this. For one thing, the icy reserve which kept all common acquaintances at a distance was deliberate and even necessary. Pitt became prime minister at 24, and held the office for more than seventeen years at a stretch. At one time he was nearly ten years younger than any of his cabinet colleagues (incidentally, he was also the only commoner in a cabinet of peers). A man so placed has to keep his end up, and the only way to do it is to make himself out even haughtier than he is (and Pitt was haughty enough from the first).

There is a very near parallel which helps us to understand this. Sir Robert Peel likewise obtained high office in his twenties and held it, with a very short break, for many years: he, too, struck everybody as reserved, self-contained, and cold. Yet Peel had a warm heart and Pitt had at least lively affections. A prime minister, at one of the busiest times of our history, cannot take much time for private life; but Pitt's personal relations did not lack intensity. They were confined, however, to his closest friends and fellow workers—he gave himself very little trouble about the world outside. One colleague criticized him for making no friends, another for giving no dinners, a third for answering no letters. When, however, he could detach himself for a few hours from business, he showed to his intimates such a ready mind and such dazzling charm as made them his slaves for life—we hear of him construing at sight a difficult passage of Thucydides which baffled even Lord Grenville, himself no mean scholar; at another time, taking out a prayer book from a bookshelf in a country house library and discoursing easily, though with evident learning, on the prose style of the English liturgy; again, at Lord Stafford's dinner table, talking about Homer so clearly and with such charm that even the ladies were interested. Nobody could tell when one of these exhibitions was going to take place: in Pitt's life there were no set pieces, like the celebrated spectacle of Charles Fox's domestic felicity at St. Anne's Hill. A prime minister has no time for such set pieces: a leader of the Opposition, in those days, had all too much.

Perhaps Pitt's character is puzzling for another reason: his heredity. We know more about his heredity than about that of any other leader in our history, the royal family always excepted. No other British minister has been the son, the nephew, and, incidentally, the first cousin of prime ministers. That sort of thing may happen amongst dynasties of Oriental viziers, but not in British parliamentary life. Pitt's father, the great Earl of Chatham, and his uncle, George Grenville, are both well known to us, and they differ remarkably from each other. From his father Pitt must have derived the unevenness of temperament which I have already described: the phrase 'always in the cellar or the garret', which was used of one of them, would equally well have served for the other. These ups and down of mind more than once drove Chatham mad, or as near mad as makes no matter: perhaps the effort to remain perfectly sane in spite of them was one of the things which brought his son to an early death at 46. Pitt also inherited, or adopted, his father's extravagance—substantially the same story about the series of roast chickens is told of father and son.

Perhaps we need not assign this kind of characteristic to unaided heredity; for William Pitt was the chosen companion of his father's old age, and may have imbibed the notion that this was the right way to order one's meals. The same thing, perhaps, may be said of his immoderate ambition and his instinct for dominating his colleagues and his followers. Perhaps, too, the old man developed his son's quickness of mind, for a boy shut up for hours with a daemonic father like the Earl of Chatham could only hope to defend himself if he could parry thought by thought with the speed of lightning.

But, despite all this, William Pitt inherited the tastes of the slow-plodding Grenvilles. For example, his favourite subject was finance, a thing which his father never even cared to understand. Chatham would never have had the patience to read political economy; he always preferred foreign policy, a subject which his son neglected as long as he could and, when he turned his attention to it, viewed sometimes in a manner which the old man would have thought downright disreputable. As Charles Fox pointed out, Chatham would have turned in his grave to hear his son describe as 'weak and childish' the idea that one nation should be unalterably the enemy of another: for Chatham it was in the nature of things that the House of Bourbon should be the enemy of Great Britain. In these respects the son of Chatham's rival, Fox, was more truly his heir than his own son.

The tastes of a Grenville at war with the temperament of a Pitt must have produced a curious mixture which not everybody could understand. Moreover, Pitt's ideas and policies were not very easy to place—they did not fit well into the accepted categories. When he was a young man entering politics, public attention was concentrated upon the struggle between the king and the leaders of an aristocratic Opposition. I suspect that Pitt never considered this subject so interesting or so important as his contemporaries thought it. His mind was far more modern than theirs: he busied himself with such things as finance and administrative reform which were, to them, almost technical matters on the fringe of politics. On these subjects he was throwing off new ideas, or adopting new ideas of others, all the time: if we look at the questions of political economy, or even that odious but necessary accessory to modern life, the income tax, we find that Pitt saw the point years, or decades, before most of his fellow politicians. But that did not endear him to them: they felt that he ought to have taken a stauncher and more consistent part in the good old-fashioned constitutional squabble of the day.

To add to their distrust, he did not even stand by his own ideas—he would not sacrifice his position for them, dropped them when they encountered opposition, and even put them in cold storage for a long time when the French Revolution made new ideas suspect and gave him something else to think about. This added to the confusion—for nobody could tell which was the real Pitt—the Pitt who took up reforms so gaily in his youth, or the Pitt who put them into cold storage with such alacrity in his middle age.

His real character is still further obscured by the misfortune which condemned him to spend half his political life at a task which he had not chosen and was not fit to handle. All his merits and all his interests were those of a peace minister; but from 1793 he had to wage a great war, and he did it badly. Here the Grenville in him undoubtedly predominated over the Pitt, for his father was the greatest war minister we have ever had. To do him justice, it is hard to say why everything turned out so badly: most of the alliances he made, most of the campaigns he directed, were reasonable schemes in themselves, but somehow they added up to nothing, and all he could do, at the end of failure after failure, was to defend himself in parliament by a great speech which might justify the past and keep up hope for the future, but won no battles. It was this long catalogue of defeats decorated in vain by oratory that made Sydney Smith describe him as a 'luminous eloquent blunderer'.

In the end, the effort was too much even for him. In those days there was no psychiatrist to diagnose a nervous breakdown, but there can be no doubt that Pitt suffered from one for years and went on leading the country in spite of it. We should not judge him a weakling. The frightful strain of waging war against half the world and holding down the refractory and defeatist classes at home made the entire British governing class feel as if it were in a state of siege, and nearly all its most brilliant members died of this strain comparatively young—Castlereagh committed suicide like Romilly and Whitbread; Liverpool had a stroke at 57; and even Canning did not reach 60. These men were the victims of the decades of crises; and Pitt was the most illustrious victim of them all. He continued for years to devise expedients against disasters he could not prevent, responding to one emergency after another with diminished vitality but almost unquenchable optimism, his pulse going up from 80 to 120 whenever one of the green dispatch-boxes was brought into the room, until, as his doctor all too truly said, he died of old age at 46.

He was on the verge of total failure—few experts believed that his ministry could have lasted another month. Yet everybody wept at his death; even Charles Fox turned 'pale as ashes'. The great diplomat Lord Malmesbury solemnly vowed that in his whole future life he would always act as he believed William Pitt would have wished. For a whole political party, almost a whole political class, Pitt became a symbol—but a symbol of what? Each of his disciples posed as his true political heir. The reactionaries and the reformers within the tory party each claimed to appropriate the whole of his political mantle. Perhaps this proves that his mind was universal; perhaps only that it was ambiguous. What was his real mind? We shall never know whether it was more than a series of responses to circumstances. But at least we can believe, as his contemporaries believed, that his struggle with those circumstances, whether well or ill conducted, was the labour of a giant. After his death, Charles Fox said that 'it seemed as if there were something missing in the world'.

X

AMERICAN VERSUS CONTINENTAL
WARFARE 1739–63

[*English Historical Review*, li (1936), pp. 429–65]

W HEN England went to war with Spain in 1739, all Europe was at peace except the emperor and the Turks. The English ministers had no temptation at first to turn the conflict with Spain into a general European war. They believed their own armies and fleets were a match for the enemy; and if they too eagerly applied to the Dutch for help, that was in part a precaution against an inconvenient mediation, or an antidote to the unpopularity which would attend the overthrow of the American equilibrium by one Power alone. They began the war without knowing whether they would find other allies, or where. This was even more true in 1755, when England was equally uncertain of foreign help, yet entered cheerfully upon a struggle, this time with the greater, not the lesser of the Bourbon Powers. In fact, the middle of the eighteenth century was the period of the English offensive, in which pessimists were prepared, and optimists even anxious, for a single combat with France and Spain.

Not everybody found this dangerous position congenial. The diplomatic isolation of England was one of the strongest reasons alleged by the Walpoles and Henry Pelham for trying to make up the quarrel with Spain; and when a remarkable mortality among the crowned heads of eastern Europe opened new prospects and uncertainties in the autumn of 1740, the English ministers began to look for allies as quickly as they could. This opportunity happened at the same time that the intervention of France in behalf of Spain became much more likely; and whatever Newcastle may have thought of that danger at a distance, his first motion, upon its approach, was a nervous scurry for allies. In this way the great debate began over the relation of England to the continent of Europe on the one hand, and, on the other, to the colonies and dependencies beyond the seas.[1]

---

[1] A great deal of the material of this article is covered by Admiral Sir H. A.

The question was posed in two forms. What were the objects for which a war was worth fighting? What was the best way to fight a war with France and Spain? Three alternative policies were possible: a continental policy, a Hanover policy, and a maritime and American policy. Both the first and the last admit of further distinctions still. A continental policy might assert an unqualified devotion to the balance of power, or it might aim only at protecting certain countries whose interests were thought to be specially connected with our own. On the other side, the zealots for America were likewise divided between conquests in North America and conquests in the West Indies. With all this choice of methods and objects, there was only one great and inevitable enemy: France, or at most the combined House of Bourbon.

Historians sometimes treat the preoccupation with the balance of power as an essentially whig principle, and the preference for colonial aims as characteristic of toryism. Whatever foundation this view may have in the history of Queen Anne's reign, it has little relevance to that of George II. There were indeed some tories who stolidly adhered to the doctrine that we should only fight at sea and for commercial or colonial objects. They continued to resist the Austrian subsidy treaty in 1741, when most of the Opposition whigs assented to it in order to make their court to the king.[2] Beckford, one of the loudest declaimers in this sense, called himself a tory at first, and Pitt's popularity with the tories may have been increased by his identification with the American policy; but Bolingbroke (who should presumably be called a tory in 1743, though a slippery one) admitted that England might sometimes be concerned in upholding the balance of power. 'Our true interests require', he told Marchmont, 'that we should take few engagements on the Continent, and never those of making a land war, unless the conjuncture be such, that nothing less than

Richmond, *History of the Navy in the War of 1739–48* (3 vols., Cambridge, 1920); Sir Richard Lodge, *Studies in Eighteenth-Century Diplomacy, 1740–1748* (London, 1930); Sir Julian Corbett, *England in the Seven Years' War* (2 vols., London, 1907); Albert von Ruville, *William Pitt, Earl of Chatham* (3 vols., London, 1907); Basil Williams, *Life of William Pitt, Earl of Chatham* (2 vols., London, 1907); and Richard Waddington, *Louis XV et le renversement des alliances* (Paris, 1896), and *La Guerre de Sept Ans, histoire diplomatique et militaire* (5 vols., Paris, 1899–1914).

[2] Chesterfield to Marchmont, 24 Apr. 1741, *A Selection from the Papers of the Earls of Marchmont*, ed. Sir George H. Rose (3 vols., London, 1831), ii. 249.

the weight of Britain can prevent the scales from being quite overturned. This was the case, surely, when we armed in the Netherlands, and when we marched into Germany.'[3] There were whigs like Joseph Yorke who could applaud Newcastle's insistence on the continental war as 'recalling our wandering thoughts to the true principles of the Revolution'; but Pitt and Temple, Bedford and Halifax were also whigs, yet they were all zealots for America. In fact, there is a complete confusion of whigs and tories on this point, which illustrates the general uselessness of those superannuated labels.

The doctrine of the balance of power was inherited from the days of William III and Marlborough, when it met a genuine need and could easily be realized in practice. It had descended, with a great deal of paltry rhetoric about the 'common cause' and the 'ambitious House of Bourbon', to be used as a cant term by secretaries of state, who did not inquire too closely whether it retained any sense or utility. It was not, however, devoid of either, although the reiteration of it is wearisome in Newcastle's dispatches. France still desired to be the arbiter of Europe,[4] though she pursued the aim with patience and finesse, instead of the cruder and bolder methods of Louis XIV. She was no longer equal to her former reputation in war, nor did her cunning in negotiation achieve any very useful results between the days of Fleury and those of Choiseul; but she still had some ostensible claim to be considered the first nation in Europe, and so far the balance of power may have been the right one for her nearest rival.

Almost all Englishmen assumed that France was the nation against whom the balance of power was invariably to be maintained. For some time after the Peace of Utrecht, the whig ministers had tried to establish the system in a more universal and speculative form; its object, they said, was to control and

³ Ibid. ii. 314.

⁴ The instructions which Bussy, as a senior clerk in the French Foreign Office, drew up in 1740 for his own use as minister in England, represent the jealousy of England against France as one of prestige rather than interests, and refer to 'the ambition of England, all the more irritated at seeing France the sole arbiter of the universe, because she cannot conceal from herself that her own imprudence has excluded her from any share in that honour' (A[rchives des] A[ffaires] É[trangères, Paris], Mém. et Doc. Angleterre, 40, f. 85). This piece of professional vanity was justified at the moment of writing, for Fleury then had Europe at his feet; a year or two later it was out of date.

weaken the strongest state in Europe, whatever that state might be. In the name of this doctrine they justified their understanding with France and their abandonment of the Austrian alliance, for Austria, rather than France, was then to be considered as the greatest and therefore the most dangerous Power in Europe. The renewed competition of French commerce and the successes of Cardinal Fleury were later held to discredit this view, and when the Spanish war broke out Walpole's enemies attacked him with a great display of historical detail for strengthening our inevitable enemy and weakening our natural ally. The great topics were the Treaty of Hanover in 1725 and the neutrality of England in the war of the Polish Succession. Had we ranged ourselves on the side of Charles VI at those two crises, we might have obliged Spain to abandon the right of search. At any rate we should have had a grateful and vigorous ally instead of having to face France and Spain without one useful friend in the world. So the Opposition argued, and the reasoning with which the Walpoles tried to prove the inexpediency of war at the present juncture was interpreted as the conclusive proof of their past mistakes. In this light the death of Charles VI in the autumn of 1740 was to be considered a blessing in disguise. He owed us no goodwill, and was not likely to have done anything to help us had he lived. When his inheritance came to be disputed, there must be at least one party to which we could attach ourselves if we needed allies and if we believed that they were worth the trouble we must take on their behalf.[5]

The practical difficulty of keeping the balance even was greater than either the ministry or the Opposition believed. It had much increased since the war of the Spanish Succession. Then the foundation of all such calculations had been the rivalry of Habsburg against Bourbon; but this traditional policy had lost some of its recommendations in the strange diplomatic convolutions of the last twenty-five years. Not only was Charles VI an exacting ally, whom we had sometimes had occasion to offend; but the Habsburgs had not lately been reckoned a fair counterweight to the Bourbons, and could still less be so, now that a Bourbon possessed the throne of Spain.

Writers on the balance of power sometimes confused and

5 *Parliamentary History*, xi. 635 and 1067 (Carteret), 645 and 1087 (Newcastle), 1121 (Hardwicke), 1270 (Pulteney), 1308 (Sandys), 1337 (Stephen Fox).

sometimes distinguished two ways of preserving it. We might either support the strongest single state against France, or try to unite all against her. In the first case it was not so easy as it had once been to choose our ally, in the second it was infinitely more difficult to effect the combination. Statesmen and pamphleteers made the mistake of thinking that another Grand Alliance could be formed against France, as in King William's reign. When Newcastle heard that Fleury had sent his fleet to the West Indies to protect the Spanish colonies against us, he suggested at once that 'some kind of concert might be set on foot with the Dutch, the emperor, the czarina, the king of Prussia, the king of Poland, the landgrave of Hesse, &c., to form a kind of grand alliance to oppose the ambitious views of the House of Bourbon'.[6] He would at all times have had great difficulty in collecting such an omnium gatherum, but as the emperor was not yet dead, he can hardly be blamed because he did not foresee the inevitable conflict between Austria and Prussia over Silesia. Yet he should have known better than to repeat the mistake so often. In 1748 he would have welcomed a Prussian alliance, but as a supplement to that with Austria, not a substitute for it.[7] It was not to be had upon such terms.

Seven years later he made an astonishing blunder of the same kind. He concluded a treaty with Russia, in order to deter Frederick II from attacking Hanover. This and other measures having produced overtures from Frederick, Newcastle made a treaty with him too, hoping that Russia would make no objection, as if she had no ends of her own to serve by her arrangement with us, beyond the subsidy she was to receive. He was then very indignant when both Russia and Austria renounced our alliance as soon as Prussia showed signs of acceding to it. (It is true this was not an act of sudden impulse, nor prompted by hostility to Prussia alone, but Newcastle ought to have reckoned on a continuance of the Austro-Prussian antagonism.) Finally—and this was the crowning mistake of a long career of diplomatic ineptitude—it was Newcastle who induced Bute to make the fatal overture to Austria in January 1762, which did as much as anything else to make

---

[6] Newcastle to Harrington, 6 Sept. 1740, British Museum, Add. MSS. 32695, f. 7. Newcastle's passion for attempting to square the circle is perhaps explained by his timid maxim 'that he that is not for us is against us', a principle which seems to have inspired his domestic politics as well, and to account for his pursuit of unanimity, as vain in the House of Commons as in the concert of Europe.

[7] Lodge, op. cit., p. 360, n.

Frederick II an intractable and untrustworthy associate.[8] New-castle believed the rest of the world would be as much concerned and frightened by the Bourbon Family Compact as he was him-self, and that Austria would at once come round from her French alliance and fall into the arms of England.

This sort of conduct might be called a continental policy, but it was in truth the most barbarous insularity. It assumed that the other Powers of Europe had no occupation in life but to fear and resist the House of Bourbon, and would sacrifice any private aims for this. Newcastle may have been right in thinking that such resistance was the supreme and general concern of all Europe, just as the younger Pitt may have been right in believing that it was everybody's duty to oppose Napoleon. Newcastle may have seen the interests of other countries better than they could see them for themselves; but he did not understand that while this general concern of Europe happened to correspond with our private interest—almost the only interest of any kind which we had on the continent—the same fortunate coincidence could not be expected in other countries. What was the House of Bourbon to Poland or Sweden or Prussia? Certainly a very powerful agent for good or evil, but not the immediate and inevitable enemy to the public welfare. The self-centred diplomacy of England was too slow to see the growth, especially in Germany and Italy, of local conflicts as necessary and important to those who were engaged in them as our struggle with France was to us. It therefore made the mistake of thinking that it had only to raise the cry of 'the liberties of Europe in danger' to obtain the harmonious support of Powers which could never remain long or sincerely on the same side of any question.

Newcastle was not the most intelligent, though he was far the most experienced foreign secretary of his generation. The same unenlightenment is to be found among pamphleteers and

---

[8] Compare the first and second drafts of Bute's dispatch to Yorke of 12 Jan. 1762, Add. MSS. 32933, ff. 82, 221; Newcastle to Bute, 7 Jan., f. 84; to Yorke, 8 Jan., ff. 112–16. These overtures to Austria do not wholly justify Frederick's disingenuous behaviour to England. He did not hear of them until the beginning of April 1762, by which time he was far advanced in a secret and disloyal nego-tiation with Russia, of which the English ministry would have disapproved the terms if it had known them. Bute's and Newcastle's blunder was therefore his excuse rather than his reason (*Politische Correspondenz Friedrich's des Grossen* [46 vols., Berlin, 1879–1939], xxi, nos. 13590, 13594).

parliamentary orators. They could not get the Grand Alliance out of their heads, and ignored the incompatibilities of foreign states, however fundamental. Frederick II, in their opinion, was merely shortsighted, and Maria Theresa merely obstinate, in continuing to quarrel over Silesia when they ought to have been making common cause against France. Both Walpole and Carteret were criticized severely for their inability or omission to reconcile Austria with Prussia and Bavaria, and later ministers were condemned in the same way for policies which perpetuated, by trying to exploit, the rivalries of those countries.[9]

Perhaps the argument was never put more intelligently than by Israel Mauduit in his famous *Considerations on the Present German War,* published in 1760. He assumed that there was only one way to fight France in Europe: a revival of the Grand Alliance. England could not profitably be connected with the continent unless the continent were connected with itself. This was particularly true of Germany, which united might be a match for France, but was no more than a battlefield, and an inconvenient one for us, when divided. Mauduit saw the conflict between Austria and Prussia as a German civil war, which we only aggravated and prolonged by taking sides in it; our part should have been that of mediation, that peace might be restored as soon as possible and both the rivals induced to direct their arms against France.[10] The only fault of Mauduit's theory was that it was too speculative. There was no such thing as Germany at that time; indeed, in this sense there was no such thing as Europe; for this reason all the attempts to form a sacred league against France were bound to fail.

The policy which Mauduit attacked may have been illogical, but it was the only one possible. The most practicable way of maintaining the balance of power was not by combination, but by supporting the strongest nation that could be found to resist France. Nearly everybody believed this to be Austria; that was the 'good old system' to which Newcastle was attached, as an

---

[9] *Parl. Hist.* xii. 255 (Carteret), 348 (Henry Pelham), 925 (Bance), 961 (Waller), 979 (Quarendon); xiii. 156 (Pitt), 175 (Winnington), 192 (Lyttelton), 260 (Dodington), 384 (George Grenville), 409 (Murray); *A Compleat View of the Present Politicks of Great Britain, in a Letter from a German Nobleman to his Friend in Vienna* (1743), p. 34; *An Englishman's Answer to a German Nobleman* (1743), p. 17; *The Case of the Hanover Forces in the Pay of Great Britain* (1743), p. 48.

[10] *Considerations on the Present German War,* pp. 2–17.

alternative to his dreams of a Grand Alliance. Most speakers and writers treated Austria as the natural ally, a fact which helps to explain the sentimental cult of Maria Theresa in the early years of her reign. When her bravery developed into an exacting though pardonable obstinacy—when, in fact, she refused to make the sacrifices required by our schemes of a Grand Alliance— Carteret's patronage of her began to be looked upon as romantic knight-errantry; but here the English public was the victim of its own confusion of thought. If the league of all Europe against France was the object, certainly Maria Theresa's firm resistance to Prussia was inconvenient and perhaps even selfish; but if we were to support the strongest power available, it was absurd to invite her to weaken herself.[11] Circumstances forced the English government into an uneasy combination of these policies; it refused to abandon Austria, but pressed her to part with territories, first in order to bribe her allies and then in order to put an end to the war by contenting her enemies. Friendship does not flourish upon such terms, and the breach between England and Austria was prepared long before 1756, in spite of Newcastle's blind tenacity to the 'good old system'. The alliance was unnatural, or at least no more natural than any other, when Austria began to withdraw from western politics and to canton herself in Germany and Italy.

The Prussian alliance, which then succeeded the Austrian, might be in some respects a better one for England. Prussia was a nearer neighbour to Hanover, to whom she could do either good or harm; indeed, the opponents of the continental war represented the help we gave to Frederick II as a tribute paid to induce him to keep his hands off Hanover.[12] In view of the way in which the diplomatic revolution came about, the accusation has some justice. Some English ministers, notably the Walpoles, had already begun to prefer Prussia to Austria by 1740, but the alliance was never popular until it was made. Though the 'Protestant hero' then became twice as great a favourite as the gallant queen of Hungary ever had been, some of the older politicians,

[11] This point is made in *An Englishman's Answer to a German Nobleman*, loc. cit.

[12] *Considerations on the Present German War*, p. 38. In fact, when we began to quarrel with Frederick in 1762, Newcastle suggested that perhaps he would seize Hanover in revenge (Newcastle to Legge, 18 Feb. 1762, Add. MSS. 32934, f. 411).

especially Newcastle and Granville, kept in their hearts a secret attachment to the 'good old system'; their futile return to their old flame had deplorable results in the last year of the war.

Not everybody believed that the balance of power was a legitimate object of English policy. Temple declaimed against 'the phantom of keeping your power on the Continent', and Pitt said in 1755, 'We have suffered ourselves to be deceived by names and sounds, the balance of power, the liberty of Europe, a common cause, and many more such expressions, without any other meaning than to exhaust our wealth, consume the profits of our trade, and load our posterity with intolerable burdens'.[13] According to the politicians of this school, the balance of power had nothing to do with us, so long as we had a superior navy to guard us from invasion. We were a great commercial nation, uninterested in conquest; an expensive continental policy could only load our trade with taxes which would disable it from competing with its nearest rivals.[14] Others would admit that the balance of power was worth a certain price, but a very low one. If we were to be the sole paymasters of the alliance against France, the expense would be intolerable; it would be less so if the Dutch would share it with us. This was one of the reasons why we usually tried to involve the Dutch in our general wars against France, and why those wars became more onerous and unpopular when they ceased to take part in them.[15]

Again, the relation of England with her allies, and the argument for interference in continental politics, must depend on the way in which the alliance was formed. There was a great difference between entering into a continental war as principals and as auxiliaries. For a war which we provoked in the defence of our own interests, we should have to pay more heavily than for one in which we conferred a favour by taking part. The government usually argued that we must set up our standard on the continent in order that the oppressed enemies of France might rally to it;

---

[13] *Parl. Hist.* xv. 357 (Beckford), 530 (Temple); John Almon, *Anecdotes of the Life of the Right Hon. William Pitt, Earl of Chatham* (6th ed., 3 vols., London, 1797), i. 241.

[14] *Parl. Hist.* xii. 336 (Pulteney), 1161 (Lonsdale).

[15] Ibid. 913 (John Philips), 950 (St. Aubyn); xiii. 384 (debate on Grenville's motion), 1052 (Powlett). The Dutch are defended against the aspersion of backwardness in *A Letter from a Member of the States-General in Holland to a Member of Parliament in England* (London, 1743).

that we must act first, to encourage others.[16] The Opposition distinguished applying to the other Powers of Europe from being applied to by them. If we first appealed to them in the name of the balance of power, they would exploit our necessity; we should commit ourselves to paying them to look after their own interests. If they sued to us for help, we could limit our obligations and our expense.[17] Some orators went farther, and suggested with perverse flippancy that we should be justified in provoking quarrels on the continent when it suited our interest.[18] The English government was far from acting upon such cynical principles, but continued its inept effort to glue the whole of Europe together by subsidies and cant into a coalition against France.

The adversaries of the continental war founded their argument on a further assumption. The balance of power, they said, could very well look after itself. We were not the only nation to be afraid of France, and when the others came to see their true interests they would be just as anxious for a Grand Alliance as we were. Instead of interfering in their politics or pressing them for help, we should stand aside and let the course of events bring them to their senses. In this spirit Lee and Vernon argued that we ought not to have stopped the war in 1748 on account of the distress of the Dutch, because if the French had pursued their conquests in Holland any farther, they would have made enemies within the Germanic body, and so the balance would have righted itself.[19] Temple used the same argument in 1755, when he hinted that Hanover could and would be defended against French aggression by the affronted solidarity of the empire. Mauduit and other writers of this school suggested that, if we left France to make herself thoroughly odious in Germany, we should the sooner be able to raise up a league against her.[20]

They assumed two things. First, that France could never use enough force to overcome the repugnance of Europe to her domination, that the more she exerted herself the stronger the reaction

---

[16] *Parl. Hist.* xii. 149 (Cholmondeley), 174 (Walpole), 614 (Winnington), 942 (Yonge); xiii. 178 (Winnington).

[17] Ibid. xii. 928 (Bance), 1034 (Pitt); xiii. 159 (Pitt), 425 (Waller); xiv. 159 (Velters Cornwall), 175 (Samuel Martin), 197 (Beckford).

[18] Ibid. xv. 345 (Potter), 356 (Beckford), 370 (Egmont).

[19] Ibid. xiv. 339 (Lee), 602 (Vernon).

[20] *Considerations on the Present German War*, p. 12; the *Monitor* of 6 Sept. and 8 Nov. 1755; *Parl. Hist.* xiv. 163 (Velters Cornwall).

would be. In the second place, they flattered themselves that everybody was afraid of France and nobody had any reason for jealousy or dislike of England.[21] That was because they thought only in terms of territory and political independence; we desired no possessions on the continent, therefore we could not be dangerous to any state. They reckoned without the commercial jealousy which France did her best to exploit. If trade is riches and riches are power, then we were the strongest nation in the world. Since our own jingo pamphleteers boasted of it, it is no wonder that the French propagandists made the most of it.[22] The excesses of our privateers, and the official encroachments of our navy upon the rights of neutrals, sharpened this feeling into something like hatred, especially among those maritime peoples whom we least wished to see subject to French influence. It was therefore idle to imagine that Europe, left to itself, would always resist France and court England.

The advocates of continental measures were not quite content with declaiming about the liberties of Europe, or with assuming that France must be fought wherever we could encounter her. They tried to meet the Opposition on its own ground. They denied that a commercial country like England could be indifferent to the fate of Europe. France was admittedly our rival in trade, and we could only keep our customers by safeguarding their political independence. What if one sole monarch of Europe should force all the nations bordering on the sea to shut their ports to English trade? The hint of a 'continental system' was thrown out by Hardwicke as early as 1738, and was later developed into a stock argument by government pamphleteers.[23] Frenchmen saw the same point; Silhouette recommended it to the attention of his superiors in 1739, and Choiseul began to execute the scheme in 1762 when he tried to make Portugal exclude English shipping from her ports.[24] Both Pitt and Newcastle saw the danger that France might treat other states in the same way and shut the whole of Europe against us from Genoa to the

[21] The *Monitor* of 22 Nov. 1755.

[22] *Britons Awake, and Look About You, or Ruin the Inevitable Consequence of a Land War, whether Successful or not* (1743), p. 13; *Le Politique Danois* (Copenhagen, 1756), pp. 19–52.

[23] *Parl. Hist.* x. 1156 (Hardwicke); xii. 1173 (Hardwicke); xiv. 167 (Fox), 184 (West); *The Conduct of the Ministry Impartially Examined* (1760), p. 38.

[24] Silhouette to Amelot, 26 Nov. n.s. 1739, A.A.É., Angleterre, 405, f. 292.

Elbe.[25] What would be the value of prizes or American conquests if their produce could not be re-exported abroad? They would glut the home market and ruin the English producers; England in fact would 'starve by satiety' as Napoleon later intended.[26]

The mercantilist assumptions of the age strengthened this argument. If prosperity could only be achieved by a favourable balance of trade, foreign exports were necessary. If England and her overseas possessions became a closed system exchanging goods only within itself, it could not grow any richer.[27] The colonial and maritime party made a feeble attempt to repel this reasoning by pretending that we had an unfavourable balance of trade with those parts of Europe from which France could exclude us in this way. They were thinking chiefly of Germany, 'from whose Bourne, like that of Death in Shakespeare, no British Guinea ever returned'.[28] That was not true. The trade statistics of the day may not prove very much as to the value of the imports and exports, but they were the only ones that contemporaries had, nor can they be mistaken beyond a certain degree. The figures given by Whitworth appear to show that our exports to Holland never exceeded our imports thence by less than three to one, and that our exports to Germany were worth, on an average, half as much again as our imports. What is more, our exports to Germany usually went up when a German war was at its height.[29]

[25] Newcastle to Hardwicke, 15 Nov. 1761, Add. MSS. 32931, f. 47; to Yorke, 8 Jan. 1762, 32933, f. 113; Horace Walpole, *Memoirs of the Reign of King George III*, ed. G. F. Russell Barker (4 vols., London, 1894), i. 129.

[26] *A Compleat View of the Present Politicks of Great Britain*, p. 65.

[27] *The Important Question Discussed* (1746), pp. 4–6, 13.

[28] *A Second Letter from Wiltshire to the Monitor, on the Vindication of his Constitutional Principles* (London, 1759), p. 12.

[29] The following abstract is taken from Charles Whitworth's *State of the Trade of Great Britain* (1776). Whitworth's figures were based on the reports laid before parliament. They are useless as a guide to the value, but are generally held to reflect accurately the rise and fall of the quantity, of goods imported and exported in this period:

	Exports	
	to Germany	to Holland
	£	£
1731–40, average (peace) . .	1,111,174	1,867,142
1741–8 (war)	1,519,478	2,390,669
1749–55 (peace) . . .	1,345,212	1,978,351
1756–62 (war) . . .	1,616,537	1,764,480

The effect of the figures given for Holland is perplexing; they do not rise in the second war, except at the very end: from which we might infer that it was a war with Spain which caused the exports of Holland to go up, and that the increase

Adam Smith afterwards attributed this to the war itself. Contemporaries offered the same explanation, though in a somewhat crude form; they suggested that it was due to the enrolment of manufacturers into the French army, which reduced the industrial power of our rivals. Some of them used this as an argument for the continental war.[30]

The universal domination of Europe by France might have a yet more fatal consequence. Perhaps the English navy was equal to those of France and Spain, though by no means everybody admitted this; Admiral Norris, for example, did not.[31] It could not be a match for those of the lesser Powers as well, Holland, Denmark, Portugal, and perhaps Sweden. If France held undisputed control of Europe by land, she would be able to make herself equal to us at sea by this method.[32] The failure of Choiseul's Family Compact discovered a weakness in the argument. If France meant to press into her service the navies of the smaller Powers, she must do so before her own was ruined; that of Spain was of little help to her in 1762, because her own had ceased to exist. But the reason why the colonial and maritime party in England proposed to abstain from interference on the continent was that they might destroy the French navy first of all. It would, therefore, be a race between the French domination of the land and the English domination of the sea. The calculation of the colonial

represents goods shipped to Spain by way of Holland. But this impression is contradicted by the fact that the rise does not take place in the first war until 1743, when a war with France was also expected. If, therefore, it was caused by the cessation of direct trade between England and Spain, we must assume that between 1741 and 1743 France, not Holland, was the intermediary. That is possible, but there may be something in the correspondence between the Dutch and German figures. In Germany, too, it is 1743 which marks the beginning of the great increase; and again in the Seven Years War the exports do not rise to great heights until the last two years. The normal trade of Holland with England consisted largely in distributing English goods to Germany and the north, so any alteration in the figures is likely to be due to events in that part of the world.

[30] *Parl. Hist.* xiii. 128 (Carteret), 316 (Bathurst). The author of the plan for carrying on the war, printed in Almon's *Anecdotes of the Earl of Chatham*, i. 262, says that 'in England, the manufactures, more especially the woollen, sell at higher rates when at war with France, than in times of peace', and Kinnoull found in 1759 that the Yorkshire woollen manufacturers were doing so well during the war that they might be inclined to captious criticism of the terms of peace (Kinnoull to Newcastle, 28 July 1759, Add. MSS. 32893, f. 331).

[31] Norris's diary, 22 Sept. 1740, Add. MSS. 28133, f. 60.

[32] Newcastle, notes for a speech, Add. MSS. 32996, ff. 315 seqq.; *Parl. Hist.* xiv. 686 (Henry Pelham); xv. 629 (Chesterfield).

party in England assumed that the second must happen at least as soon as the first.

The amateur strategists of England had to take one thing more into account. England or Ireland might be invaded. This was a favourite plan of the French government, but the English colonial and naval party denied that it could be executed; so long as we were superior at sea to France and Spain, it was logically impossible.[33] The advocates of continental measures replied that, if France dominated all Europe, we should not long remain superior to the fleet which she could bring together; moreover, command of the sea is always uncertain, especially in the Channel, where the same wind would in some circumstances blow the French forces towards our coasts while it held our own fleet in port. There might be no genuine instances of this, for the Armada was dispersed by a storm, King William III was not properly resisted, and Monmouth had landed almost like a smuggler, without fleet or army; but it could still happen. A momentary loss of command or lapse of vigilance would give the enemy his chance; perhaps his flat-bottomed boats might cross the strait under cover of a single night.[34]

This was not a great danger, considered in the light of strategy alone. Our fleet could never be blown off its station long enough to let a great invasion through; and what harm could a small one do? Here politics entered into the question. If Englishmen had been united and loyal, ten thousand Frenchmen landed in England could have done nothing but get themselves taken prisoners; but there was disaffection and Jacobitism in Scotland and the south-west, however the Opposition leaders might pooh-pooh it.[35] Walpole was really afraid of it, and the panic of 1745 justified him. There was, therefore, some colour for the opinion that though a great invasion could not take place and a small one could not succeed by itself, it was the duty of the government to see that nothing of the sort was even tried.[36]

After the collapse of Jacobitism, this might have ceased to be true, but another argument took its place. English ministers as well as French were impressed by the delicate and fragile structure

---

[33] Ibid. xiii. 502 (Strange); *The Present Ruinous Land-War Proved to be a H——r War* (1745), p. 18.

[34] *Parl. Hist.* xi. 1027 (Hardwicke), 1028 (Abingdon).

[35] Ibid. xii. 614 (Winnington), 621 (Carew).

[36] Ibid. xi. 650 (Newcastle), 944 (Pulteney); xii. 911 (Yonge).

of our credit and finance. A small invasion might bring it to the ground by a Stock Exchange scare, and paralyse the whole machine. Even Pitt admitted this. 'Paper credit', he said, 'may be invaded in Kent'; he described 'the consternation that would spread through the City, when the noble, artificial, yet vulnerable fabric of public credit should crumble in their hands'. This fine piece of mischievous rhetoric, with its 'striking and masterly picture of a French invasion reaching London',[37] probably conduced as much as anything else to the panic which inspired Newcastle to so many mistakes.

Panic was the real danger, and the real remedy a tonic for the nerves. The militia was such a tonic. Its value in the field might be doubtful, but it reassured the propertied classes of England by making them proud of themselves, and alone accounts for the vast difference between the invasion scares of 1756 and 1759.[38] The militia had always been popular with the Opposition leaders. They represented it as a safeguard of British liberty which would make the unpopular standing army and the policy of the balance of power alike unnecessary. Nevertheless the ministers of the old school continued to believe that the best way to stop France from invading us was to raise up trouble for her in Europe.

The advocates of continental measures made little impression on the public rage for a maritime war. This can hardly be accounted for but by prejudice and rant. The appeal to the demonstrable necessity of European trade ought to have had some weight; but public opinion suffered from a curious blindness on this subject. Many orators and pamphleteers seemed to think we could live by American trade alone. As Hervey complained in the House of Lords, the Opposition talked as if 'there is not a shilling comes to us by our trade with any quarter of the world but with America'.[39] Bedford spoke of it in 1739 as 'almost the only profitable trade which this nation enjoys, unrivalled by others', a curious opinion from the man who thought in 1762 that we were in danger of over-colonizing. Even Hardwicke, who had no motive for exaggerating in this respect, once said that the North

---

[37] Horace Walpole, *Memoirs of the Reign of King George II* (3 vols., London, 1846), ii. 87.

[38] A difference which Pitt belittled out of consideration for his colleagues, but cannot have failed to have seen (West, House of Commons report, 13 Nov. 1759, Add. MSS. 32898, f. 223).

[39] *Parl. Hist.* x. 785.

American colonies alone 'constitute one-half, at least, of the trade of this Kingdom'.[40] That was nonsense. In 1760, when the exports to the colonies reached an unprecedented figure, they were still hardly more than a quarter of the whole export trade; the colonial imports bore a somewhat higher proportion, but even when the West Indian figures were included, they did not approach a half.[41]

It is difficult to see why the colonial trade was valued so much beyond its real importance. The chief ostensible reason was, that it was the only one for which we need not depend on the good graces of foreign governments; the only one which, in a mercantilist age, we could not lose to foreigners. Particular colonies were prized for particular merits, military or economic: the West Indies for the re-exports of their produce which had once swelled the favourable balance of trade; the northern colonies for their large population able to bear arms in American expeditions; the fisheries for the training of seamen. Colonies were also a profitable and perhaps a safe field for the investment of capital. All this barely explains why the colonial trade should have been regarded as the one certain salvation of the country in spite of its insignificant proportion to the whole overseas commerce. This exaggeration led the nation to sacrifice other trades to its security in the war of Jenkins' Ear. Not only was the interruption of the trade to Old Spain—so far as it really was interrupted—borne for this sake, but the losses of English shipping in the war seem to have fallen very severely on the European trades in general.[42]

[40] Ibid. x. 1040; Hardwicke to Joseph Yorke, 5 Jan. 1758, Add. MSS. 35357, f 223.

[41] Whitworth's figures. T. Malvezin gives in his *Histoire du Commerce de Bordeaux* (4 vols., Bordeaux, 1892, iii. 322–3) some interesting statistics which bear on the proportion of the colonial trades to other foreign trades in France. I do not know from what authority he took them, nor whether they include overland trade in 'Europe'; but they show the comparative insignificance of the colonies. Even if the East India trade is included, the trade of the French dependencies does not seem to have exceeded a third of the total imports or a fifth of the total exports, in any of the periods for which he gives averages, before 1763–76.

[42] The figures given by the *Gentleman's Magazine* (xi. 689, xiii. 23) are bad, but I know of none better:

In 1739   9 ships were taken in the American trades, 33 in others.
In 1740   34 „   „   „   „   „   „   85   „
In 1741 108 „   „   „   „   „   „   63   „
In 1742   75 „   „   „   „   „   „   67   „

These figures are probably too low for the shipping of the American colonies,

England had other reasons for concerning herself with the continent, besides the fetish of the balance of power. There were certain parts of Europe in whose security we were supposed to have a special economic or strategic interest. These were Portugal, the Netherlands, and, some said, Hanover. Portugal was valued chiefly as the European terminus of the considerable trade which we carried on with Brazil, and, through its dependency of Nova Colônia do Sacramento, with Buenos Aires and Chile. Since this trade brought in gold, it was particularly valuable during a German war, which was supposed to cause an export of bullion to the continent.[43] For this reason one of the favourite schemes of France for putting military or diplomatic pressure on us was a threat to Portugal. It was not executed during the war of 1739. In the next war it could not be done by France alone; but when Spain took her part in 1762 one of the most important points of Choiseul's strategy was the invasion of Portugal. He also intended an expedition against Brazil, which might have the same effect upon the trade and revenues of England that an attack on the Spanish West Indies had on France: to dry up the sources of our wealth. This last scheme was never executed, because it was only designed a few weeks before the preliminaries of peace were signed.

Portugal only appeared upon the scene in the last year; but the problem of the Low Countries was a chronic one. From the days of Edward III to the German invasion of Belgium, the Low Countries have always been of the first importance to the military and

from which full and reliable information was not so likely to be had as from Europe; but for some time, while Vernon was in the West Indies, the losses there were very slight. It should also be remembered that the average size and value of American shipping was small; only the ships which traded from Europe to America would be worth as much as those in the European trades. A deputation which professed to represent the merchants of London, but consisted almost entirely of West Indians, told the Admiralty in Apr. 1747 that 1,212 English ships had been lost in the French war, of which 800 were in the plantation trades (P[ublic] R[ecord] O[ffice], Admiralty, 3/57, minute of 14 Apr.). Only 311 prizes, worth 11,128,676 livres, or about £500,000, were brought into Martinique, which was the chief port for privateering in the French colonies (A[rchives] N[ationales, Paris], Colonies, C 8, B 21). Not many prizes can have been taken into the other colonies, but as the ships bound to and from the colonies were oftenest taken in the Channel, 800 is not an incredible figure. Yet the proportion of two ships lost in the plantation trades for every one in all others differs very materially from the figures of the *Gentleman's Magazine*, and is not in itself very probable.

[43] Hardwicke to Newcastle, 1 Apr. 1762, Add. MSS. 32936, f. 261.

naval security of England, and for a long time they also har-
boured her chief commercial rivals in north-western Europe. It
has always been a maxim of her policy to prevent the nation of
whom she is most afraid from possessing them; it was particularly
so at this period, when their defence was supposed to be ensured
against France by the Austrian alliance and the Dutch barrier
fortresses. The sovereignty of most of Belgium was meant to bind
Austria closer to England, but had rather the reverse effect.[44] Both
England and Holland had their commercial difficulties with the
Austrian Netherlands, and the political relations which arose out
of the Barrier Treaty were not much more satisfactory. The gratitude of Austria was very much attenuated when she ceased to be
interested in western Europe. She showed this by her secret treaty
with France in 1757, when she promised to give up Ostend and
Nieuport to Louis XV if he would help her to recover possession
of Silesia. Even while the gratuitous interference of France in
German affairs kept Maria Theresa loyal to our alliance, she
brought difficulties on us by her inability to defend the Netherlands against the French armies, so that we had to ransom them
for her by restoring Cape Breton at the Treaty of Aix-la-Chapelle.

The Dutch, too, were at least as much a liability as an asset.
Perhaps the English ministry had not realized their financial and
military weakness, and their political timidity, when it spent all
its efforts to drag them into the war of the Austrian Succession.
Even then, there were people in England who doubted the wisdom of it; the participation of the Dutch would draw on them an
invasion from France, and the war would become a land war in
the most dangerous part of Europe.[45] This caution was lost on the
ministers, especially the Pelhams, who overthrew Carteret in 1744
because they would not carry on the continental war unless the
Dutch joined in it.[46] Fortunately, they could not execute their

[44] Chesterfield prophesied that it would do no good; see his letter to Newcastle,
6 Dec. 1745, *The Letters of Philip Dormer Stanhope, 4th Earl of Chesterfield*,
ed. Bonamy Dobrée (6 vols., London, 1932), no. 896.
[45] Hop to Fagel, 25 Oct. 1740, P.R.O., State Papers, 107/46. Long afterwards,
Pitt blamed Carteret's efforts to force the Dutch to enter the war, and Halifax
said in 1755 that he hoped the government would not press them to take any
step which would involve them in a land war, for then we should have to contribute more to their defence than they could possibly do to ours (*Parl. Hist.*
xv. 638).
[46] See the document of 1 Nov. 1744, printed by P. C. Yorke, *Life and Correspondence of Philip Yorke, Earl of Hardwicke* (3 vols., Cambridge, 1913), i. 333.

plan quickly, because it took years to persuade the Dutch to any active measure; meanwhile the French carried the war into Flanders and reduced the barrier fortresses. The Opposition made this an excuse for coming to terms with the Pelhams. They might not have approved the way in which the war had been begun, but since it was now being waged for the Dutch barrier they could justify themselves to their constituents as fighting for a real English interest:[47] a significant incident, which shows how popular was the distinction between general and local interference on the continent.

This might be a political success for the Pelhams, but it was a military disaster. The war went from bad to worse in Flanders, and the crowning misfortune was the co-operation of the Dutch, which came about gradually in 1747 and gave the French army an excuse for invading them. It was their bankruptcy and their military failure which forced Newcastle to put an end to the war at once.[48] So far from bringing us any strength, the Dutch alliance nearly proved our Achilles' heel. The English government ought to have known it long before; indeed, Chesterfield, who had been ambassador at The Hague, did know it, and thought a permanent neutrality of the Austrian Netherlands the best thing that could happen.[49]

Many people thought that this fiasco had furnished a conclusive argument against any dependence on continental allies; but it did not even cure Newcastle of his passion for the Dutch. There was a moment when he desired in good faith the succour of six thousand men which we required of the States-General in the spring of 1756, though the ministry as a whole had ulterior motives and would have been embarrassed if the demand had been complied with.[50] Not only did Newcastle continue to hope

---

[47] *Parl. Hist.* xiii. 1055 (Pitt), 1056 (Barrington), 1250 (the abstract of the 'new courtiers'' argument). The Dutch barrier fortresses were not situated in Dutch territory, but in the Austrian Netherlands. Hence it came about that the French reduced them two or three years before they began to threaten the frontiers of the Dutch Republic itself.

[48] Lodge, op. cit., chap. vii.

[49] Chesterfield to Newcastle, 24 Oct. and 6 Dec. 1745, 20 Mar. 1746, Chesterfield, *Letters*, nos. 881, 896, 923; to Trevor, 20 May 1746, no. 934; to Dayrolles, 17 July and 2 Oct. 1747, nos. 1304, 1408; *An Apology for a Late Resignation* (1748), pp. 5 seqq.

[50] Newcastle to Yorke, 10 Feb. 1756, Add. MSS. 32862, f. 430; Walpole, *Memoirs of the Reign of King George II*, ii. 184.

intermittently that the Dutch would take an active part in the Seven Years War; the English government, the English minister at The Hague, and the English party in Holland did their best to promote, with inept and hide-bound devotion to tradition, an increase of the Dutch army which was not only likely but designed to embroil the States-General with France. How much wiser was Pitt when he said he would rather feed the war in Germany than have it carried into Flanders.[51] When Pitt's influence was removed, Bute and Newcastle tried in 1762 to revive the phantom of Dutch participation. It was all of a piece with Bute's plan of a continental war contracted to the defence of our immediate interests in Europe; but for Newcastle it was a consequence of the Family Compact, and of his belief that all the Powers of Europe could be united against the House of Bourbon because the House of Bourbon would at once dictate with theatrical haughtiness to all the Powers of Europe.[52]

The most vexed question of all was Hanover, with which England had no connexion but their common sovereign. I have distinguished Hanover politics from true continental politics, because they sometimes had different effects. In the early days of the war of the Austrian Succession, the Opposition tried to prove that the measures which were meant to be taken for the defence of Maria Theresa were warped by the sinister influence of Hanover. The most conspicuous example is the convention of neutrality in 1741, which certainly rendered Hanover itself useless to Maria Theresa.[53] George II was afterwards accused of withdrawing for the defence of Hanover the troops which were to have been sent to Austria; of precipitating a war in Flanders for the sake of an excuse to hire Hanover troops; of advising Maria

[51] Walpole, op. cit., iii. 18.

[52] The suggestion that the States-General should be roused by jealousy of the Family Compact to resist the House of Bourbon is in the first draft of Bute's dispatch of 12 Jan. 1762 to Yorke (Add. MSS. 32933, f. 82). It was, therefore, probably his own. Newcastle's contribution was the fatal hint of treating Austria in the same way, and the idea that the commercial jealousy of the Dutch could be excited against the clauses in the Compact which dealt with exclusive privileges in trade (Newcastle to Yorke, 8 Jan., Add. MSS. 32933, f. 113). Newcastle had noticed in November that Bute was especially struck by the question, what would become of Holland if we abandoned the continent (Newcastle to Hardwicke, 15 Nov. 1761, Add. MSS. 32931, f. 47).

[53] *Parl. Hist.* xii. 255 (Carteret), 269 (Argyll), 285 (Bathurst); see the account of the Neutrality in Paul Vaucher, *Robert Walpole et la Politique de Fleury, 1731–1742* (Paris, 1924), pp. 394–407.

Theresa, against her real interest, to continue the struggle against Frederick, in order that he might have an excuse for acquiring Prussian territory for Hanover.[54] Some of these accusations were true, others tortuous and absurd.

The difference between the Hanover and continental policies was apparently more obvious than ever at the opening of the Seven Years War. The hope of a grand alliance against France had entirely vanished, because we found we could expect no help from Maria Theresa or the Dutch Republic. Newcastle had, therefore, to abandon continental measures for the time being, and declare for a purely naval and colonial war.[55] Nevertheless, as the king's minister he was forced to provide something for the defence of Hanover. He therefore encouraged George II to conclude and renew subsidy treaties for its protection. He thought it unfair that he should be attacked for incurring a continental war when he had taken particular pains to avoid it, and justified what he had done as a mere Hanover policy.[56] The justification was worse than the offence. There might be something to be said, as Pitt afterwards admitted, for a scheme which united against France some of the greater Powers of Europe; there was no excuse for amassing a heterogeneous German force for the protection of Hanover.

Moreover, this particular way of distinguishing Hanover and continental measures was unreal. The ambitions of the electorate might traverse the proper conduct of a continental scheme, but Hanover could not be defended without involving Germany in the war. This was an aggravation of Newcastle's crime in the eyes of his enemies, but in the end it saved his policy from failure. He came to terms with Prussia in order that she might keep her own hands off Hanover and discourage France from entering the

---

[54] *Parl. Hist.* xii. 870 (Barnard), 925 (Bance), 956 (Waller), 997 (Quarendon); xiii. 157 (Pitt), 193 (Lyttelton); *A Vindication of a late Pamphlet, intitled, The Case of the Hanover Troops* (1743), p. 51; *A Letter from a Member of the States-General in Holland to a Member of Parliament in England* (1743), passim; *The Present Ruinous Land-War Proved to be a H——r War* (1745), pp. 32 seqq.

[55] Newcastle to Holdernesse, 2, 11, and 18 July 1755, Add. MSS. 32856, f. 448, 32857, ff. 1, 183; Holdernesse to Newcastle, 30 July, Add. MSS. 32857, f. 446; Newcastle to W. Bentinck, 16 Oct., Add. MSS. 32860, f. 64; Bentinck's reply, 31 Oct., f. 256.

[56] Newcastle to Hardwicke, 3 Sept., Add. MSS. 32858, f. 413; to Hartington, 20 Sept., Add. MSS. 32859, f. 160; his notes for a speech, ? Nov. 1755, Add. MSS. 32996, ff. 315 seqq.

Empire to attack it. This stroke cost him, it is true, the tepid and useless friendship of Maria Theresa, also that of Russia; but it gave England a better ally, with whose help an impracticable defence of Hanover was turned into a glorious continental war.

No doubt there was a great deal of factious noise in the perpetual clamour against Hanover. Perhaps the majority of English people had not actively desired the accession of George I; and the whig schisms in the reign of Walpole had created a new Opposition which was willing to strike at the minister through the king. All the ministers of George II—Walpole, Carteret, and even Newcastle—depended on his favour much more than constitutional historians have usually admitted. They were sometimes forced to purchase their influence by improper compliances with his passion for his electorate, and thus to give frequent occasions to the criticism of unreconciled enemies and dissident friends of the dynasty. The former could only express their animosity against the king, and the latter could best create embarrassments for the ministers, by harping on the sinister influence of Hanover upon English policy.

There were also genuine reasons why the connexion of England with Hanover was a misfortune for both parties to it. The Act of Settlement laid it down that England should undertake no war for Hanoverian objects; but it did not provide for the case of an attack made upon Hanover by the enemies of England for no other reason than the identity of king and elector. Yet this was what happened in 1741 and 1756. There might be some colour for it the first time, for it was the king of England's interference in German politics that provoked Maillebois's invasion; but in the Seven Years War, France proposed to attack Hanover solely in order to avenge herself for England's aggressions at sea and in America. It was easy to say that the elector of Hanover ought not to pay for the king of England;[57] but what was the elector of Hanover to do? If he concluded a neutrality for his German dominions, as he did in 1741, he incurred great unpopularity among his English subjects and was accused of betraying their allies on the continent. Yet he could not defend himself against the whole power of France, with his own soldiers or those he

---

[57] The expression used by George II. Bussy to Amelot, 6 Sept. 1741, in J. B. G. de R. de Flassan, *Histoire générale et raisonnée de la diplomatie française* (2nd ed., 7 vols., Paris, 1811), v. 135.

could hire out of his electoral revenues; and if he used the money
and diplomacy of England for these purposes, he involved her in
the continental measures which it might be her interest to avoid.

The disadvantage to England was even greater. Either she must
allow herself to be drawn into that full system of continental
alliances which some believed to be the inevitable consequence
of any step taken for the protection of Hanover, or she must try
to defend it by herself. That was almost as difficult, expensive,
and elaborate a task as a general war on the continent, for Hanover had no natural frontiers.[58] Thus whatever form the defence
of Hanover might take, it must deprive England of all the military and diplomatic advantages of an island. This was particularly resented as a grievance in 1755, when we were beginning a
war with France which had nothing whatever to do with the
continent, and was not meant to be fought there. If England was
to be reduced to terms, or involved in a general European war,
on such an occasion as this, by the pressure of France upon Hanover, there would never be a time, so long as the connexion of the
kingdom and the electorate subsisted, when we could pursue un-
hampered our real interests in a maritime and colonial war.[59]

Pitt, Temple, and Bedford proposed to cut the knot by abandoning Hanover to its fate during the war, and procuring compensation for it at a peace. Perhaps they would purchase its
recovery by restoring to France some colonial conquests; perhaps
they would give it a money indemnity out of the revenues of
England.[60] Shrewder observers foresaw that the reluctance to
sacrifice English interests to Hanover would only be postponed,
not overcome, by this method; the statesmen who would not

[58] Holdernesse believed that 'defending Hanover only will be attended with
very great difficulty and perhaps with as much expense as a more extended and
more useful plan' (Holdernesse to Newcastle, 30 July 1755, Add. MSS. 32857,
f. 446), and Pitt dismissed the idea of doing so as laughable. The military weakness of Hanover was one of the stock themes of the Opposition (Walpole,
Memoirs of the Reign of King George II, ii. 60).

[59] *Britons Awake, and Look About You*, p. 46; *Parl. Hist.* xv. 533 (Temple's
protest), 640 (Halifax); Walpole, op. cit., ii. 51 (Dodington). Even the defenders of Newcastle's policy had to admit that Hanover 'took off from our
insularity'.

[60] *Parl. Hist.* xv. 530 (Temple); Hardwicke to Newcastle, 9 Aug. 1755, Add.
MSS. 32858, f. 76; Potter to Temple, 5 Oct. 1755, *Grenville Papers*, ed. W. J.
Smith (4 vols., London, 1852–3), i. 146; see Dodington's plan of 'leaving Hanover
in deposit', in his letter to Bute of 16 Jan. 1761. John Adolphus, *History of
England* (7 vols., London, 1840–5), i. 571–2.

defend Hanover at England's expense would hardly give up the colonial acquisitions on which they had set their hearts, in order to buy back the hated electorate. This prophecy was right; for Pitt, who in 1755 would compensate Hanover but would not defend it, declared in 1761 that he would defend it but would never hear of compensation for it if it were lost or damaged.[61] Newcastle was always afraid of the political dilemma with which the government would have to deal if Hanover should be conquered; but the French never had very much hold on it at any time after 1758. There was, therefore, no question of ransoming it. George II, however, wanted more; he expected some territorial compensation for such inconvenience as Hanover had suffered in the war. That both Pitt and Newcastle vowed he never should have; but this ambition had the effect of attaching him to the party which would rather continue to conquer the French colonies than make peace. He appears to have seen that he would never get anything for Hanover until England could afford to be generous. He was probably mistaken in thinking that she would in any circumstances make a present to Hanover; but his illusion had the effect of ranging him, for a time, on the side of Pitt against Newcastle.[62] In the end, this difficulty proved unimportant. At the beginning of George III's reign Hanover ceased to have any influence on English policy. The king and his confidants ostentatiously proclaimed their indifference to it, and had it been in danger during the last year of the war they might have indecently sacrificed it to their popularity.

The antithesis of America and the continent was not only expressed in discussion of the legitimate objects of war; it came out also in a similar controversy over the strategy. For example, nobody could dispute that the origin and motive of the Seven Years War was commercial and colonial rivalry; but that did not conclude the question, how it was to be conducted, and whether a diversion on the continent was good or bad policy. The parties

[61] *A Full and Candid Answer to a Pamphlet entitled, Considerations upon the Present German War* (1761), p. 33; Newcastle's memorandum of 10 Apr. 1761, Add. MSS. 32921, f. 381.

[62] Newcastle to Hardwicke, 17 Sept. and 19 Oct. 1758, Add. MSS. 32884, ff. 33, 436; Hardwicke to Newcastle, 22 Oct., 32885, f. 38; Devonshire to Newcastle, 10 July 1759, 32892, f. 500; Newcastle to Stone, 1 Aug., 32893, f. 406; to Hardwicke, 31 Aug. and 19 Sept., 32895, ff. 83, 490; 31 Oct., 32897, ff. 513–15; 16 Nov., 32898, f. 285.

to the debate were the same as in the other, but the arguments were different.

The upholders of the American war began with the truism that the military and naval efforts of the country should be directed to their real object, instead of pursuing it by the roundabout way of a war elsewhere.[63] The war had been begun in North America, and its real design, so far as the government could be said to have one, was to drive the French from certain disputed territories there and in the West Indies. Indeed, public opinion, which was more conscious and explicit on this subject than the ministers who conducted the war in its first stages, intended nothing less than the expulsion of the French from all North America. What more natural than to concentrate the attack there? Indeed, how else could the object be achieved? If the German war was a diversion, as some of its supporters claimed, it was a diversion chosen and started by France to distract us from the objects in which we were interested and the kind of warfare in which we were at home.[64] So far as the war had a diffused secondary object, it was the destruction of French trade; this, too, could only succeed if it was pursued directly.

A continental war could only be undertaken by the distrusted and despised army, unpopular outside the circles of the court; a maritime and colonial war was to be preferred because we were in our element and the French were out of theirs.[65] So at least the argument went; but there was some doubt of its truth. By no means all the English successes of the Seven Years War were achieved in America; by no means all the failures in Europe. Even an American war could not be fought by sailors alone. The long series of military defeats in its earlier years proved that regular soldiers were not at all at home in the backwoods; nor were the efforts of the colonists proportionate to a population twenty times as large as that of Canada. The English navy was more numerous than the French, and far more money was spent on it; but it is doubtful if it had much other advantage. If the commanders of French squadrons—d'Antin, Bompar, Du Guay Lambert, and Blénac—lacked enterprise and moral courage, one

---

[63] Walpole, *Memoirs of the Reign of King George II*, ii. 56 (Pitt); the *Monitor*, 6 Dec. 1755.

[64] *Considerations on the Present German War*, pp. 2, 32, 116.

[65] *Parl. Hist.* xii. 913 (John Philips); xiii. 233 (Waller); xiv. 601 (Vernon); xv. 355 (Beckford).

could find English parallels such as Lee and Cornelius Mitchell; and was there ever a more celebrated case than that of Byng? The French captains showed as much address and gallantry as the English, in the presence of equal or superior forces. Newcastle was reduced to despair by the punctual and neatly concerted movements by which, so long as Machault was in charge of the Marine, inferior French squadrons got out of port, crossed the Atlantic, joined and reinforced each other, relieved and protected their colonies, and slipped home without interruption. It was a type of war for which Newcastle was unfit, and he had not made a fair trial of it; but he had a little justification when he complained that our boasted superiority at sea did not offer any certain means of bringing the enemy to instant submission or preventing him from transferring his superiority on land from Europe to America.[66]

The advocates of a continental war argued that nothing but neglect of her navy for her army could prevent France from becoming equal to us at sea, as she had been in King William's war. Complete freedom from all danger on the continent would enable her to do so in a few years.[67] This was to assume that military and naval power were interchangeable at will. However, there was at least this much truth in the suggestion: the starvation of the French navy for the sake of the army was one of the greatest causes of our naval victories.

In the spring of 1760 a crisis arose which illustrates the competition between army and navy for the resources of France. Berryer, minister of Marine, wanted to relieve Martinique from the danger of an English attack. He had already demanded in December 1759 an appropriation of forty million livres for this and other services, but though his projects had been approved, they had not been executed for want of the money. If the English had attempted the island in the winter campaigning season, it had nothing but its own resources to defend it. The budget of the Marine had now been reduced to thirty millions, out of which

[66] Newcastle to Hardwicke, 4 Oct. 1755, Add. MSS. 32859, f. 361. Newcastle even seems to have been frightened by the 'immense' French fleet (see his letters to Hardwicke, 28 Dec. 1755, Add. MSS. 32861, f. 487, and to Devonshire, 2 Jan. 1756, Add. MSS. 32862, f. 6). See also the speeches of his supporters, *Parl. Hist.* xv. 340 (Conway), 362 (Horace Walpole).

[67] Ibid. xii. 909 (Yonge), 974 (Horace Walpole); xiii. 409 (Murray); xv. 362 (Horace Walpole), 369 (Egmont).

twenty-one had to be deducted for the ordinary expenses of the colonies, for stores sent to Canada, for old debts, and for some articles which had nothing to do with the Marine. That left only nine million livres, or half a million sterling, for the ordinary expenses of the navy. This was a very small sum compared with the £3,640,000 voted for the English sea service in the same year (and that did not include the payment on the navy debt and the 'Ordinary of the navy', which amounted to nearly a million and a quarter more). Berryer laid the deplorable case before his fellow ministers. Martinique was one of the most important colonies; it was the military and commercial capital of the Windward Islands, and its fall would be a serious blow to the prestige of France. There could be no two opinions about the necessity of saving it; but how could that be done?

The ordinary peace-time budget of the Marine had been so inadequate between 1748 and 1755 that it did not enable the Marine to pay off the debt of thirty millions contracted in the preceding war, which therefore still subsisted. The necessary supplies could not be bought for readiness at the outbreak of the Seven Years War, with the result that heavier expenses had to be incurred after it began. Nothing was ever ready in time, or up to the standard necessary for success. Stores were bought too cheap, insufficient labour employed at the arsenals, new constructions prevented, old ones suspended, repairs badly done; the marines reduced, departments closed, officials turned off, pensions denied. Some said the Marine should try to pay for current operations and let the old debts look after themselves; but this was impossible, for arrears of pay could not be kept up indefinitely. Berryer finished this jeremiad with some general remarks:

We must not flatter ourselves that a navy which has been long neglected and in the greatest disorder can resist, with very inadequate resources, one which has been manned, armed and supplied long beforehand, and has besides 150 million livres a year spent on it to keep it in commission; and since the occasion offers, I will add that we do not go the right way about it. We make plans, and only then do we fit out the fleets; it seems to me that, on the contrary, we ought to have the fleet ready and then make the plans. Besides, we ought to be sure of our ways and means before we get the fleets ready at all. To explain more precisely, I believe that France will never succeed in making war with advantage, or even on an equality, against a maritime power such as England, unless the French navy is in commission all the year round like the English; without that, all plans and expeditions are liable to fail. The reason is obvious; for when the French navy wants to make an expedition it is forced to let the world know it four or five months in advance; the English soon hear of it, and are in a condition to prevent it by blockading the ports, and in fact to frustrate any measures that may be taken, while in the period for which the French fleet is out of commission, the English fleets, convoys and coasting trade sail safely by without being molested.[68]

This lamentable deduction of the consequences of insolvency is perhaps exaggerated, for Berryer was aware of his own insufficiency and made the worst of his task. His paper was communicated to three soldiers—Belleisle, Soubise, d'Estrées—and to Puysieulx, the minister of finance. Only Puysieulx was wholly in favour of the expedition to Martinique, and offered to provide the necessary twelve million livres by cutting the expenses of other departments. He said:

I do not know of any real enemies of France except the English. Because they are fortunate and have got the upper hand of us, are we to abandon everything to them? Is it not humiliating to think that the loss of Martinique will transfer to them a trade worth 70 million livres, or two-thirds of the interest of their national debt?

The three soldiers acknowledged the importance of Martinique, and wished something might be done to save it; Soubise concurred half-heartedly with Puysieulx, but Belleisle and d'Estrées were prepared to content themselves with some half-measure. One of them suggested equipping some vessels at Brest for six months, in the hope that they might be able to cruise in the Channel for the protection of the coasts and trade, or even that their existence might intimidate the English into keeping a large force at home. Failing that, something might be done with the famous flat-bottomed boats, which had terrified Newcastle out of his senses the year before but were now powerless, since the calamitous defeat of the French navy at Quiberon, to effect a really formidable invasion. Belleisle, the minister of war, pointed out that his departmental estimate for this year had originally been 190 million livres. He had reduced it to 145 millions, by retarding certain payments, and the contrôleur général had slashed it down again to 120 millions. Farther he would not go, and if the Marine could not relieve Martinique without encroaching upon the finances of the army, it must content itself with something less. The expedition did not sail.[69]

This controversy would have delighted and justified the English advocates of a continental war; for it was obvious that the decrepitude of the French navy was chiefly caused by want of money. Want of spirit too, perhaps; for when Choiseul succeeded the doleful and frugal Berryer, the naval affairs of France took a brisker turn, in spite of the difficulties to which Berryer called attention.[70] Yet even Choiseul could not raise the Marine at once from the debility to which years of starvation had reduced it. Besides, the suspension of payments on the French government's bills of exchange from the colonies gave the continental politicians of England an argument against their adversaries. When the latter asserted that the continental diversion made no real impression on France, the former replied that she had already defaulted.[71]

England was never reduced to such an alternative between her army and her navy; but the land and sea wars competed for her resources as they did for those of France. A maritime war was believed to be cheaper to us than any other. It could be pursued for many years without straining public credit. The financial dangers of a continental war were demonstrated by the crisis of 1748, when the subscribers to the loan had the greatest difficulty in paying their instalments and might never have succeeded in completing them if peace had not intervened.[72] This would have realized a danger which the Opposition always prophesied,

[69] Replies of d'Estrées, 16 Mar. 1760; of Puysieulx, 17 Mar.; of Soubise, 22 Mar.; of Belleisle, 26 Mar. (ibid.).

[70] Choiseul succeeded in sending Blénac off to the West Indies, but could not get d'Aubigny out of Rochefort to follow him. Ternay took St. John's, Newfoundland, but it was soon recaptured. Choiseul's schemes for 1762 are to be found in the Plan de campagne par mer pour l'Année 1762, A. N., Marine, B 4, 104, and in his dispatch to Ossun of 5 Apr. 1762 (A.A.É., Espagne, 536).

[71] A Full and Candid Answer to a Pamphlet entitled, Considerations upon the Present German War (1761), p. 11; The Conduct of the Ministry Impartially Examined (1760), p. 44.

[72] This was used as an argument to justify the peace in 1748 (Parl. Hist. xv. 331 (Murray)), but was later turned by Temple and others against the continental policy (ibid., 621). In fact, the movements of the stocks were striking. The 3 per cents. fell from 86¾ in Apr. 1747, when there was a hope of a peace, to 74 in Mar. 1748, just before the conferences began; by the end of April they had risen to 86¼ and in June, after the preliminaries were signed, to 92½.

namely that we should spend so much on an inconclusive effort upon the continent as to disable ourselves from carrying on our own war at sea.[73] Various amateurish calculations were made, which showed that, while the respective costs of keeping up an English and a French warship were roughly the same, an English soldier in Germany was twice as expensive as a French one. This belief that we got better value for money in a naval war was heightened by the hard bargaining, not to say exorbitance, of our subsidized allies, among them the king himself as elector of Hanover. It created the legend of 'the German gulph, which cries "give, give", and is never satisfied'.[74] Another considerable argument was the drain of bullion for the upkeep of armies in Germany. A naval war spent money at home, and even brought some into the country by prizes; our expenditure in our own colonies only increased their power of purchasing English goods.[75]

Mercantile considerations like these appealed no doubt to a nation of shopkeepers; but the adversaries of the continental war were on still stronger ground when they asserted, like Legge, that 'no nation can afford a greater quantity of war of any species, than it is able to pay for, and that if we add greatly to our expenses at one end of the scale and are not able to abate at the other, we shall soon be bankrupt'.[76] The politicians who conducted the Seven Years War were haunted by the fear of a necessary option to be made between its two branches, and this financial danger enabled each party in the ministerial coalition to denounce the expensiveness of measures which it disliked for other reasons.

It was impossible to come to any agreement about the financial aspect of the struggle between England and France. There was none as to the premisses, which were founded upon ignorance and guesswork on both sides. The question was, which country had the greater resources, and how would they be affected by the war? If either could afford to outlast the other, its interest would be to engage in a contest of expense. As Choiseul put it, the longest purse must win; but each nation imagined itself to possess it, so that Count Viry, who managed the peace treaty of 1762, remarked

[73] *Parl. Hist.* xiii. 425 (Waller), 503 (Strange); Legge to Newcastle, 15 Feb. 1762, Add. MSS. 32934, f. 351. Grenville took the same view (Hardwicke to Newcastle, 14 Apr., Add. MSS. 32937, f. 103).

[74] Bolingbroke to Marchmont, 9 June 1741, *Marchmont Papers*, ii. 258.

[75] *Britons Awake, and Look About You*, p. 58; *Parl. Hist.* xii. 924 (Bance).

[76] Legge to Newcastle, 4 Sept. 1758, Add. MSS. 32883, f. 276.

that the war would soon come to an end if each side would give
up the vain hope of ruining the other financially.[77] Some Frenchmen were obsessed by the precariousness of the English credit
system, and recommended a continental war as the shortest way
to overload and destroy it.[78] This reasoning was accepted by many
Englishmen, who therefore urged the necessity of avoiding such
a war; but some were of another opinion and justified the continental war on the ground that it would exhaust the resources of
France first.[79]

Again, there was some doubt how far a purely maritime war
would affect the two nations. Most Englishmen were agreed that
it would be fatal to France, by destroying her shipping and her
trade, and drying up her sources of revenue so that she could no
longer support her campaigns in Europe. There were Frenchmen
who took the same view. It was true that, as England had much
more shipping than France, her losses would be absolutely
greater; but while English shipping might be reduced, that of
France would be annihilated.[80] This argument, however, was
contradicted by others who thought the absolute losses more
important as they would conduce to bankruptcy and shrinkage
of revenue.[81] Besides, would French trade be destroyed because
French shipping was so? This turned on the rights which England was prepared to accord to neutrals, and their courage in
claiming them.[82]

[77] Stanley to Pitt, 12 June 1761, in F. Thackeray, *A History of the Right Hon.
William Pitt, Earl of Chatham* (2 vols., London, 1827), i. 525; Viry to Solar
(private), 27 Mar. 1762, A.A.É., Angleterre, 443.

[78] Silhouette to Amelot, 24 Dec. 1739, A.A.É., Angleterre, 405, f. 368; Bussy
to Amelot, 17 May 1741, 412, f. 50.

[79] Yorke expressed both these opinions within little more than a year. Yorke
to Newcastle, 18 June 1756, Add. MSS. 32865, f. 344; 15 July 1757, 32872, f. 91;
Walpole, *Memoirs of the Reign of King George III*, i. 129–30.

[80] On this matter, Silhouette and Bussy took different sides in the letters
quoted above; Silhouette attached more importance to the relative losses of English and French shipping, and Bussy to the absolute losses of the latter. D'Argenson reported in 1739 that the French and Spanish navies were thought equal to
a defensive war against England, during which the French privateers could 'soon
cause the insurance on English ships to rise to 50 per cent., which is the ther-
mometer of a maritime war', always provided the rest of Europe was not inspired
by jealousy of the House of Bourbon to arm against it. *Journal et Mémoires du
Marquis d'Argenson*, ed. E. J. B. Rathery (9 vols., Paris, 1859–67), ii. 307.

[81] Bunge to Höpken (intercept), 31 Jan. 1756, giving the supposed views of the
French court, Add. MSS. 32862, f. 301; *Parl. Hist.* x. 1192 (Hervey).

[82] This point was taken into consideration in the debate of 14 Nov. 1754 (*Parl.
Hist.* xv. 333 seqq.; speeches of Beckford, Horace Walpole, and Egmont).

There was another thing to be considered: the mercantilists were always afraid that a temporary diversion of trade might become a permanent loss. One must, therefore, take into account not only the damage to the trade of each country during the war but the situation after it. Much of the English commerce and navigation was ordinarily carried on for other peoples, or supplied them with goods which our rivals would be glad to offer them. That of France and still more of Spain, on the other hand, was more confined to their own coasts and dominions, or consisted in the export of goods which could not equally well be obtained elsewhere. The latter must revive at a peace, and could be reserved once more for native merchants and shipowners, even if it had to be thrown open to neutrals in war-time. The former, once lost, was gone for ever.[83] Lastly, there were points which escaped most people's notice. All the foreign trade of England was overseas trade; that was not true of France. Moreover, France was a self-contained country whose foreign trade played a smaller part in her whole economy than did that of England.

There was so little material for a solid judgement of these problems that both sides of the question were supported in both countries. Each had its advocates and opponents of continental war; but the diplomatic conjunctures of Europe tempted both to engage in it. To trace the process by which the maritime wars of 1739 and 1755 became general all over Europe would be beside the point here. Both England and France came to lay more and more stress on the continental side of the action.

In spite of the fanatics for America, we had allies in both these wars, and the fact raised a new set of debates. What kind of help should we give them? The maritime party maintained that we could do them more good by activity in our proper sphere than by meddling in theirs. If we destroyed French trade and seized the French colonies, we should hamstring France so that she could not afford to play the tyrant in Europe.[84] This indirect salvation never satisfied our allies; they demanded something in hand. Then the question arose, whether men or subsidies? Even if we set forth armies on the continent, the territories of our allies were sometimes invaded; must we then make peace? Here again

[83] *Parl. Hist.* xi. 944 (Pulteney); xii. 253 (Talbot).
[84] Ibid. xiv. 163 (Velters Cornwall), 198 (Beckford); the *Monitor* of 8 and 15 Nov. 1755.

M

the maritime party was ready with an answer. Let us sacrifice our allies for the time being. To defend them in their own countries would be expensive and useless. We must therefore leave them 'in deposit'. Our strength and money would be better spent in amassing cheap conquests outside Europe. The superfluity of these would be enough to ransom our allies at the peace, and perhaps to procure them a compensation for their sufferings. In this spirit Pitt proposed to leave Hanover 'in deposit'. Nivernois found in 1762 that nobody in England would mind if Lisbon fell; instead of redeeming Portugal with Cuba, we should leave it in the possession of Spain for a year, while we conquered Mexico. Then we should buy the freedom of Portugal by restoring Mexico, and keep Cuba as pure gain. To the allies thus left in pawn, this must have appeared to be the most heartless commercialism that ever called itself strategy; no doubt the maritime party in England thought it merely good business.[85]

These questions gave rise to more than pamphlet controversies; there was a real struggle over them in the cabinet from the beginning of the Spanish war. Even before the troubles on the continent began, Walpole was questioning the wisdom of sending all our forces to the West Indies, because he was afraid of an invasion. Newcastle overrode him, and remained passionately keen to promote the American expedition, even after that venture had been frustrated and rendered ridiculous at Cartagena. Slowly, however, the interest of the ministry and even the public was beginning to turn from American expeditions to the contest over the Austrian succession. Hardwicke told Newcastle that 'It looked last year as if the old world was to be fought for in the new; but now the tables are turned, and I fear that now America must be fought for in Europe. Whatever success we may have in the former, I doubt it will always finally follow the fate of the latter.' Even then Newcastle was for hurrying out reinforcements to Vernon and making another attempt in the West Indies;[86] but he soon acquiesced in Hardwicke's reasoning. When the continent was quiet, English

[85] Viry to Solar, 10 July 1762, A.A.É., Angleterre, 446; Nivernois to Comte de Choiseul, 15 Sept., vol. 447. Frederick II suggested in Feb. 1762 that the King of Portugal had better retire to Brazil, so that Spain would gain very little and England lose very little by the conquest of his country (*Politische Correspondenz*, xxi, no. 13468).

[86] Hardwicke to Newcastle, 17 Aug. 1741, Add. MSS. 32697, f. 426; Newcastle to Harrington, 20 June, 4 July, ff. 215, 310; to Hardwicke, 15 Aug., 35407, f. 68.

statesmen could make good resolutions to have nothing to do with it; but they could not keep them when a disturbance arose and allies went begging.

When Carteret succeeded Walpole, the change was complete. He might profess to be the slave of the English merchants,[87] but that was a piece of popular affectation which never sat worse on anybody's shoulders than on his. He was a typical continental statesman, who only liked and understood the highly artificial business of juggling electors, grand dukes, and empress-queens into uneasy and astonishing alliances. The political associates over whose shoulders he had just climbed into power naturally reminded him of the cry of 'Take and hold'; yet though Carteret repelled the charge of neglecting the Spanish war for the German, he satisfied the public not by American adventures, but by a strong reinforcement in the Mediterranean which blocked up the Spanish forces in Italy.[88]

No more was heard of America in Carteret's time. The Pelhams hardly gave it another thought, until the capture of Louisbourg. This seems to have inspired Bedford, the first lord of the Admiralty, with a passion for North America; he planned an expedition to Quebec for 1746. Newcastle conspired to prevent it. He believed it would determine the Dutch (who were not yet technically at war) to make a separate peace.

> 1st, as the Dutch will think it a proof that we are not disposed to peace, but are resolved to continue the war, and that in a manner, that will not promise a speedy end of it. 2dly, that by sending our troops to America, we disable ourselves still more from sending any to their assistance, and 3rdly that if we make these conquests, we shall be disposed to keep them, which will be in a degree as disagreeable to them as to France herself.[89]

It may have been Newcastle who was responsible for some of the delays which prevented the forces from sailing until it was too late in the year to go to America at all; Bedford seems to have suspected something of the sort.[90] Next year Newcastle had got

---

[87] Bussy to Amelot, 17 May, n.s. 1742, A.A.É., Angleterre, 414, f. 431.

[88] Bussy to Amelot, 29 Mar., n.s. 1742, A.A.É., Angleterre, 409, f. 274; 28 June, n.s. 415, f. 62; *Parl. Hist.* xii. 1083 (Carteret), 1109 (Hervey), 1141 (Chesterfield), 1154 (Newcastle).

[89] Newcastle to Hardwicke, 2 Apr. 1746, Add. MSS. 35408, f. 220; 21 May, 32707, f. 230.

[90] This may be an exaggerated deduction from a peppery letter written by

over his fear of the effect upon our allies, to whom he thought to justify the enterprise as a severe blow to the French trade and finances.[91] Besides, he was no longer so anxious for peace, and having convinced himself that the conquest of Canada was strongly desired by the public, he had to fear criticism from an even more dangerous quarter than the allies if he gave up the attempt. He believed that the popularity of the government and the war depended on it, and would be injured by its abandonment. That was enough for Newcastle; he and Bedford stood out for the expedition against the rest of their colleagues, and were only frustrated by the professional opinion of Admiral Warren.[92]

Newcastle's record in the war of 1739 thus offers no ground for condemning him outright as a slavish devotee of continental politics. In 1755 he was converted once again to the American and naval war. That, indeed, was only because, as the Duke of Cumberland quite truly said, 'he could get nobody to take his money', or, as he put it himself, the weakness of the Dutch and the bad behaviour of Maria Theresa left him no choice but to give up continental politics for the time being.[93] It was, therefore, no true conversion, and Newcastle went back upon it as soon as he saw a chance of forming a system on the continent.[94]

During the Seven Years War Newcastle did not constantly

Bedford to Newcastle's secretary, 10 Nov. 1746 (*Correspondence of John, fourth Duke of Bedford*, ed. Lord John Russell, 3 vols., London, 1842–6, i. 182). Pitt speaks of Bedford as the only supporter of the Canada expedition in the ministry; he might know, being secretary-at-war, but he was not in the effective cabinet (ibid., p. 131).

[91] Draft declaration of (?) Jan. 1747, Add. MSS. 35409, f. 16.

[92] Newcastle to Sandwich, 23 Dec. 1746, Add. MSS. 32806, f. 298; 31 Jan. 1746–7, 32807, f. 43. In this correspondence with Sandwich, Newcastle doubtless overrated the fervour of his concurrence with Bedford, for Sandwich was Bedford's disciple and confidant.

[93] *Diary of the late George Bubb Dodington*, ed. H. P. Wyndham (Salisbury, 1784), 22 July 1755, pp. 346–7; Newcastle to W. Bentinck, 16 Oct. 1755, Add. MSS. 32860, f. 64.

[94] In Jan. 1756 Newcastle was already less convinced of the impossibility of a continental war, partly because of the Prussian alliance, and partly for the curious reason that France appeared to desire a purely maritime war against us; he argued that if it was to her interest it could not be to ours (Newcastle to Devonshire, 2 Jan. 1756, Add. MSS. 32862, f. 6). Newcastle expressed a strong preference for a continental plan after his experiences of 1756; see his letters to Yorke, 11 June 1756 and 19 Aug. 1757, Add. MSS. 32865, f. 261, 32873, f. 174; to Anson, 7 July 1758, 32881, f. 189. But though he sometimes disparaged the naval war, he usually took care to refer to the German operations as a diversion.

obstruct Pitt's American projects. He and his party in the coalition bickered with Pitt about the kind of help which should be sent to Germany, and disliked the descents upon the coast of France. That was only contrasting one kind of continental war with another, for the descents were chiefly important to Pitt because they diverted French troops from Germany.[95] Newcastle never tried to stop the conquest of the French colonies; he sometimes proposed it himself, or believed himself to have done so. It is easy to be misled into a one-sided view of Newcastle's policy by his constant whinings and whimperings for continental operations during the coalition ministry. He only meant to correct Pitt's inclination to neglect that side of the war. He was not responsible for the conduct of the whole war, but only for seeing that Pitt conducted it. He would not have exclaimed so vehemently on behalf of his favourite measures if he had not believed them to be slighted by his partner. Pitt insisted on an ostensible preference for the American war, as Newcastle did for the German. Symbolical action was immensely important to both of them; each was always looking out for an opportunity to establish his doctrine by implication from a trifle, or to repel an attempt of the other to strengthen his own in the same way.

There was nevertheless a real difference between Newcastle and Pitt, but it has been obscured by the imaginary distinctions which Pitt and his admirers drew in order to justify his conversion to the German war. In fact that conversion was natural enough. Responsibility sobered the declamatory patriot until he saw the necessity of what he had denounced. He found himself in charge of a war in which England had already got, as much by blunder as design, an important ally in Germany. Measures were already taken for an army of observation. Pitt could hardly have retreated abruptly from these preparations already made; he wisely made the best of them, and invented a new doctrine to excuse them. If, he said, we were to have continental allies at all, we should rather connect ourselves with some great Power like Prussia, than compile a nondescript force of mercenaries from all the small principalities of Germany.[96] This was good sense, but it

[95] Hardwicke seems to have misunderstood when he imagined that the chief object of these expeditions was to destroy ships and dockyards (Hardwicke to Newcastle, 9 Oct. 1757, Add. MSS. 32874, f. 489; Newcastle to Hardwicke, 14 May 1761, 32923, f. 68).

[96] Compare Pitt's language of 1755 (Hardwicke to Newcastle, 9 Aug. 1755,

was hardly the language he had talked two years ago, when he merely denounced the treaties as likely to lead us into a new continental war.

Five years afterwards, he was probably thinking of the same thing when he said, in a famous speech, 'As Germany had formerly been managed, it had been a millstone round our necks; as managed now, about that of France'.[97] That might be true, but he did not deserve all the credit of it, for he had not made the Prussian alliance. If he was thinking of distinctions in the strategy of the war, there again they were less important than they looked. Newcastle's treaties were designed, perhaps ineptly, for the same purpose as Pitt's 'containing operations': to keep Europe quiet while we pursued our proper aims in America.[98] At one time and another, Pitt prevented Newcastle from making concessions to Germany; but he afterwards made most of them himself. Indeed, he seems to have admitted the unimportance of the differences between himself and Newcastle, when he said of his colleagues that 'he borrowed their majority to carry out their own plan'. His hero-worshippers have thought it necessary to ignore this admission and to claim the merit of consistency where inconsistency would have been more meritorious still. Pitt was a great man; not necessarily a good or a clever man, still less a consistent man. His greatness consisted in learning the lesson, not in having nothing to learn.

If there was a difference between Pitt and Newcastle, it consisted in Pitt's efficiency and driving force, and still more in the fact that he had a purpose where Newcastle had none. If Newcastle, like Pitt, had meant to drive the French out of North America, he would have been inexcusable if he had not carried on the war in the way that Pitt did; but he meant nothing of the kind. He had drifted into the war he hardly knew how; he wished to put general pressure on France in order to make her give up her pretensions and practices on the North American frontier. As his object was not North America but peace, it is no wonder the war was, for him, a general war with France, not a war for North America.

Add. MSS. 32858, f. 76) with that of 1757 (Walpole, *Memoirs of the Reign of King George II*, iii. 17–18).

[97] Walpole, *Memoirs of the Reign of King George III*, i. 83.

[98] Newcastle to Holdernesse, 9 May 1755, Add. MSS. 32854, f. 460.

Everything helped to reconcile Pitt to the German war. His colleagues in the coalition put few intentional difficulties in the way of his American schemes. As long as Pitt could have no excuse, and give none to others, for complaining that America was neglected, he could afford to feed the war in Germany with the overplus of our strength. After the essential objects of the war had been achieved in America, Pitt could see as well as Newcastle that France must be prevented from redeeming them by important conquests in Germany. That was Choiseul's calculation and, after 1759, his only hope;[99] therefore, until we could make peace, we must defend the front in Germany and prevent him from making an impression on it. Indeed we must do more: a defensive campaign was not enough. Positive victories were needed which would both cause Choiseul to lose heart, and clear the French troops out of such territories of our allies as they still held.[1]

In another way, though with a worse grace, Pitt's colleagues satisfied the requirements of his strategy. He had been impressed by the need of a militia at home, and had overcome the political objections of Hardwicke and Newcastle. Having done so, he could afford to lavish soldiers on Germany as well as America, and to disperse his fleets to all the quarters of the world.

The connexion between Germany and the militia is pretty clearly shown by the compromise of 1760; Pitt consented to send more soldiers to the continent if Newcastle and Hardwicke would procure the passage of his cousin's bill for continuing the militia.[2]

Pitt had a still stronger justification for revising his opinion on

---

[99] Choiseul to Bussy, 19 June 1761, A.A.É., Angleterre, 443; Stanley to Pitt, 12 June 1761, printed in Thackeray, *History of William Pitt*, i. 525–6; Choiseul to Ossun, 17 Apr. and 16 May 1762, A.A.É., Espagne, 536. Choiseul still treated the German war as a thing of secondary importance in 1759; he told Bernstorff that a detachment of the army would ruin the Elector of Hanover's possessions for several generations, but the main effort of France would be an invasion of England; a few months later he said that as the German war was useless as a diversion from America and did no good to the allies, and as France did not want any conquests in that part of the world, he was willing to bring it to an end when England would (Choiseul to Bernstorff, 29 July and 23 Sept. 1759, *En Brevvexling mellem Grev J. H. E. Bernstorff og Hertugen af Choiseul, 1758–66*, Copenhagen, 1871, pp. 46–74).

[1] Newcastle to Bedford, 15 Jan. 1760, Add. MSS. 32901, f. 276; to Devonshire, 8 Apr., 32904, f. 259; to Pitt, 1 June, 32906, f. 408; to Hardwicke, 21 July, 32908, f. 399; to Hardwicke, 13 Sept., 32911, f. 269.

[2] Barrington to Newcastle, 18 Apr. 1760, Add. MSS. 32904, f. 424.

the continental war; he was not merely converted from America to Europe, but combined them. Having conducted the war during four years, he had come to understand the connexion between all its parts. He saw that a diversion in Germany kept busy French troops and money that would otherwise be employed in Flanders, Portugal, America, or an invasion. He understood the necessity of a financial strain which he believed we could bear and France could not. He insisted on the totality of the war.[3]

Newcastle came to believe in this principle almost as much as Pitt, but he never went quite so far. Pitt was not only willing to carry on a war with Spain as well as France; he was anxious to provoke it. Newcastle would not give up the German war for a Spanish one, dared not give up the Spanish war for the German, and therefore had to proclaim, like Pitt, the necessity of supporting them both; but if he could have avoided this additional war with Spain he would have done so. However, though their reasons and their spirit were very different, Pitt and Newcastle agreed in defending the policy of the whole war against the new party which had arisen for contracting it.

After the 'wonderful year' of 1759, the chief purpose of the war was achieved by the virtual expulsion of the French from North America. A reaction began to arise against the continuance of the effort. France could not yet be forced to terms which would satisfy our allies as well as ourselves; but while statesmen could see the necessity of keeping up the war until then, public opinion, less able to understand the policy of altruism, began to call a halt.[4] The financial burden was great, and the elasticity of our resources difficult to guess. Both Pitt and Newcastle scented the possibility of opposition, and each met it in his characteristic

[3] Walpole, *Memoirs of the Reign of King George III*, i. 75–76, 128–30. The language of Pitt's admirers, Beckford and Charles Townshend, was very much the same.

[4] Many pamphlets were published in this sense, but none of them made such an impression as Mauduit's *Considerations on the Present German War*. It is so much superior to the common run of eighteenth-century pamphlets that contemporaries naturally ascribed it to some very exalted author. Why anybody should have chosen Lord Hardwicke for that honour is more than I can understand. Admittedly he was the best strategist in the cabinet, but neither the style nor the ideas are his. Moreover, Newcastle wrote to Joseph Yorke that an *answer* to Mauduit (of which they both approved) was thought to have come 'from a great Hand', and Yorke replied that he believed so too. Newcastle's underlining is often mysterious, and deserves a special study by itself; but I think it possible that the '*great hand*' may have been Yorke's father, Lord Hardwicke.

way, Pitt by vehemently denouncing the Treasury for frauds and overcharges in the German commissariat, Newcastle by tentative economies, whose insignificance he was the first to admit, in the disposition of our forces in America. At this point George II died, and a new actor appeared upon the scene, resolved to take the principal part but undetermined how to play it.

Lord Bute's chief aim was popularity, not for himself but for his master. In the earliest months of the new reign, he was casting about for the most certain means of obtaining it. Public opinion was in a moment of transition. The cries of patriotism were still loud, but the complaints against the German war were increasing. Nobody could tell whether the fall of Pitt would provoke a revolution or a sigh of relief; but in most people's opinion the former was the more likely. Bute wanted to end the war, but to do so gloriously, and he had to steer between the parties of war and peace, adhering now to one, now to the other, perhaps without any more cunning calculation than a desire to play the safest cards. Already at the New Year of 1761 he had his eye on the possibility of withdrawing from the German war and carrying on more vigorously the popular part of it, expeditions to the West Indies and so forth. His friends advised him to do this as his own act, that he and the king might have the merit of it. He feared that the ministry might pre-empt this acceptable line of policy, and seems to have been relieved when he found that Pitt was 'madder than ever', and had no intention of giving up the continent. Yet he was not entirely determined, and Dodington thought him disposed to carry on the whole war, or to see difficulties in the way of contracting it.[5] Bute saw his opportunity a few months later in the approach of a war with Spain. Before it was declared—even before Pitt had resigned on account of his colleagues' refusal to declare it—Bute had foreseen that this option between the Spanish and the German wars would force the resignation of a minister who insisted on carrying on both.[6] In the end,

[5] Dodington's *Diary*, 2, 9, and 16 Jan. 1761, pp. 422, 426–7, 430–1; Dodington to Bute, 16 Jan. 1761, in Adolphus, *History of England*, i. 571–2.

[6] Bute told Newcastle that, if we had a Spanish war, we should have to give up our operations in Germany, and Pitt would probably resign on that account (Newcastle to Hardwicke, 26 Sept. 1761, Add. MSS. 32928, f. 363). Hardwicke did not think Pitt would or should do anything of the kind, for he still believed that Pitt and Temple would agree with Bute in giving up the German war, if an option had to be made. Pitt's public-spirited declarations against doing so must

Pitt left the ministry for a different reason; nor does Bute seem to have been glad of his departure.[7] Bute now had his hand on the engine which would remove Newcastle: the Spanish war or the German war, but not both.[8] It would hardly be just to accuse Bute of involving himself in the Spanish war at the end of 1761 on purpose to force this alternative upon his colleagues. He and Egremont did, indeed, provoke it by a diplomatic *brusquerie* worthy of Pitt himself, but they did so because they were afraid to yield anything which Pitt would not have yielded.

There is no need to describe again the process by which Bute edged out Newcastle and shuffled out of the Prussian alliance. He advanced slowly. In November 1761 he was angry with Shelburne for making a speech against the German war, because he was afraid his friend would appear to be flying a kite for him; but on 10 January he spoke in the cabinet for giving it up.[9] The new prospect which was opened by the accession of Peter III of Russia made him waver; for though he let it be understood that he was resolved to abandon the continental war, he opposed Bedford's motion for that purpose in the House of Lords, only, it is true, by the previous question.[10] It soon appeared, however, that Peter III was going to increase the embarrassment between England and Prussia by his wild-cat schemes in the Baltic, and Bute determined to deprive Frederick of the subsidy which we had paid

therefore have surprised Newcastle and Hardwicke after his resignation. Bute had taken Pitt's measure better than they had, perhaps because he was not obsessed, as they were, by Pitt's past record on this subject.

[7] Bute to Dodington, 8 Oct. 1761, printed by Adolphus, op. cit., i. 572.

[8] This edifying dialogue took place one day between them. Bute told Newcastle that the popular opinion was 'That we had worked Mr. Pitt out, and were now following his extravagant measures (meaning the continent measures), and that we had better have Mr. Pitt again'. Newcastle replied that people really said 'That Mr. Pitt went out because we would not declare war against Spain; and as soon as he was out, we did the same thing; and that being the case, Mr. Pitt would carry on his own measures better than anybody' (Newcastle to Devonshire, 13 Apr. 1762, Add. MSS. 32937, f. 88).

[9] Fox to Shelburne, 12 Nov. 1761, 8 Jan. 1762, in Lord E. Fitzmaurice, *Life of William, Earl of Shelburne* (2nd ed., 2 vols., London, 1912), i. 100, 103; Newcastle to Hardwicke, 10 Jan. 1762, Add. MSS. 32933, f. 179 (but a fortnight later Newcastle thought the king and Bute were still undecided; Newcastle to Yorke, 26 Jan., 32934, f. 13).

[10] *Parl. Hist.* xv. 1217 (Bedford), 1218 (Bute), 1220 (Protest); according to Fox, George III was very angry with those who spoke on Bedford's side against Bute (Memoir, in *Life and Letters of Lady Sarah Lennox, 1745–1826*, ed. Lady Ilchester and Lord Stavordale, 2 vols., London, 1901–3, i. 60).

him since 1756.[11] He went no farther; he did not abandon the German, as distinct from the Prussian war. In fact, 1762 was one of the most successful campaigns of the English army under Prince Ferdinand; but the controversy over the Prussian subsidy was enough to bring on the quarrel of Bute and Newcastle.

At first it was George Grenville who forced the pace. Newcastle wanted peace, and believed that the best way to get it was to carry on the war on all fronts, continental as well as American. Grenville wanted not peace but conquest and dignity; he therefore advocated a kind of war which could be carried on for ever. Newcastle thought him ripe for giving up the German war in November 1761, though he defended it in the House of Commons as an unwelcome moral obligation.[12] (This point of view explains the efforts of the ministry to prove Frederick in the wrong; only so could his moral claim be repudiated.) George Grenville represents a more definite kind of policy than Bute. While Bute shuffled confusedly between war and peace, Grenville always knew what he wanted. He was for limiting the war to the sea, the colonies, and such European countries as Portugal, where England had a special economic interest. In these fields, he was ready to fight Spain as well as France. This was the Opposition cry of 1755, revived as the policy of the government. It was now Pitt who claimed that America had been conquered in Germany, and Grenville who denied, with a show of pedestrian reason, that we owed Wolfe's victory or Hawke's to anything but English valour.[13] George Grenville stole the suit of clothes which Pitt had deliberately discarded as too small for him. In the end he wore it alone; for Bute, having turned out the war minister and the peace minister, did not mean to suffer the dictation of his new colleague, whose programme was the limited war, and turned back to his original policy of peace at almost any price. In the spring of 1762, however, Bute took Grenville's part against Newcastle. It is a

[11] Newcastle to Devonshire, 13 Apr. 1762, Add. MSS. 32937, f. 85; Hardwicke to Newcastle, 14 Apr., f. 103; Yorke to Newcastle, 16 Apr., f. 141; Newcastle to Rockingham, 4 May, 32938, f. 50; Bute to Mitchell, 26 May 1762, printed in Andrew Bisset's *Memoirs and Papers of Sir Andrew Mitchell* (2 vols., London, 1850), ii. 294–302.

[12] Newcastle to Hardwicke, 9 Nov. 1761, Add. MSS. 32930, f. 374; to Yorke, 16 Nov., 32931, f. 60; West, House of Commons reports, 9 Dec. 1761, 32932, f. 74. See also the correspondence of Newcastle and Legge upon this subject, Add. MSS. 32934, ff. 351 and 410.

[13] West, report of, 9 Dec. 1761, Add. MSS. 32932, f. 74

degrading story, for the silly old man deprived himself, by shameful half-surrenders, of all the merit of his final stand for his principles. He had already abandoned Frederick before he fell, and the German war for which he sacrificed his place was a thing without substance or outline. The events of that year proved that it was not impossible to fight a German campaign without co-operating with Frederick; but Newcastle had no clear idea how to do it.[14]

Perhaps these quarrels between the isolationists and the interventionists have little relevance for our own time; but they illustrate the dilemma which English foreign policy has often had to deal with in the last two centuries. There is a third light in which they could be considered. England has often had to decide how much of her colonial conquests she would restore to her enemies in order to procure for her allies the recovery of their lost territories or the satisfaction of their legitimate ambitions. It was of no use to conclude a war of intervention by an isolationist peace, as Lord Bute did in 1762. But that is another story, which has often been told.

[14] For example, his chief objection to depriving Frederick II of his subsidy was a fear that it would look like abandoning the German war, which he was resolved to continue; he thus distinguished between the two and thought one was possible without the other (see his letter to Hardwicke, 25 Feb. 1762, Add. MSS. 32935, f. 74). Hardwicke kept him true to his ally for a time; but when Newcastle resigned, it was not because the ministry had decided not to pay the subsidy, but rather because he insisted on an additional vote of credit in order to show the world that we should continue to carry on the *German* war (Newcastle to Mansfield, 2 May 1762, Add. MSS. 32938, f. 18; to Yorke, 14 May, f. 239).

XI

THE MANNING OF THE NAVY IN THE WEST INDIES 1702-63

[*Transactions* of the Royal Historical Society, 4th series, xx (1937), pp. 31–60]

THE manning of the navy in the West Indies presented a great administrative difficulty to the English and French governments in the eighteenth century, and brought them into conflict with several important interests. These conflicts are worth examination, because they throw light upon the problems which arose when the claims of war and business had to be adjusted to each other.

The naval squadrons, the privateers, and the merchantmen in the West Indies were all sure to lose a great number of men, not so much to the enemy as to rum and the climate. These adversaries made their most violent attacks in the first months, but they seem to have continued their work steadily after the first paroxysm. The losses which resulted from these causes could not easily be made up, for neither the shipping nor the plantations afforded a large reserve of white men able and willing to go to sea. The French privateers overcame the difficulty by employing free negroes and even slaves; but if we may judge by the remarks of governors and admirals, this practice was not common among the English privateers and almost unheard-of in the Royal Navy.[1]

---

[1] Admiral Frankland condemned the use of the 'woolly race' in vessels of war, and wished to discourage it by selling all negroes, free or slave, found on board French privateers. Governor Thomas would not allow this, probably because the negroes on the English privateers would be treated in the same way (Frankland to Clevland, 28 Apr. 1757, and his reply to charges, 20 July, P[ublic] R[ecord] O[ffice], Admiralty Papers, 1/306). The English must therefore have employed some negroes, especially at Jamaica; indeed, the *Dowdall* privateer of Jamaica had fifteen negroes in her crew, and the *Queen Anne* had twenty. The owners themselves lamented the necessity of filling up their crews in this manner, and ascribed it to Admiral Davers's press-gang, which took up all their white sailors (Second petition of the Manning party, 28 Nov. 1745, with annexed affidavit of Curtin, P.R.O., Colonial Office Papers, 137/57; Trelawny to Lords of the Admiralty, 21 Dec. 1743, Adm. 1/3817). However, we may infer from the general tone of surprise and disapproval that negroes were seldom enlisted in the crews of English privateers. Governor Robinson of Barbados expressly said so, and

The merchant shipping from Europe was reputed to need more hands on the return than on the outward voyage, because it came out half-loaded and went home with a full freight in a good or normal year. Besides, some ships carried out a few servants or emigrants, who might help in the work on board; no assistance of the kind was to be had on the voyage home. On the other hand, the slave traders nearly always had some hands to discharge in the West Indies, because they did not need nearly so large a crew to carry home a cargo of sugar as for supervising and controlling the slaves in the middle passage.[2] Whether the slave traders' surplus equalled the deficit of the other sugar-ships, there is no means of telling for this period; nor can we know what relation either figure bore to the ordinary mortality of seamen in the West Indies. But it appears from certain complaints of the merchants that

argued from it that the English would lose rather than gain by an agreement to exchange free negroes taken in privateers (Robinson, answers to queries, 20 Feb. 1746/7, C.O. 28/46). This is what might be expected, for there were fewer free negroes in the English islands than in the French, and the owners of valuable slaves would hardly expose them to capture at sea when they could employ them profitably on land. The fate of free negroes taken in arms at sea was very hard. Sometimes the colonial authorities agreed to respect their freedom if it could be lawfully proved; Trelawny and Larnage made such an arrangement in 1746 (Larnage to Maurepas, 13 Mar. 1746, A[rchives] N[ationales, Paris], Colonies, C⁹A 68). But the English courts obstructed this humane disposition. John Hudson Guy, Chief Justice of Jamaica, declared that a letter of a Spanish governor was not enough to prove the freedom of a negro. The Vice-Admiralty Court of New York invented another way to produce the same result. It accepted the Governor of Havana's certificate, but decided that the English purchasers had bought the prisoners in good faith and ought not to suffer by the mistake; therefore the negroes were not to have their freedom until the purchase-money had been refunded, presumably by themselves (C. M. Hough, *Reports of Cases in the Vice-Admiralty of the Province of New York*, New Haven, 1925, pp. 29–31). A grotesque example of the arguments employed in court against the negroes' freedom is to be found in the speech of Peter Vezian, quartermaster of the *Revenge* privateer, at New Providence. This speech may indeed be a mere literary composition invented or half-remembered after the event (J. F. Jameson, ed., *Privateering and Piracy in the Colonial Period*, New York, 1923, pp. 407–10). Some governors refused to make any arrangements for exchanging prisoners of this colour, fearing to be imposed upon by certificates of freedom falsely obtained from the enemy's authorities. Even where the governors and courts agreed to respect the freedom of negroes and mulattoes, they had still to reckon with the admirals. Frankland took the law into his own hands so far as he could, by selling as slaves all the free negroes taken by the ships under his command. Commodore Douglas followed his example, and told the Governor of Martinique that he could treat English negroes in the same way.

    [2] Trelawny to the Lords of the Admiralty, 21 Dec. 1743, Adm. 1/3817; Holmes to Pitt, 29 Oct. 1761, Adm. 1/236.

there was sometimes a great shortage of hands, even in time of peace.

War increased the competition, by adding a number of privateers to the bidders for seamen. Not all the privateers who cruised in the West Indies fitted out there, and even those who did so might draw some of their men from other parts of the world; for instance, many of the privateersmen of Martinique were non-resident. Yet there must have been some additional demand for men in the islands themselves; moreover, the royal squadrons in the West Indies were always strengthened during a war, and their needs were proportionably increased.

Desertion and inveigling were therefore very prevalent. In the French islands, the captains of vessels whose crews were reduced by mortality suborned the sailors of other vessels by excessive wages, which they paid in advance. Those whose crews were inveigled in this way were forced in their turn to seduce the crews of yet others. The captains could not well help themselves; some people thought the sailors more worthy of punishment, for they exacted five or six times their ordinary wages for the run home. There was an order of 1721 for annulling such bargains with deserters; but the sailors always made their new captains engage to indemnify them against it. Complaints of the same kind abounded in the English colonies. The seamen sometimes asked and obtained as much as forty pounds for the run home. They were commonly encouraged and concealed by the innkeepers, who were sometimes accused of 'working up' the seamen's demands 'for their obtaining the payment of the large scores, they have debauched them into the expence of', or keeping the seamen hidden 'in order to make great and unreasonable profit of them'. These landlords played, no doubt, into the hands of those merchants who were ready to pay for it, like those of Cork, of whom it was said: 'The merchants encourage the landlords to trust and keep them ready till they are wanted for privateers or merchant ships, when those who want them pay the debt which they have contracted and have security for their proceeding the voyage.'[3]

[3] Samson to Maurepas, 15 May 1745, A.N., Colonies, C⁹A 67; Vernon to Trelawny, 24 May 1740, P.R.O., State Papers, 42/85; Preamble to the Barbados Act of 30 Oct. 1754, C.O. 30/10; *Tomlinson Papers*, ed. J. G. Bullocke (Navy Records Society, 1935), pp. 185–6.

Governor Trelawny of Jamaica, in one of his quarrels with admirals, asserted that the press-gang itself was the cause of all these nuisances. That was not quite true, as we can see from the peace-time legislation of the colonies. Some masters of merchant ships at St. Kitts petitioned the governor in 1735 for a law to prevent the keepers of punch-houses from harbouring their seamen and inducing them to desert. An act of Antigua, made in 1739, recited that the traders had lately suffered from the desertion of their sailors and the extravagant demands of those whom they were forced to hire in the deserters' room. It prohibited the payment of any lump sum or gratuity for the run home, and imposed penalties on innkeepers who kept sailors on their premises after eight o'clock at night, and on masters of vessels who took them into service without a certificate of discharge from their last ship. The legislature of Barbados passed a very similar act in 1754. Both these laws, made in time of peace for the benefit of the masters of trading ships, contain provisions for search warrants and for compelling the seamen to take service, which the naval commanders-in-chief might well have envied.[4]

Where their own squadrons did not demand too much, those commanders might well have co-operated with the merchants in rounding up seamen. Admiral Vernon actually did so, before he broke with Trelawny. He felt for the merchants of whom the seamen demanded extravagant wages, and suggested that if the civil power were 'exerted with vigour in taking up all the idle seamen on shore at once, and delivering them into his Majesty's service', he would 'take care the merchant shall be assisted with them at reasonable terms, or find those to spare them in their rooms that will be glad to do so'. This scheme was executed. At the Leeward Islands, Captain Holburne performed a curious service to a merchant captain who had been obliged to promise excessive wages for the run home. He used his authority to annul the bargain by having the men pressed into his own ship, and lending some of his own crew instead. The aggrieved sailors, however, threatened to go to court, and the owners' representatives thought it prudent to pay them their full hire.[5] So long as there were

[4] St. Kitts Council Minutes, 29 May 1735 (St. Kitts Administrator's Office); Antigua Act of 1739, C.O. 8/7; Barbados Act of 30 Oct. 1754, C.O. 30/10.

[5] Lascelles and Maxwell to the owners of the *Royal Captive*, 24 Oct. 1746, Letter Books of Messrs. Wilkinson and Gaviller, vol. iii. [For these papers, and their fate, see below, p. 198.]

enough seamen to go round, the merchants could only gain by such alliances with the navy, which would lower wages artificially. In the French ports, if we may judge by the records of Bordeaux, the ship-owners relied greatly upon the interposition of the *Commissaires des classes* to force the seamen to take less wages than they asked, presumably by threatening to draft them into the king's service if they held out.[6] That kind of arrangement was only possible where the state had an absolute claim to the service of the whole sea-faring population. The government might be held to have such a claim in England, but was in process of losing it in this period, particularly in the colonies.

We cannot enter here into a general discussion of the press-gang; but we must notice its operation during these wars, and the way in which the colonies came to be exempted from it.[7]

Why had the navy to rely on the press-gang at all? Because it offered less rewards than the privateers and imposed more hardship than the merchant service. Wages naturally rose on the outbreak of war. The government made some attempt to keep pace with this rise by increasing the bounties to volunteers. It allowed the privateers and merchants to employ a high proportion of neutral sailors in their crews.[8] At the same time it tried to suppress competition by enacting that nobody should pay a seaman more than thirty-five shillings a month. This prohibition was not to apply to 'voyages from any parts beyond the seas, to any other parts beyond the seas, or to Great Britain'. Therefore, though it might have kept down wages on voyages which started in Great Britain, it did nothing to check the practice of demanding excessive lump sums for the run home from the West Indies. It must rather have stimulated desertion in the islands, from ships whose crews were engaged at a monthly wage for the whole navigation

---

[6] Directors of the Chamber of Commerce of Guienne to Maurepas, 10 Oct. 1744, 9 and 30 Mar., 25 May 1745, Archives de la Gironde, C., 4263, ff. 7, 13, 15, 19. It was in order to prevent these powers from being abused for private interests that an Ordinance of 1693 forbade the *Commissaires de la Marine* to own shares in privateers; they were still allowed, however, to take shares in the enterprise of fitting out for privateering frigates borrowed from the crown (Lebeau, *Nouveau code des prises*, 3 vols., Paris, 1798–1801, i. 176, 196).

[7] There is a good essay on this subject by Professor Dora Mae Clark in the *Essays in Colonial History presented to Charles McLean Andrews* (New Haven, 1931), pp. 198–224.

[8] 6 Anne, c. 37; 13 Geo. II, c. 3; 29 Geo. II, c. 11; *Gentleman's Magazine*, xxvii. 140. These foreign seamen were exempted from impressment by 13 Geo. II, c. 17.

out and back, to others where the sailor could make a new contract to which the act did not apply. This, at least, must have been its effect if it had any; but by most accounts it was a dead letter, and in 1745 a certain Mr. Chitty proposed to frame a new law for the same purpose.[9]

This clause therefore failed to keep down wages in the merchant vessels and privateers, so that the government had to take other measures for the purpose of attracting or compelling sailors to enrol themselves in the Royal Navy without raising their pay. It was the great argument for the press-gang, that it effected this economy. Indeed, if George Grenville was to be believed, the pressed men were detained for months, or even years, without receiving any wages at all. This abuse was explained by the fact that no seaman was entitled to pay until he was entered on the books of a ship of war; so long as he was only a supernumerary, he was victualled but not paid. A ship's press-gang often brought in more men than she wanted. The captain kept the whole catch as supernumeraries until he had chosen out the best to be entered on his books; then, instead of letting the remainder go, he turned them over to another who did the same thing. Thus the least promising sailors might be tossed about from ship to ship for a long time without acquiring a title to a day's wages.[10] Grenville's Navy Act of 1758 contained a clause to remedy this cruel custom.

Delay in the payment of their wages was perhaps the greatest hardship which the seamen suffered in the Royal Navy. There were two reasons for it. In the first place, parliament did not always vote quite enough for the current service of the navy, which therefore fell into arrears. When the government had to choose between leaving unpaid debts which would bear interest, and falling behind with seamen's wages which bore none, it

---

[9] 14 Geo. II, c. 38; Admiralty Minutes, 20 Feb. 1744/5, Adm. 3/50. Tomlinson, in his otherwise enlightened *Essay upon the Manning of the Navy*, proposed to return to the practice of limiting wages in the merchant service (*Tomlinson Papers*, pp. 128, 181).

[10] *Parliamentary History*, xv. 844. Speeches in parliament are never very reliable authorities for this kind of fact, even when they are correctly reported. Grenville was at this period a member of that quasi-Opposition which aimed at out-ranting Pitt, so his statements on a popular grievance are to be accepted with caution. But he had been a Lord of the Admiralty, and an active one, for some time; nor can he be accused, in general, of distorting facts. See also *A Letter to the Mayor of ——, . . . by a Member of Parliament* (London, 1758), passim, especially pp. 11–12.

naturally chose the second. Some acts were passed at the beginning of George II's reign for the better payment of the seamen's wages, but according to Grenville they had no effect after 1733. In this respect the crown was less tender to its employees and their dependants than the owners of privateers, who often advanced money to the families of their seamen during the cruises.

The fear of leaving his family in want for months or years might well deter a sailor from volunteering for the fleet.[11] This was obvious, but the official mind was less able to conceive how men who had several years' pay owing to them could be so silly as to forfeit it by deserting. The legislators indulged in some rather cruel cynicism on this subject. The adversaries of Grenville's Navy Bill argued that the less, and the more slowly, the seamen were paid, the better—not only because they wasted their wages intemperately when they received them, but because they were less likely to desert when there was something owing to them. Keep it from them to the last, and they would stay to get it. 'Their growing wages is a deposit which detains them, it is a bank which they do not forget, which keeps them cheerfully together.'[12] The commanders in the West Indies were genuinely surprised when the seamen despaired of receiving their due, and deserted their 'bank' for a merchant or privateer who would offer them something in hand. Sometimes the inducement justified the risk by almost any standard; in time of war, for example, the masters of merchant vessels offered forty or forty-five pounds for the run home, which was more than a year's pay in the Royal Navy; but Commodore St. Lo remarked in 1728 that men who had three years' wages owing would even desert for ten pounds and ten gallons of rum.[13]

Naturally the naval commanders deprecated any measure which made for the more regular payment of wages. Admiral

[11] Lascelles and Maxwell engaged a man to go out to be coachman at Barbados, whose chief reason for leaving England was the hope of escaping the press-gang. He was afraid he would not get his wages paid in the navy for two or three years; and as he had been a sailor, he probably spoke from experience (to Jonathan Blenman, 8 Apr. 1755, Letter Books of Messrs. Wilkinson and Gaviller, vol. vii).

[12] See the whole debate, *Parl. Hist.* xv. 839 seqq. For the effect of delay in the payment of wages on the manning of the French navy, see Berryer's letter to La Clue, 21 Apr. 1759, A.N., Marine, B² 363.

[13] St. Lo to Burchett, 10 Nov. 1728, Adm. 1/230; Davers to Corbett, 22 June 1746, Adm. 1/233.

Cotes reported in 1759 that the act of parliament, which directed pay-tickets to be made out for seamen sent to the hospital, had made it very difficult to prevent them from running away to serve on the homeward-bound merchant fleets—'If the seamen think they will save their wages or part of them by a ticket so made out, they will certainly desert more frequently than they do at present.' The only remedy was to remove from the hospital to the ships almost every man who could stand, until the convoy had sailed and it was once more safe to trust the sailors ashore. Vernon had already experienced the same difficulty at the hospital, 'not less than five hundred having deserted from the hospital in Port Royal since my being in command, which I believe have all been seduced out, and gone home with the homeward bound trade through the temptation of the high wages and thirty gallons of rum; and being generally convey'd drunk on board their ships from the punch-houses where they are seduced'. He thought this breach of duty should be discouraged by a rigid execution of the rule that deserters should forfeit their wages, as the hope of some indulgence in this respect was a great inducement to desertion. Commodore Knowles went further and suggested that 'unless some method is found out to deprive the seamen of their prize-money as well as their wages, when they desert, there will be no keeping them, especially when it happens their prize-money amounts to more than their pay, . . . for it being adjudged matter of private property, their attorneys will receive it, whereas if it became forfeited, when they ran away from His Majesty's service, and was appropriated to some fund, and the captains of ships directed, never to pay the whole sum (if considerable) at one payment, it would be a strong tie on the men, and certainly keep them in the service'. In fact this was provided for by an act of 1744.[14]

The long wait for pay and prize-money brought into being a class of usurers and ticket-holders who traded on the seamen's

---

[14] Vernon to Corbett, 5 Sept. 1742, Adm. 1/232; Knowles to Corbett, 10 July 1744, Adm. 1/2007; Cotes to Clevland, 20 Apr. 1759, Adm. 1/235; *A Letter to the Mayor of* ——, . . . *by a Member of Parliament*, pp. 54–56. Since Knowles reappears in several different capacities in the essay, it is necessary to explain that he served in the Leeward Islands, 1743–5, acting as commodore in the winter months; in 1746–7 he was in North America, partly as Governor of Louisbourg and partly as commodore; and early in 1748 he arrived at Jamaica as rear-admiral in command of the station.

need for ready money at a heavy price. The immense discount on seamen's pay-tickets was cited more than once as the chief reason for the fewness of volunteers. Grenville's Navy Act of 1758 was meant to do away with all these disgraceful evils; but if it was effective in some ways, it did not free the Royal Navy from its dependence on the press-gang for many years to come.[15]

In fact, all other ways of manning the squadrons failed, and there was no recourse but to pressing. It was an old custom, and so long as the navy could not or would not keep its men by offering them advantages, it was a necessary one. Even the government would admit that it was objectionable where it interfered seriously with trade or privateering; but certain rules had been laid down which were thought to mitigate its inconveniences.

Except in very special emergencies when every other consideration must give way to the national danger, the press-gangs were expected to spare the outward-bound shipping so far as possible. To disappoint a voyage already as good as begun, by depriving the vessel of hands, was a manifest blow to trade. To press men at the end of a voyage already as good as concluded was thought somehow to be less harmful. Hence the rule imposed on the commanders in the West Indies, not to press hands at all from shipping ready to sail.[16] The colonial governments sometimes strained this rule; that of Massachusetts seems to have regarded as outward bound a vessel which had any prospect of ever leaving the harbour again.[17] Though this New England logic was inconvenient to the naval commanders, it had some justification.

---

[15] Tomlinson wrote that in spite of the act, 'We found seamen *full as averse* to enter voluntarily in the Navy as if no such Act had passed' (*Tomlinson Papers*, p. 121, note).

[16] This rule was sometimes broken, as by Kerusoret at Cap François, who pressed from some ships which were actually under sail with his own permission (Fleury to Massiac, 5 Feb. 1759, A.N., Colonies, C⁹A 103). The press-gangs sometimes took men from the outward-bound ships in the Thames, to the great loss of the ship-owners. Henry Lascelles had to explain to some correspondents in Barbados the delay of their ship; the captain 'had all his hands on board, and was ready to depart, but that very morning there were number of press boats appeared all at once in the Poole, and swept away every man they could meet with, not excepting Mates. Captain Williams had some little notice of it an hour or two before, altho' it was so unlooked for, an sent his people ashoar, but this will not avail him much, for they dare not appear on board and it has detained him as well as many others in the same readiness' (to Clarke and Whitaker, 12 June 1741, Letter Books of Messrs. Wilkinson and Gaviller, vol. i).

[17] This, at least, was Forrest's contention in 1745 (see his letter to Corbett, 26 Nov. 1745, S.P. 42/30, f. 117).

Where there was no great reserve of sailors to be drawn upon, it made little difference whether a ship's hands were pressed just after she arrived or just before she was ready to start, unless there was a question of catching a convoy. If the master had time to seduce some deserters from another merchant, he could pass on the inconvenience of short-handedness to somebody else, but the nuisance to the community remained exactly the same. Therefore, although Trelawny made a mistake in ascribing desertion and inveigling solely to the press-gang, it must have caused particular instances of them and increased them in general, at whatever stage of the voyage the pressing took place. Moreover, it was very hard on the sailors to be hurried away on a new service before the old voyage was finished. Some writers, like Tomlinson and Hanway, thought the men's lives were shortened by this continuous employment without any rest or relief on shore.[18]

The Admiralty, however, made no objection to pressing from incoming vessels. The rule in the West Indies was to take one sailor in five, except from slave traders, who were to contribute one in three because a great part of their crews was superfluous after they had arrived in the islands. The merchants accepted this proportion as reasonable and customary; in fact it was part of the agreement made (and broken) by the admiral and the merchants at Jamaica in 1745. In the Seven Years War, when the colonial governments had some say in the matter, the proportion was altered at Jamaica to one in seven.[19]

The right of pressing men at the end of a voyage was not always exercised very wisely. On one occasion a slave ship was in serious danger of a revolt among the cargo, because the crew was reduced by the press-gang before the voyage was really finished. Though such a ship might be able to spare seamen after her arrival, she could obviously afford to do so less than any other kind of vessel while she was still on her voyage.[20] Other ships appear to have been stranded because their men were pressed before they quite

---

[18] *Tomlinson Papers*, pp. 123, 124 note.

[19] Vernon to Burchett, 19 July 1740, Adm. 1/232; Deposition of Manning, 10 Nov. 1745, Adm. 1/233; Jamaica Council Minutes, 11 Oct. 1759, C.O. 140/38; see also C[alendar of] S[tate] P[apers], Col[onial Series, America and West Indies], 1702–3, no. 124, by which it appears that one in five was the rule at Jamaica in Benbow's time.

[20] Admiralty Minutes, 21 Jan. 1743/4, Adm. 3/47; Orders to Davers, 10 June 1745, Adm. 2/64, p. 225.

reached port.[21] Yet if the men-of-war waited for the shipping to arrive, they were cheated of their men. Not only privateers, but trading vessels too, landed as many of their crews as they could spare in an out-bay just before they reached a place where they knew they would meet a press-gang. Vernon ordered Captain Mitchell to meet ships to windward of Port Royal and escort them into harbour in order that their whole crews might be taxed for the usual proportion of men.[22] The navy combined the press-gang with the protection of trade in other ways: when the commander of a homeward convoy neared England, he set to work to press as many men as he could from the ships under his care; no doubt this is the reason why the merchantmen always proved so elusive and refractory going up the Channel.[23]

These were only incidents of a system which was for some time tolerated as a necessity. At one point, however, the system itself was attacked. The colonists disliked measures which would endanger the plenty of their markets by discouraging the North American traders from frequenting them. The press-gang was commonly held to have this effect. As Brigadier Wentworth pointed out to Vernon, any trade between Jamaica and the northern colonies must be carried on in the shipping of the latter, since the West Indians had almost ceased to possess small vessels, and could neither man nor equip them to such advantage as the North Americans.[24] It was therefore most important not to frighten the North American traders away. The cry was raised several times in Jamaica that the admirals' insistence on their right to press out of North American vessels would produce, or was already producing, a famine. Even before the Spanish war broke out, Trelawny wrote home in 1739 that pressing was sure

[21] Lascelles and Maxwell to Samuel McCall, 13 May 1755, Letter Books of Messrs. Wilkinson and Gaviller, vol. vii; *Tomlinson Papers*, p. 177.

[22] Vernon, orders to Mitchell, 26 June 1742, S.P. 42/90, f. 209; Robinson to Newcastle, 25 June 1743, C.O. 28/46; Orders to Ogle, 2 Mar. 1742/3, Adm. 2/59, p. 349; Davers to Corbett, 5 Aug. 1745, Adm. 1/233.

[23] Rodney, orders to O'Bryan, 13 July 1762 (P.R.O., Rodney Papers, vol. 2, p. 294); Ourry to Clevland, 13 July 1762, Adm. 1/2246; see also the very detailed description in the *Tomlinson Papers*, p. 185, and *C.S.P. Col.*, *1710–11*, no. 172 (i), in which the Lords of the Admiralty describe the way men were pressed at the return of their ships from the colonies. Yet the seamen sometimes refused to sail without convoy (Henry Lascelles to Ruth Miller and George Maxwell, 20 Apr. 1741, Letter Books of Messrs. Wilkinson and Gaviller, vol. i). Perhaps an outward convoy was not so dangerous to their liberty.

[24] Wentworth to Vernon, 12 July 1742, C.O. 5/42.

to discourage the North Americans from bringing their provisions to Jamaica. A controversy on this subject produced a famous scuffle between Trelawny and the admirals in 1742. Trelawny continued to complain of Admiral Sir Chaloner Ogle, after Vernon had gone home, and the pressing of North American seamen was one of the chief ingredients of the complicated dispute between Admiral Davers and the merchant Edward Manning.[25] This dispute was the more bitter because it was not only the consumers who were afraid that the press-gang would cause a famine in this way. The re-exporters of North American produce to the French and Spanish colonies felt their interests to be threatened likewise.[26]

Why were the North Americans so easily discouraged and so peculiarly afraid of pressing? Davers might well ask this question; and no doubt there was some exaggeration in the descriptions of their unique sensibility. Yet there may have been reasons for it, as Trelawny dimly apprehended. The distinction between seamen and landmen was probably less marked in America than in Europe. The sailors of the mother-country were a professional class to whom it was no hardship to spend most of their lives at sea and to return home seldom. The more elastic and less specialized manner of living in North America brought forth jacks-of-all-trades who were ready to make occasional voyages at sea, but kept their connexions with the land and sometimes a share of the land itself. In England the seamen were a part of the wage-earning class, which could only leave behind dependants. North America had hardly yet developed such a class, and some of those who went to sea left behind them affairs which needed their own attention. This, I think, is what Trelawny meant by saying that 'they have most of them small familys and propertys at home, and when they are press'd their desire is so strong to return to their families and the life they were us'd to, that they desert the

[25] Trelawny to Wager, 8 Aug. and 22 Sept. 1739, Library of Congress, Vernon–Wager MSS.; Wentworth to Vernon, 5 and 12 July 1742, C.O. 5/42; Vernon to Wentworth, 6 and 14 July 1742, ibid.; Trelawny to Newcastle, 29 July 1742 and 10 Nov. 1744, C.O. 137/57; Trelawny to the Lords of the Admiralty, 21 Dec. 1743, Adm. 1/3817. See my book, *War and Trade in the West Indies* (Oxford, 1936), pp. 119, 121–3, for further details of the Manning-Davers controversy.

[26] Jamaica Council Minutes, 2 Dec. 1745, C.O. 140/31; second address of merchants favourable to Davers, 6 Feb. 1745/6, Adm. 1/233.

first opportunity they have or for the most part die soon if they can find no such opportunity'.[27]

Trelawny professed to see the result of Vernon's and Davers's press-gangs in the brisk trade which the North Americans carried on with the Dutch colonies of Curaçao and St. Eustatius. He said he could produce instances of masters who could not get seamen for voyages to the English colonies while others, bound to the foreign islands, had all the hands they wanted, so that those who meant to navigate to the English dominions had to pretend to put up for the foreign.[28] Vernon would have said this was putting the cart before the horse; the real reason for the scarcity of provisions in Jamaica was the additional demand of the several fleets and armies in the West Indies, which raised the price in the foreign islands as well as in Jamaica.[29] There was more truth in Trelawny's contention that pressing drove the men themselves to Curaçao, which had always been a resort for miscellaneous seamen because of the opportunities of advantage and employment in the hole-and-corner trade which the Dutch merchants carried on with the Spaniards. This was an old complaint; a witness said before the House of Lords in 1707 that there were 1,100 English seamen at Curaçao, of whom 600 belonged to Jamaica.[30] This cannot be ascribed entirely to the pressing, for the French islands suffered from it as well as the English, although the press-gang was not so much used there. But there is no doubt that the press-gangs diverted trade from the ports chiefly frequented by men-of-war to others where they seldom came. Vernon attributed the dispersion of trade among the outports of Jamaica to this cause. The Boston merchants complained of the advantage which Newport derived from its freedom from the press-gang.[31] A doggerel

[27] Trelawny to Newcastle, 29 July 1742, C.O. 137/57.

[28] Trelawny to Newcastle, 10 Nov. 1744, C.O. 137/57; second petition of Manning party against Davers, 28 Nov. 1745, and annexed affidavit of Henry Ram, C.O. 137/57; petition of Drake and Long to the king, 1746, S.P. 42/89.

[29] Vernon to Wentworth, 14 July 1742, C.O. 5/42.

[30] *Hist. MSS. Comm., House of Lords MSS., new series*, vii. 227; *C.S.P. Col., 1704–5*, no. 437. The Jamaica privateers said in a later controversy that the act of 1708, which remedied the situation, resulted in the return of hundreds of seamen to Jamaica (*C.S.P. Col., 1710–11*, no. 170 (iii)).

[31] Trelawny to Lords of the Admiralty, 21 Dec. 1743, Adm. 1/3817; Shirley to Newcastle, 31 Dec. 1747, C.O. 5/901. Dudley reported the same thing in Queen Anne's reign, but he attributed the popularity of Rhode Island to other causes besides immunity from the press-gang (*C.S.F. Col., 1702–3*, no. 1094; *1704–5*, no. 410).

ballad-advertisement for a Bristol privateer tells the same story:

> Here is our chief encouragement, our ship belongs to Bristol,
> Poor Londoners when coming home they surely will be press'd all:
> We've no such fear when home we steer, with prizes under convoy,
> We'll frolick round all Bristol town, sweet liberty we enjoy.[32]

Trelawny suggested that the infrequency of the men-of-war's visitations accounted partly for the popularity of New Providence in the Bahamas as a resort for privateers.[33] Perhaps he was right; but the other advantages of the situation would have been enough by themselves to make it a good place to dispose of prizes.

The competition of privateers for sailors was probably much severer than that of the merchant ships, and they were much better able to elude the press-gangs. Certainly the naval commanders in the West Indies were bitterer against them, and regarded them as a greater nuisance. In fact they seem almost to have thought that the merchant ship-owners were potential allies, or at least as great sufferers as themselves by the unscrupulous practices of the privateers.[34] This animosity against the privateers probably had some other causes, which this is not the place to discuss.

For various reasons privateering was much more attractive than service in the Royal Navy. Many stories are told of the way the privateers stole each other's sailors and seduced men out of the king's ships.[35] They regarded the king's men-of-war as fair game, and stuck at nothing to get their men out of them. Details of this would be tedious; it was always happening, and in every possible way. The naval commanders could sometimes, but not always, come to some agreement with the privateers. Commodore Warren claims to have succeeded in doing so at New York, but Knowles failed in the West Indies. They promised Warren not to sail from any port where his ships lay without letting him know, in order

---

[32] J. W. Damer Powell, *Bristol Privateers and Ships of War* (Bristol, 1930), p. 140. Laporte-Lalanne complained that the 'Frères de la Coste', who did all the coasting trade of St. Domingue, were beginning to disappear in order to escape Périer's press-gangs (to Machault, 5 June 1756, A.N., Colonies, C⁹A 99).

[33] Trelawny to Newcastle, 4 Nov. 1745, C.O. 137/57. An instance of this at Bermuda is given in Popple's letter to Newcastle, 26 May 1741, C.O. 37/29.

[34] Knowles to Corbett, 15 Oct. 1744, Adm. 1/2007.

[35] *The Voyages and Cruises of Commodore Walker*, ed. H. S. Vaughan (London, 1928), pp. 41 seqq.; J. F. Jameson, op. cit., pp. 382–91.

that he might have their vessels searched for deserters. In return, Warren presumably undertook not to press their men—and indeed, if they loyally observed their covenant he would have little need to do so, for his sailors would be deterred from deserting him by the knowledge that no resistance would be made to a search and that he would therefore be able to fetch them back. Some other commanders exercised the same right without exciting any outcry; but when Knowles proposed a similar arrangement to the privateers of Barbados they rejected it.[36]

The privateering interest was popular at home, and in the sugar islands it was probably more influential than the merchant service, because many owners of privateers were resident there, whereas most of the trading ships were owned in England. The admirals often complained of the protection afforded by the public authorities to privateers.[37] Sometimes the authorities were themselves interested in the privateers, especially in the French islands. Latouche-Tréville, captain of the *Zéphire*, applied in vain for men to Givry, the Intendant of Martinique, who was concerned in five privateers and protected all sailors who engaged in that service.[38] The French officials who invested in privateers represented this as a patriotic demonstration intended to stimulate the public spirit of the inhabitants; but it is hard to believe they meant to lose by it. The English governors seem to have been more cautious. Some of them were suspected of an interest in privateering, but the imperfect lists transmitted to the Admiralty do not bear the suspicion out.

The privateers did not rely entirely on their popularity and influence with the governments and magistrates. At the last resort they took up arms or raised mobs. Knowles encountered a storm in Antigua when he tried, largely out of ignoble revenge, to press privateers' crews. They overpowered his press-gang and ran away with its boat; when he retaliated the next day by confining one of their lieutenants, they spirited up such a crowd that the governor had to ask him to release the man. Soon afterwards they got Knowles himself arrested and imprisoned for some days, and followed this up with a writ of *habeas corpus* in order to get

[36] Warren to Corbett, 8 Sept. 1744, Adm. 1/2654; Knowles to Corbett, 15 Oct. 1744, Adm. 1/2007; Jameson, op. cit., p. 415.
[37] Davers to Corbett, 22 June 1746, Adm. 1/233; Knowles to Corbett, 15 Oct. 1744, Adm. 1/2007.
[38] Latouche-Tréville to Machault, 16 Jan. 1757, A.N., Marine, B⁴ 77.

another pressed man released. Having frightened off the governor from interfering, on the pretext that this was a common-law matter with which he had no concern, they pursued Knowles's prosecution to the conclusion—a foregone one with a colonial jury—of a heavy fine. The tactful Warren arrived on the scene and patched up the affair by buying the privateers' vessel at an exaggerated price for the government service. Unfortunately the Admiralty rejected this rather shabby accommodation, and either Warren or Knowles must have been left a loser. A similar combination of violence, prejudice, and chicanery prevailed elsewhere. There were riots and prosecutions at St. Kitts. The Governor of Barbados only prevented a pitched battle between the sailors and the mob by calling out the militia, in whose ranks the hot-headed could be brought under some discipline.[39] This was nothing to the more celebrated tumults at Boston in 1745 and 1747. In the first of these, two townsmen were eventually killed in a scuffle, and in the second, the governor had to retire to the castle, the militia hung back from doing its duty, and the furious admiral was only just restrained from bringing his guns to bear on the town.[40]

There were no such disorders in Jamaica, but the controversy was the same. Admiral Ogle promised Trelawny to take no men from privateers; but he broke his word, exasperated no doubt by the ingenuity with which they seduced his sailors. According to Trelawny, this discouraged the privateers so much that the number of privateering vessels fell from thirty to three. Davers was charged with pressing privateers' crews; but it is plain from the documents which his enemies quoted that he must have had particular reason to suspect certain privateers of seducing or concealing his men.[41]

The naval commanders were so much irritated by all these embroilments that the more hot-headed openly wished the number of privateers could be reduced, or at least that no new com-

[39] Knowles's memorial to the Admiralty, 1743, Adm. 1/2006; Knowles to Corbett, 17 Mar. 1743/4, 15 Oct. 1744, Adm. 1/2007; Warren to Corbett, 24 May 1744, Adm. 1/2654; Robinson to Newcastle, 10 May 1744, C.O. 28/46.

[40] Shirley to Newcastle, 1 and 31 Dec. 1747, C.O. 5/901. For an account of armed disturbances between sailors and press-gangs at Cork, see Adm. 2/371 (Lords of the Admiralty to Bedford, 8 Dec. 1758). See also Damer Powell, op. cit., p. 206, and Gomer Williams, *The Liverpool Privateers* (London, 1897), pp. 157–9.

[41] Trelawny to Newcastle, 12 June 1744 and 4 Nov. 1745, C.O. 137/57.

missions should be granted. Knowles and Lisle at the Leeward
Islands tried to convert Governors Robinson and Mathew to this
view. Robinson actually ceased for a time to grant commissions
at Barbados, but Mathew tried to avoid a definite attitude; however, his caution did not save him from unpopularity in Antigua,
where he was suspected of taking Knowles's part.[42]

In so far as the privateers helped to destroy the enemy's trade
and enriched the nation by their prizes, they seemed to deserve
encouragement; besides this, they sometimes afforded some protection to our own trade. The Admiralty did its best to have them
exempted from the press, but does not seem to have meant that
exemption to be universal. On the one hand, it instructed Captain
Thompson, at New England, not to press from letter-of-marque
ships actually employed in service against the enemy. A captain
in the Downs, however, was ordered to press one man in six from
homeward-bound privateers but not from the outward-bound.[43]
Although the commanders in the West Indies were told to use
their power of pressing circumspectly, they were not forbidden
to take any men at all from privateers, but only commanded to
respect the protections granted by the Admiralty. Such protections were often issued for the crews of particular ships, but conditions were generally attached to them; a certain proportion of
the men must be landmen, and the owners had sometimes to give
up some of their sailors to the government in order to buy a protection for the rest.[44] Sometimes the Admiralty had to break
through its own protections, but a commander on a colonial
station would hardly dare to disregard them.[45]

[42] Lisle to Mathew, 24 Oct. 1743, Adm. 1/2041; Mathew to Lisle, 25 Oct., ibid.;
Lisle to Corbett, 25 Oct., ibid.; Antigua Assembly Minutes, 21 June 1743, C.O.
9/15; Knowles to Corbett, 15 Oct. 1744, Adm. 1/2007; Robinson to Newcastle,
24 Mar. 1744/5, C.O. 28/46.

[43] Corbett to Thompson, 27 Oct. 1741, Adm. 2/474; Orders to Windham,
12 Aug. 1745, British Museum, Add. MSS. 19031, f. 192.

[44] James Wymble received one for 150 men in 1740, on condition that half of
them should be landmen (Minute of Lords Justices, 25 Sept. 1740, S.P. 43/99).
When the French navy was hard pressed for sailors, it too obliged privateers to
take a proportion of landmen (Chamber of Commerce of Guienne, minutes,
29 Nov. 1758, Archives de la Gironde, C. 4256, f. 75). Henry Lascelles and son
complained of 'the great expence in procuring protections which oblige us to
find the Government with one man in four' (to Thomas Applewhaite, 17 Mar.
1739–40, Letter Books of Messrs. Wilkinson and Gaviller, vol. i).

[45] St. Lo, however, did so in 1728 (St. Lo to Burchett, 24 June 1728, Adm.
1/230). The French government, like the English, was sometimes reduced to
pressing from privateers, limiting their numbers or even suppressing them

The navy was not always left to its own discretion in this matter. The abuses of the press-gang united two of the most popular influences in England against it—the privateering interest and the American trade. The privateers had been fighting hard for favourable legislation throughout the reigns of William III and Anne. They gained their point in 1708, and one result of their triumph was an act of parliament which appeared to abolish the press-gang in America.[46] It made one important exception: it was not to prevent the forcible recovery of those who should thereafter desert from the men-of-war. The commanders of privateers and merchant vessels were expected to satisfy themselves that the seamen whom they hired were not deserters. They had to carry attested lists of their crews, and produce them on demand to any captain of a man-of-war, in order to show whether they had any deserters on board. The squadrons in America were thus to be protected as before against the loss of their crews by desertion, but could not draw on the merchant ships to replace the ordinary mortality. For this purpose the navy had to send over reinforcements.

This popular law was in some respects vague and impracticable. For example, who could tell whether a merchant captain had taken enough care to be sure that he was not hiring a deserter from the king's service? The penalty for secreting deserters could only be exacted from masters of ships, for which reason the Attorney-General of Barbados refused to prosecute an innkeeper; but it was the innkeepers who most and oftenest deserved punishment.[47] There was a further doubt whether the act only prohibited the naval commanders from pressing on their own account, or restrained the civil authorities as well from empowering them to press. This question arose in New York; the English law officers advised that the act did not tie up the hands of the colonial governments from assisting the navy in this way. This was a strange opinion, and contrary to the apparent sense of the act, which it deprived of almost all force and meaning. Before ever

altogether (Chamber of Commerce of Guienne, minutes of 29 Nov. 1758 and 22 Apr. 1762, Archives de la Gironde, C. 4256, ff. 75, 166; memorial of the Nantes Chamber to Massiac, 28 Oct. 1758, C. 4321, no. 52).

[46] 6 Anne, c. 37. For the discussion of pressing which preceded this act, see the *House of Lords Journals*, xviii. 373 and 406; also *Hist. MSS. Comm., House of Lords MSS.*, new series, vii. 226–7, 231, 309–10.

[47] The Case of Jonathan Blenman, Add. MSS. 32921, f. 29.

the act was passed, the officers of the navy had been instructed to procure the governors' consent for sending out their press-gangs. What difference then did the act make in practice, if the same thing was lawful after it was passed?—except, of course, to provide a statutory penalty where there had been none before. The law officers' opinion does not seem to have had any practical consequence; the Admiralty and the Board of Trade continued to assume that pressing was entirely out of the question during the rest of the war of the Spanish Succession.[48]

Even more disastrous was the uncertainty about the duration of the act's validity. The Admiralty asked the law officers several times, in later years, whether it had expired with the war during which it was passed, or subsisted without limitation of time. The law officers always reported that it had expired, and that pressing was once more legal without any restriction. This opinion was received in the West Indies, but the people of North America did not choose to attend to it. As they truly said, an opinion of the law officers was not a legal determination, and they preferred to maintain that the act was still in force.[49] It is not easy to see why the courts never pronounced decisively on this question, for the captains of the navy were often prosecuted in the colonies, and one would have expected them to appeal. Perhaps they were prevented from doing so by a circumstance first heard of in the war of the American Revolution. Admiral Sir Peter Parker was then frequently condemned in Jamaica to pay fines for transgressions of this act, but never succeeded in appealing because the governor was instructed to allow no writ of error for under £300, and the maximum penalty provided by the act was £50.[50] However this might be, the state of the law remained uncertain. The validity of the act was generally affirmed in North America but denied in the West Indies.

When the quarrel between Edward Manning and Admiral

[48] C.S.P. Col., 1702–3, nos. 124, 888, 1179; 1704–5, no. 910; 1708–9, nos. 747 (iv and v), 753; 1710–11, no. 112; see also Dora Mae Clark, op. cit., pp. 208–9.

[49] Antigua Assembly Minutes, 24 Nov. 1743, C.O. 9/15; Trelawny to the Lords of the Admiralty, 21 Dec. 1743, Adm. 1/3817; letter of Blenman in Barbados Council Minutes, 21 Sept. 1744, C.O. 31/23. Some people of Barbados asked the governor for warrants of arrest against the officers of the navy under this act, but he would not sign them (Robinson to Newcastle, 10 May 1744, C.O. 28/46; Auchmuty to Corbett, 27 Nov. 1746, Adm. 1/3881; Lords of the Admiralty to Newcastle, 15 Mar. 1742/3, S.P. 42/26, p. 24).

[50] Parker to ? Sandwich, 23 Sept. 1780, Adm. 1/242.

Davers reached its height at Jamaica, the West India interest in London could contain itself no longer. The colonists had borne with the press-gang in Vernon's time because their enthusiasm for the war was not spent, and, useless as his expeditions proved to be, he could at least claim that he wanted the men for a definite public purpose. Even Vernon wore out the patience of Jamaica in the last months of his stay, and Trelawny, who was on the worst possible terms with him, taxed him with exercising his right to press for the sole end of displaying his authority.[51] This accusation could even more plausibly be made against Ogle, who never did anything at all, and Davers, who never did anything in particular. At the same time Knowles had aroused resentment in the Leeward Islands which Warren could not quite assuage, and the uselessness of the Royal Navy for any important purpose had never been more conspicuous than under Vice-Admiral Townsend and Commodore Lee.

The West India interest therefore resolved to make a protest. It sent a deputation to the Admiralty in the spring of 1746 to announce that it meant to ask parliament to revive the act of 1708. The Admiralty was not unsympathetic to the proposal, or perhaps knew it could not defeat it; but it induced the merchants to accept two important modifications.[52] The first was, to confine the privileges of the act to the West Indies alone. No reason appears why the board should have ruled out North America so decisively, unless it was because the First Lord meant to send a great expedition there that year. The West Indians themselves were generally made to bear the blame of this restriction, which certainly looked as if it was due to favouritism or their sinister influence; but the Admiralty Minutes prove beyond doubt that the proposal came from the board. The Admiralty made a great mistake if it thought to facilitate in this way the raising of men in the northern colonies. Their inhabitants were very much annoyed, as well they might be, seeing that they had been protected, like the rest of the king's

---

[51] Trelawny tried to prove this by asserting that the press-gang produced very few sailors, and those of the most useless kind, since the crews of the little North American craft were quite unfit for men-of-war (Trelawny to Lords of the Admiralty, 21 Dec. 1743, Adm. 1/3817). This can hardly have been true, for no admiral would have found it worth his while to press on such terms. But we do hear sometimes of press-gangs which lost more men than they took.

[52] Admiralty Minutes, 17 and 22 Mar. 1745/6, 10 Apr. 1746, Adm. 3/53; Petition of the West India Agents, 9 Apr. 1746, *House of Commons Journals*, xxv. 117.

subjects, by the act of 1708. Knowles attributed the violence of the Boston riots to this motive; but he was seldom at a loss for a wrong explanation of the disorders which were due to his own tactlessness.[53] Moreover, this injudicious partiality did not remove the doubt in North America whether the earlier law still subsisted; and, above all, the framers of the act of 1746 made one extraordinary omission: they left the question of its permanence unsettled once again. Thus the same controversy raged over its survival as over that of the act of 1708, and factious people in the colonies were able to assert or deny it as it suited their purposes. In general, however, the act of 1746 was considered to be in force throughout the Seven Years War.[54]

Another important change was introduced into the act in 1746. It permitted the naval commanders in the West Indies, with the consent of the governors and councils, to press men in case of the actual or threatened invasion of the colonies or any other great emergency. They were to take no more men than would make up their 'usual or sufficient complement' and were to release them at the end of the special service for which they had been pressed.

The press-gang might therefore be legalized by the consent of the colonial authorities, and everything depended on the way in which they interpreted their powers. In the past, the governors and councils had usually distinguished between a press ashore and a press afloat. Even before the act, a press ashore could only be made with the consent of the governors and councils, and they had generally given it. They had been quite ready to let the navy have the 'straggling seamen' or the 'idle and vagabond persons not indented, hired or contracted servants, nor sailors already engaged to serve on board any ship or vessel'.[55] In fact, the civil power had actually co-operated in rounding up such people and sending them on board the king's ships. (The degree of co-operation might vary from colony to colony; for example, the government of Jamaica often ordered the magistrates to take up stragglers by their own authority, but the Attorney-General of Barbados persuaded the governor that the civil magistrates ought

[53] Knowles to Corbett, 18 Jan. 1747/8, Adm. 1/234. But it is fair to Knowles to add that Governor Shirley, a far more judicious man, bore him out (Shirley to Newcastle, 1 Dec. 1747, C.O. 5/901).
[54] Except by the incurably factious Attorney-General of Barbados (Barbados Council Minutes, 19 Jan. 1757, C.O. 31/28).
[55] Jamaica Council Minutes, 7 Aug. 1739, 6 Feb. 1739/40, C.O. 140/30.

not to take an active part, but only at most to keep order while the press-gangs did their work.[56]) On the other hand, the colonial governments would not sanction a press afloat among the crews of vessels in harbour.[57] After the act of 1746 was in force, the colonial legislatures continued to go by the same rules as before. That of Antigua distinguished in 1757 between taking up stragglers and pressing men afloat. In the same year the governor and council of Barbados permitted Commodore Moore to press on terms which amounted to the same thing; he was obliged to relinquish at once any seaman whom a privateer or merchant captain claimed as part of his crew. According to Moore, this qualification made the permission quite useless.[58] In general, outside Jamaica the acts of 1708 and 1746 seem to have had the effect of abolishing the press afloat.

A great deal turned on the definition of an emergency under this act. The council of Jamaica refused to let Commodore Mitchell press any men for an ordinary cruise in 1747, though it empowered the governor to lend him some soldiers to man his ships (an expedient which was quite often used in the West Indies both before and after the act).[59] Knowles, who was on much better terms with Trelawny than his predecessors, got a general permission to press for two months as many men as would make up his complement.[60] In the next war the Jamaica government seems to have made a sort of standing order for pressing one man in seven out of all incoming merchant ships; thereby the intention of the act was almost frustrated. The authorities of the other islands seem to have insisted somewhat more strictly, though by no means pedantically, on having an emergency proved, and attended particularly to the clause which provided that the men should be discharged at the end of the service for which they

[56] Barbados Council Minutes, 21 Sept. 1744, C.O. 31/23.

[57] The council of Jamaica had done so in 1726, but that was in a special emergency when the squadron had to be enabled to undertake a service of great strategic and political importance (*C.S.P. Col.*, 1726–7, no. 374, i).

[58] Antigua Council Minutes, 6 July 1757, C.O. 9/23; Workman to Moore, 26 Oct. 1757, Adm. 1/307; Moore to Clevland, 29 Oct., ibid.

[59] Trelawny to Wager, 8 Aug. and 22 Sept. 1739, Vernon–Wager MSS. The heavy mortality and the act of 1708 had forced the Jamaica squadron to rely very much on the soldiers in Queen Anne's war. The governor reported again and again that the regiment suffered great fatigue in performing this service, without which the ships could not leave harbour (*C.S.P. Col.*, 1702–3, nos. 1055, 1119; 1704–5, no. 164; 1706–8, no. 1223; 1708–9, nos. 68, 174, 339, 542).

[60] Jamaica Council Minutes, 29 Apr. 1747, 24 May 1748, C.O. 140/32.

were pressed.[61] Sometimes they also took advantage of the men-of-war's necessities, or of the power which the act had put in their hands, to dictate or suggest the service to be undertaken—thus recovering indirectly the right of giving orders to the commanders, which they had lost in Queen Anne's reign.

The officers of the navy disliked the act and asked for its repeal. Yet in spite of their jeremiads they very seldom had to make one crew out of two, or keep an empty ship in harbour.[62] Some of the few occasions when this happened were before the act of 1746 and cannot be attributed to it. The clauses empowering or obliging the crown to send over reinforcements of seamen from England do not appear to have been very important.[63] In Queen Anne's reign the Admiralty, instead of complying with the law in this respect, had threatened to withdraw the ships stationed in the colonies when their crews became too small.[64] We hear nothing of such a childish revenge after the act of 1746.

The difficulty created by the limitation of the press-gangs was ordinarily overcome in two ways: by the routine replacement of ships in the colonial squadrons by fresh ships from England, and by the control of returned prisoners of war. The exchange of prisoners had many inconveniences: the 'Flag of Truce' vessels which carried the prisoners to and from the enemy's colonies used the pretext for driving an illicit trade with the enemy, and the Frenchmen who were thus returned to Martinique and St. Domingue furnished the privateers of those islands with an unfailing supply of recruits, to the very great detriment of English trade in the West Indies. Nevertheless, the practice might also serve to replenish the crews of our own men-of-war. However, it did not always have this effect. The French governors, especially those of St. Domingue, too often sent away their English prisoners

---

[61] Jamaica Council Minutes, 11 Oct. 1759, 13 Nov. and 16 Dec. 1761, C.O. 140/38 and 140/42. Earlier in the war the council had insisted, like those of other colonies, on proof of an emergency and the limitation of the period for which the pressed men were to be kept on board (Council Minutes, 25 Oct. 1756, C.O. 140/38).

[62] Knowles to Corbett, 18 Jan. 1747/8, Adm. 1/234; Frankland to Clevland, 16 June 1757, Adm. 1/306; Moore to Clevland, 29 Oct. 1757 and 13 Oct. 1758, Adm. 1/307.

[63] Only once, at Antigua in 1757, did a colonial legislature invoke this part of the act by ordering its agent to petition the Admiralty for supernumeraries to reinforce the squadron (Antigua Council Minutes, 3 Feb. 1757, C.O. 9/21).

[64] C.S.P. Col., 1708–9, nos. 376, 649.

to North America in the 'Flag of Truce' vessels which came from those parts; they justified this on the principle of 'humanity', for many of the Englishmen were natives of North America, and those who were not would be quite as glad to escape from the men-of-war who were waiting to press them at Jamaica and in the Leeward Islands.[65] Moreover, even if the French authorities consented to return the English prisoners to the nearest West India islands, the navy did not always profit by them. Most of the cartels for exchange of prisoners were negotiated by the governors; their subordinates received the returned Englishmen and allowed them to disperse themselves into taverns or other hiding-places where the press-gangs could not find them. Besides this, the prisoners of war sometimes took possession of the vessels which carried them, and put themselves on shore at outlying bays, beyond the reach of the press-gangs. Sometimes this was done with the connivance of the master of the vessel which carried them, but the prisoners often had to revolt in good earnest.[66]

To avoid these difficulties, the admirals usually tried to make their own cartels with the French authorities, and to have the prisoners conveyed in ships of war or under a strong guard. By these methods the navy made sure of its men.[67] Finally, by the Order in Council of 25 March 1761, the navy undertook the entire

[65] See the correspondence of Admiral Knowles with Governor de Vaudreuil on this subject: Knowles to Vaudreuil, 23 Jan. 1748, A.N., Colonies, C⁹A 73; Vaudreuil to Knowles, 6 Feb., ibid.; Vaudreuil to Maurepas, 22 Feb. 1748, vol. 74; Knowles to Chastenoye, 29 Feb. 1748, vol. 72.

[66] Knowles to Corbett, 15 Oct. 1744, Adm. 1/2007; Warren to Corbett, 22 Dec. 1744, Adm. 1/2654; Holmes to Bart, 8 Aug. 1761, Adm. 1/236; *Valeur*, Derny, High Court of Admiralty Papers, 42/50; *Charming Elizabeth*, Fay, High Court of Admiralty Papers, 42/59. For similar complaints about French seamen, see Samson to Maurepas, 15 May 1746, A.N., Colonies, C⁹A 67. The custom of pressing returned prisoners into the king's service was not unknown at home in England. On 6 July 1757 the Admiralty decided not to use this method, but it changed its mind within a month and ordered all such prisoners to be secured (Minutes, 6 July and 4 Aug. 1757, Adm. 3/65).

[67] The Admiralty encouraged its commanders in the West Indies to get control of the returned prisoners if they could. (Orders to Lee, 15 Mar. 1744/5, Adm. 2/63, p. 340; to Legge, 12 Sept. 1747, Adm. 2/70, p. 275; Lee to Corbett, 9 July 1745, Adm. 1/305; Douglas to Clevland, 29 Nov. 1760, Adm. 1/307.) In 1748 it asked Newcastle to make the colonial governors acquiesce (Lords of the Admiralty to Newcastle, 5 Feb. 1747/8, S.P. 42/33, f. 23). Putting a guard on Flags of Truce was not an infallible precaution against attempts to escape, for English privateers sometimes boarded the vessel, overpowered the guard, and removed the prisoners to enlist them in their own crews (L'Abarer to Pocock, Dec. 1747, Adm. 1/2289; Pocock to Corbett, 12 Jan. 1747/8, ibid.).

management and expense of the prisoners in the colonies, and thus at last exercised a control which it had possessed much earlier in the ports of Great Britain and Ireland.[68]

From that time until the end of the Seven Years War, the naval authorities seem to have possessed at least some of that command over the services of the sea-faring population, of which the limitations upon the use of the press-gang had deprived them. Moreover the press-gang itself, limited in the manner which I have described, continued to exist; and in spite of all the mitigations which the acts of parliament applied, it put the ship-owners to infinite inconvenience—more, perhaps, in England than in the colonies. It raised wages, delayed and frustrated voyages, and exposed the merchant vessels to danger by depriving them of their men.[69] The liberty of employing foreign seamen up to three-quarters of the crew appears to have been a very slight compensation for all these evils. Yet the navy had to rely upon the press-gang for many years to come, and the West India colonists were lucky to have procured for themselves mitigations of the system which were not enjoyed by the North Americans or by their countrymen at home.

[68] See also Admiralty Minutes, 3 Apr. 1761, Adm. 3/68.
[69] The correspondence of Messrs. Lascelles and Maxwell is full of complaints of the press-gang: see their letters to Benjamin Charnocke, 11 Feb. 1743/4; to Pantaliam Fernandez, 17 Feb. 1755; to Jonathan Blenman, 21 Apr. 1755; to Thomas Stevenson, 30 Apr. 1755, &c.—all in the Letter Books of Messrs. Wilkinson and Gaviller.

XII

A LONDON WEST INDIA MERCHANT HOUSE
1740–69

[*Essays presented to Sir Lewis Namier*, edited by Richard Pares and A. J. P. Taylor (London, Macmillan, 1956), pp. 75–107]

BEFORE the great German air-raid of 29 December 1940 there stood, in a little court off the south side of Great Tower Street, a brick house built late in the seventeenth century.[1] The front room on the first floor was laid out and furnished, apparently about the time that the house was built, as a counting-house, with a long counter and panelled compartments. There was an inner room, to the right of the counter, with a fireplace surrounded by beautiful wood-carving. These were the offices[2] of Messrs. Wilkinson and Gaviller, a West India merchant house which could trace its existence back to the day, in March 1740, when Henry Lascelles and his son Daniel wrote the letter which was copied into the first page of the oldest surviving letter book.

More than twenty years ago the partners of the house kindly allowed me to spend a whole winter and spring working through their oldest archives. In this article I propose, with their permission, to describe the first thirty years of this house's history, which is all that I had studied before the Germans came and the beautiful office with the counter, the carved fireplace, and, worst of all, the archives, went up in flames.[3]

A few years ago, in the second half of *A West-India Fortune*,[4] I gave an account of a very similar merchant house, that of the

---

[1] The house is briefly described in *Royal Commission on Historical Monuments (England); London*, iv (1929), p. 185.

[2] Not their first offices: George Maxwell describes himself in his will as 'of Mark Lane, merchant'.

[3] I should consider it a piece of useless ostentation to give continual footnote references to documents which no longer exist, but when occasion offers conveniently, I shall try to give the date of any letter which I quote verbatim from my transcripts, so that, when I shall have deposited these transcripts in some public place, the more important quotations may be verified. [These transcripts are now in the Pares Collection in Rhodes House Library, Oxford.]

[4] [London, 1950.]

Pinneys of Bristol. I must refer to that book the reader who wishes to see the business of such a house fully described. This will enable me to pass over quite briefly those things in which the business of the Lascelleses resembled that of the Pinneys. On the other hand, I shall dwell particularly upon the differences between the business of a London house, dealing mainly with Barbados in the middle eighteenth century, and that of a Bristol house dealing mainly with Nevis from 1783 to 1850. Much is to be learnt from the differences between the two ports, the two islands, and, above all, the two periods. Many important changes in West Indian history are reflected in them.

The Lascelles family had been connected with Barbados nearly half a century before 1740. Edward Lascelles was on the island in 1698; he seems to have been a merchant, for he had a wharf and dealt largely in wine; he also had something to do with the money affairs of the warships on the station. In 1700 he was a member of the island's assembly. He must have returned to London soon afterwards. In 1706 he is described as a London merchant trading to Barbados. He was also the absentee owner of an estate on the island. He continued for twenty years to write occasional letters about the politics of the island and the African trade.[5]

There was also a Philip Lascelles, who traded from London to Barbados in 1702.[6]

Henry Lascelles was living on the island before 1714, married a Barbadian lady, and became collector of customs. He was a friend of Governor Lowther, whose defence against criticisms he undertook on a visit to England in 1720. Naturally, in that age of faction, he got into trouble during the next régime, that of President Cox, who accused him of various irregularities in the administration of the customs and of the $4\frac{1}{2}$ per cent. export duty. According to the president, he had connived at illegal trade with Frenchmen, had obstructed prosecutions for customs offences and, 'being one of the chiefest shippers of sugars to private persons as well as the King, ships the good sugars received for duty to his private correspondents at high prices, and buys French sugars at low rates and ships to the King for duty'.[7]

---

[5] *Calendar of State Papers, Colonial Series, America and West Indies, 1697–8*, nos. 144, 739; *1701*, nos. 343, 1159; *1706–8*, no. 540; *1708–9*, no. 321; *1719–20*, no. 30; *1726–7*, no. 83.   [6] Ibid., *1702*, no. 814.

[7] Ibid., *1714–15*, no. 654, vi; *1717–18*, no. 742, xv; *1719–20*, nos. 459, 563, 575; *1720–1*, nos. 687, 713, 754.

In 1730 he turned over the collectorship of customs to his brother Edward, but continued, at any rate until 1734, to collect the $4\frac{1}{2}$ per cent. duty and to reside on the island as a merchant. There is no means of telling whether it was Henry or Edward whom Governor Lord Howe called in 1733 'as considerable a merchant as any'. In any case Henry was back in London before the end of 1739.

Henry Lascelles was not only a whig, but a personal adherent of Sir Robert Walpole. This brought him certain advantages: for example, in 1740, by speaking personally to the prime minister, he obtained the privilege of transhipping some prize Spanish tobacco contrary to the letter of customs regulations. After Walpole's fall, however, he had to pay for his politics. Those members of the new ministry who had been no friends to the old minister tried to injure and to punish his friends and dependants wherever they could. Robert Dinwiddie, the surveyor-general of customs for the southern district of America, went to Barbados in order to rake up what charges he could against the Lascelles brothers and their friends. According to a letter from George Maxwell to Edward Lascelles, 4 July 1744,

This matter has been brewing ever since the fall of the Earl of Orford, and your Brother became obnoxious to the New Ministry, I believe from some publick Declarations in favour of the old to which he was oblig'd. Not only the Treasury was put into other hands, but some new Commissioners of the Customs were made, whereof Capt. Mead was one. The Majority at the latter Board are people of no importance, and Mr. Hill had formerly great sway there, which Mr. Mead has now in full possession. Ld. Wilmington who was at the head of the former was old and disregarded, and therefore the latter Board exerted a greater Power than belong'd to them, especially in the instance of Mr. Dinwiddie, and although at the old man's death the Treasury underwent a second change and came again into the hands of those that had been of the old Ministry, yet these did not care to intermeddle or discourage an Inspection proposed and countenanced before their time for the great Clamour of the necessity of it and for the same reason I fear the present Lords of the Treasury will not now interpose in the matter.

Dinwiddie suspended Edward Lascelles and Arthur Upton, the collector and comptroller at Barbados, and surcharged Henry Lascelles's own account with some monies due, as he said, for former irregularities. Henry Lascelles could not get his revenge until the end of 1744, when matters began to take a better turn for him. Lord Carteret, who seems to have encouraged his prosecutors, was dropped from the ministry which his friends, the Pelhams, now dominated. To make quite sure of success, Lascelles entered the House of Commons himself. On 23 April 1745 William Smelt, member for Northallerton, was appointed receiver-general of His Majesty's Casual Revenue at Barbados;[8] a new writ was ordered and Henry Lascelles was elected in his stead. Probably at the same time, he bought the borough of Northallerton outright; I do not know what he paid for it, but the price was less, perhaps much less, than £13,000. It is very probable that he bought his way into parliament expressly to get himself rehabilitated and his brother restored; at any rate, when the negotiations for the latter of these objects were hanging fire, his partner observed, 'we expected no sort of disappointment after being chosen member for Northallerton'. With these advantages Henry Lascelles gained his object in the long run: in November 1745 the Treasury ordered the Customs to stay process against him, though the matter dragged on for many years, and in 1747 Edward was restored by the good offices of Henry Grenville, the new governor of Barbados, who had a brother in the ministry and a friend, George Lyttelton, at the Treasury Board. Henry Lascelles stayed in parliament until 17 March 1752, when he resigned in order to get his son Daniel elected.[9]

Daniel Lascelles is a colourless figure compared with his father. He was not exactly a sleeping partner in the house, but he never wrote its letters and did not always see them before they were sent off. For this reason the letter books tell us hardly anything about his politics. He held the seat for Northallerton until 1780. His elder brother, Edwin, was also member for Northallerton in the parliament of 1754, but in 1761, as befitted the head of a rich family,[10] he sat for the county seat of Yorkshire. In 1780, at a

---

[8] *Calendar of Treasury Books and Papers, 1742–1745*, p. 841.

[9] Ibid., pp. 528, 695, 716, 731. This affair is treated at length by Mr. Louis K. Koontz in his life of *Robert Dinwiddie* (Glendale, Calif., 1941), pp. 67–94. Mr. Koontz scarcely seems aware of the political aspects of this prosecution. According to Miss Betty Kemp, Lascelles was the first M.P. to accept the Chiltern Hundreds, or a similar office, for the purpose of getting out of parliament altogether, not for that of changing his constituency (see *Essays presented to Sir Lewis Namier*, London, 1956, p. 208).

[10] Probably he was not his father's eldest son but, to judge from the will of

political crisis, he was turned out; his brother Daniel immediately obliged him by retiring from Northallerton in order to let him in.[11]

George Maxwell was not Barbadian born. He went to the island in 1721 or 1722—possibly a significant date, for the losers in the South Sea Bubble were fleeing in all directions at that time in order to recover their injured fortunes by means of salaried office in the colonies. He became searcher of the customs at Bridgetown, the chief port of Barbados, and so served for many years under Henry Lascelles. He does not seem to have made a large fortune in Barbados. He rented a plantation; there is no evidence of his possessing one, and if he once described himself as having been the owner of one hundred slaves, he may only have meant that he controlled them as renter, not as owner. He borrowed £1,000 from Henry Lascelles in 1741, and if he in turn made loans to his fellow planters, we know that the money was not his own but that of Lascelles. It is obvious that it was as Lascelles's junior partner that he returned to London in the autumn of 1743. In his letters to his friends in Barbados, he wrote as if he were in a foreign land. Like other West Indians, he fortified himself against the approach of winter by 'a frequent use of the Cold Bath', apparently at an establishment somewhere in Newgate Street. He disliked the winter, above all the 'nasty smoaky Coal fires', and would have liked to purchase some Barbados sunshine at any price; the meat was 'at first over luscious' to his taste. Worst of all, like many another returned colonial, he knew hardly any face in the country except that of the king. In time he got used to England and ceased to think of 'dear Barbados' as his mother country. The close friendships which he had formed in Barbados remained with him for the rest of his life: no doubt they brought the house a large part of its business, but they were also responsible for some of its most serious financial scrapes, for he did not like to refuse a loan to an old friend. The money he lent almost certainly belonged to Henry and, later, to Daniel Lascelles. Although Maxwell was credited with a half of the house's capital in the form of debts and credits, from beginning to end of his partnership, it is unlikely

the former, the eldest brother, Henry, was either feeble-minded or in some other way unsatisfactory, for he was cut off with a mere £34,000.

[11] R. Beatson, *Chronological Register of both Houses of the British Parliament* (3 vols., 1807), i. 250; ii. 311, 326.

that he brought any money with him into the firm and he may have had obligations to his partner which rendered their financial equality a merely nominal one. In his will he called Henry Lascelles his 'dear friend and benefactor'.

When Maxwell died in February 1763 Gedney Clarke junior and William Daling were taken into partnership with Daniel Lascelles. Clarke's father had been associated with the house in various forms of business; he seems to have been an expensive, enterprising man who left his money affairs in a precarious state. The son, who had married a daughter of Henry Lascelles's brother Edward, succeeded him as collector of customs in February 1765, a post which he clearly owed to the political efforts of the Lascelles brothers, and therefore left the house in order to return to Barbados. Not long after, he got into great financial difficulties, probably inherited from his father, and went bankrupt, some said for the spectacular amount of £150,000.

William Daling had risen from the ranks; he had been a clerk in the employment of the house. We do not know how large a staff they employed. According to their own account, their business was not one of the greatest in the West India trade and they had not work for many subordinates. What there was consisted of three things: writing accounts and copying letters in the counting-house; going round to the grocers once a week in order to collect money due for sugar sold; and the 'waterside business'. Every factor had to have an agent in the custom house in order to cast up the taxes due on the sugars imported, claim deductions for prompt payment, and know when to petition the commissioners for concessions; this agent also had to watch the sugars as they came ashore, compare the invoice weights with the landing weights and have the cask examined by his own cooper where any great discrepancy occurred, in order to detect pilferage. None of this was very advanced or responsible business; none of it, therefore, qualified an underling for the higher branches of the sugar-factor's profession, namely the art of selling sugars at the right time and, above all, of making loans to the right planters. Perhaps it was for this reason that, according to the house, sugar-factors very seldom took apprentices, even when money was offered with them. William Daling, however, seems to have risen above these difficulties and became Daniel Lascelles's partner in 1763.

The chief business of a sugar-factor was to sell his correspondents' sugars, for which he received a commission. The organization of the London sugar market at this time strongly resembled that of the Bristol sugar market half a century later, which I have described in chapter ix of *A West-India Fortune*, and I shall not waste time by describing it over again here.[12]

It has sometimes been said that the factors discouraged the planters from turning their efforts from the main crop to alternatives because they were only willing or able to sell one thing. There is very little evidence of this in the correspondence of the house. There are many references to sales of rum and of the minor staples. It is true that the house did not much care for selling Barbados rum. This was chiefly because it did not meet with a ready market. Rum as a whole was, unlike sugar, an article for which the demand was intermittent and capricious; moreover, if an Englishman bought rum, he preferred that of Jamaica, which was stronger and went further in punch than Barbados rum, however well flavoured. Only once or twice in the correspondence of the Lascelles house is a general demand for rum mentioned: for example, in February 1768 they reported a rise of price 'occasioned by a great many Rums being bought up in hopes of a large consumption this year as it is the General Election year'. There was, in addition, a particular nuisance in the sale of rum: it was commonly sold on board ship in order that the purchaser might pay the duties and excise, and these importers too often delayed landing the rum, which therefore cluttered up the ship when it was ready to go into dock. The house also sold ginger and cotton, though without enthusiasm: ginger was chiefly wanted for re-export to the German market, which was often obstructed in this period by war, and West India cotton, even though well cleaned, was subject to competition from Turkish cotton. The house seems to have believed that the manufacturers could not work Turkish cotton without some admixture of West India, but the proportions between the two seem to have been arbitrary, so that when Turkish cotton was cheap the consumption of the West India article would be reduced.

Besides selling the planters' crops, the factors fulfilled their orders for every article which they wanted from the mother country. The only article which was constantly sent in bulk from

---

[12] [See the author's article, 'The London Sugar Market, 1740–1769', *Economic History Review*, 2nd series, ix (1956), pp. 254–70.]

London at this time was hoops for the sugar casks; but the house had, at one time or another, to buy luxuries and conveniences of every sort—it might be anything from a spinet to a copy of Gay's *Fables* or a rat-catching dog. The house had few dealings with provincial producers but contented itself with buying from the London tradesmen. (In this way the sugar- and tobacco-factors, like the East India Company, must have helped to sustain London industry against the competition of the provinces.)

You complain [they wrote on 21 February 1745/6 to Samuel McCall of Philadelphia] of the goods by breame being dear bought, and particularly the Cutlery of Rogers's make. We have lately heard that Rogers lives at Sheffield in Yorkshire, and as we have not had orders of any great consequence in the Course of our business for the Country made goods, we never Settled any Correspondence with Sheffield or Birmingham, but have always given them to the Tradesmen in town to furnish with town made goods. It's not to be doubted but they charge some profit in consideration for their knowledge and trouble in sending to the proper places and Makers in the Country, which we are unacquainted with, but as we deal for ready money we expect to be served at a moderate profit; however, if we had any tolerable share of orders in the Country made goods, we would go to Sheffield and Birmingham on purpose, to make an acquaintance with the artificers themselves.

Evidently the London tradesmen sometimes acted as middlemen, and the house seems to have bought even London goods of the wholesalers: Maxwell described a visit to a London textile wholesaler which he and Henry Lascelles both made in order to buy the product of the Spitalfields weavers, 'from some of whom we have found exactions, but', he added, 'as some of your orders were circumstanced in respect of lengths, we could not be so well supplied but by Browne & Co., who have a general accquaintance among all the weavers'. The partners usually bought from a restricted circle of tradesmen whom they could trust and, on the strength of this, they by no means always examined the goods, though they would usually do so if, in pursuance of their correspondents' orders, they had patronized a West End tradesman with whom they were not well acquainted.

For the goods they bought they paid cash and obtained a discount with which they credited their correspondents. From an arbitrarily chosen date (generally four months after the date of

shipment, by which time they would, on an average, have received and paid the bills) they charged their correspondents with
interest on these purchases. Some correspondents complained,
evidently believing that the house had itself bought the goods on
credit. It may be significant that most of these complaints came
not from planters but from merchants, either in the West Indies
or on the continent of North America. These merchants wrote as
if they could obtain goods at nine or twelve months' credit from
the manufacturers. It seems probable that there were, side by
side, two different systems of exporting to the colonies—that, on
the one hand, merchants in the colonies bought on credit from
British manufacturers while, on the other hand, planters bought
through factors in London who paid cash, passed on the discount,
and charged interest. On 1 February 1742 Henry Lascelles had to
answer a complaint from Samuel McCall of Philadelphia.

I have attentively looked into your Invoice and am observing your
directions as near as possible, in the orders to the Tradesmen, it will
be best buying the whole with ready money which I believe will be for
yr. Int^t, and for the time I may be in Advance for any part I can only
Charge Int^t allowing the Discount for prompt payment where any is
Customary. Richd King is the pewterer I employ, I spoke to him about
the parcel you had ordered, that I was to give him the Marks and
Numbers, I made no doubt of his providing it for you, seeing you had
writt to him, but he pretends to decline meddling with it, and says his
business is to take his orders from the Merch^t here, and not to send
his Goods abroad as if he were a Factor, so that I am to include his
Bill in your Invoice and pay him the Money here.

I doubt if a Birmingham manufacturer would have behaved in
the same way, at any rate twenty years later.

In order to send all these goods to and fro, the factors found it
necessary to hold an interest in shipping. Here the differences
between London in the middle eighteenth century and Bristol
after 1800 are considerable. The partners held shares in many
ships—indeed, in so many that they complained that their ships
got in each other's light—but these shares were seldom large (five-
sixteenths was exceptional) and only by accident, when the other
prospective owners had let them down, did the house ever own
a whole ship. One-sixteenth or one-eighth was a very usual share
and the house once owned as small a part as one-thirty-second.
The other owners were sometimes rival sugar-factors and, still

more commonly, planters. A planter who had sugars to ship might like to take an interest in a number of vessels in order to be able to claim a preference in getting his sugars aboard them. One or two vessels seem to have been entirely owned by planters or by merchants in the colonies.

This fragmentation had several consequences. For one thing, since nearly every ship had some owners in the colony, it was virtually tied to the trade of that colony and could not easily be shifted to another destination even when the colony in question had a small crop and was likely to abound in shipping. As it happens, this did not make a great difference in the case of Barbados, since the island was to windward of all others: if there was a bad crop in Barbados and news of good crops elsewhere, the owners on the spot would know this and would consent to let their ship go down for a better freight. Secondly, since the house seldom had a very large interest in any one ship, it had only a weak inducement to give the preference to its own ships at the expense of others: hence, it often gave its good offices to the vessels owned by its friends in the colonies when they arrived in London even though it had vessels of its own in the same trade. The last and most serious consequence of this fragmentation was to strengthen the importance and the power of the captains. The captain was always a central figure in this trade, for it was his personal relations with the planters that got the vessel her freight home; but when the captain was faced, not with a single owner but a collection of owners on both sides of the Atlantic, his control must have been still stronger, especially if he was an owner himself. The captain-owner seems to have had a veto on all the proceedings of the ship. In 1755, when the Seven Years War was obviously coming on, the house endured torments from Captain Holland of the *Judith*. He was too lazy to collect a crew or put up the ship for freight; he would not let the owners sell and they were reduced to blockading him by saying that she should lie by the walls until further notice. They offered that, if he would let them sell her, their share of the price should be invested in the funds for his benefit as long as he lived, but even this offer was declined. Finally they got him to consent to her sale on condition of giving him the command of a new ship (but without any share of the ownership this time). So bitterly did they remember this incident that ever afterwards they accused of 'treachery' or 'ingratitude' any owner of a ship in which they were concerned who sold his share to the captain.

They often claimed that they were only interested in shipping in order to serve their friends. If so, they did not always get value for their investment, for these headstrong captains often neglected their owners' friends when accepting goods for shipment. Sometimes this was excusable, if, for example, there was a hurry to catch a convoy. Only once or twice did a captain in the West India trade refuse to accept goods for shipment unless they were consigned to the owners.[13] A planter, for his part, was only bound morally to favour a particular ship belonging to his factors. He might reserve his early sugars for their first ship, but he could not be expected to do so unless the ship appeared punctually, and the house never liked to make a stipulation of it.

These collateral benefits were probably the chief advantage which the house made from its investment in shipping. Its books do not give enough detail to show conclusively the profit or loss that it made on ship-owning. There are particular instances of small losses or small profits—£200 or £500 per voyage; only occasionally, and then in war-time, do we hear of so great a profit as £2,000.

Ship-owners in the Barbados trade appear to have relied more than most others on freight outward from London to the West Indies. This seems to have been a peculiarity of the island, which had an unusually large white population and therefore consumed a lot of European goods. In consequence there were some occasions (especially in war-time, when fewer ships frequented the island and none could make more than one voyage a year) when a ship could be filled up entirely with high-class freight so that bricks, hoops, coal, and lime could not find room at all. More often, however, there was room for these heavy goods, unless an owner preferred seeking a profit from shipping them to the island on his own account, and refused to take those of anybody else. There are no instances in the Barbados trade of coal or lime carried out to the island freight-free. This was common later in the experience of the Pinneys, who dealt with the Leeward Islands, and even at this earlier period the Lascelles house

---

[13] I have stated on p. 210 of *A West-India Fortune* that this was quite common in the experience of this house. I find on closer examination that this is an exaggeration.

arranged for one such shipment—but to St. Christopher, not to Barbados, which points the lesson that the islands with smaller white populations were those in whose trade the outward freight was insignificant.

Even at Barbados, it was homeward freight that really counted. The house made many attempts to get as high a rate of freight as possible, but it could only persuade, not command: besides the regular ships which were tied to the trade of the island year by year, any ships from any other part of the world could go there in the hope of a great crop on a particular occasion, and lower the rate by its competition. Even the house itself might charter an additional ship, or a rival sugar-factor might do so. The house was particularly jealous of the standing competition of the North Americans, and of the slave traders who were only too glad to fill up with a cargo of sugar on the last lap of their voyage from the islands. The house often claimed, and evidently believed, that this alternative shipping was inferior and that the planters would be unwise if they trusted their produce to it. But it continued to compete with the superior London-built ships which the house put into the trade.

The rate of freight was necessarily settled in the West Indies— at any rate in Barbados. In the spring of 1746 (according to the house's letter to Thomas Applewhaite, 1 March 1745/6):

The planters and owners of ships that are here [in London] having agreed, as by the original papers enclosed, that good ships can not be sent to bring home the Crops, during the continuance of the War at a less freight than nine shillings per cwt. for Sugar, on accot of the high charges of fitting, navigating and insuring, we hope for the Concurrence of the Gentlemen of Bdos. with us in the same opinion. We do not allow the Ships from North America, by any meanes, to be upon the same footing as they are never so well found nor navigated at the same expence and therefore they do not deserve so good a freight.

This attempt to impose upon the planters evidently failed, for next year (on 13 February 1746/7) the house wrote to Foster March:

The freight must always be settled abroad and not at home. We attempted to settle it at home last year for Barbados and thought to have fixed it at Nine Shillings per cwt. but the Gentlemen there would not allow more than 7/6, and at that rate the Ships loaded, and indeed

P

high or low freights must always depend upon the plenty or Scarcity of shipping.

At the beginning of the Seven Years War the owners in London made another attempt to dictate the rate:

The present immoderate Expense that now attends the fitting out ships [so ran the house's instructions to Captain Thomas Mapstone, 16 February 1757] Provisions of all kinds being extravagantly dear, and Sailors' Wages £4 per month—a Circumstance never known before—it will be impossible to support the Navigation without some considerable additions to the homeward bound freight. And therefore, upon a meeting of the Gentlemen concerned in Ships employed in the Barbados Trade, it was unanimously [sic] to give orders to all Captains under their respective directions not to take in Sugar at less than 7/6 per cwt. Freight—the same that was paid during the last war, when the Charges did not run near so high. We flatter ourselves that the Gentlemen of the Island in general will think it very reasonable, and just, under the unhappy Circumstances of Publick affairs, and these orders you are punctually to regard.

I do not know whether they were successful in imposing their will, but if they did so, it was only in war-time. Their jeremiads about the high expense of ship-owning, especially the high wages, after the war are almost plaintive and do not seem to have produced any results. Only in the different outports of Jamaica, where there was no strong centre of local opinion and the rate of freight at the capital, Kingston, was not known, bills of lading were filled up in such a manner as to leave the rate of freight to be settled in England.

Besides selling sugars, purchasing stores, and ship-owning, the factor had to perform services of every kind for his correspondents. He invested their money for them if they had any; he dealt with government departments on their behalf; he got sugar machinery made in accordance with the models or drawings which they sent him; he interviewed suppliers of unsatisfactory goods; he prosecuted their law-suits (although the partners once said that this was not in their line, there is evidence that they feed lawyers and sometimes even attended the courts on behalf of their correspondents who sent home appeals from the colonies to England, especially in prize cases).[14] On one occasion the house

---

[14] See my book, *Colonial Blockade and Neutral Rights* (Oxford, 1938), p. 107, note 2.

even looked out for a seat in parliament for a friend who was an officer in command of the squadron on the Jamaica station.

Perhaps the best way of illustrating this diversity is to give an account of the miscellaneous commissions which the house executed in September and October 1743, just after George Maxwell had become a partner. For Mary Croasdaile of Jamaica they bought two tickets in a state lottery and received the interest on her East India Company bonds. For John Denny of Barbados they bought some more lottery tickets, also Gay's *Fables* in two volumes. For John Frere they got a gown dyed and a bell re-cast, and they interviewed a milliner on behalf of Miles James in order to complain of the inferior quality of the fur with which Mrs. James's nightgown had been trimmed. On behalf of Samuel Husbands they interviewed the secretary of the island of Barbados (whose deputy on the spot Husbands was) about the terms of the deputation. Henry Lascelles ordered a spinet for the granddaughter of William Gibbes. George Maxwell went to Thomas Alleyne's school to report on his progress; the house also put to school the stepson of the governor, Sir Thomas Robinson, and on this occasion their task was complicated by the fact that when the child arrived the school he was to have attended no longer existed. They sent out some gold coin for H. P. King; they wrote to Nicholas Wilcox that they had ordered their correspondent at Cork to send him some beef, candles, tongues, and claret, would order some Dutch clinkers from Holland when they could be sure of getting a ship to take them from England, and would speak to the coppersmiths about some work that he wanted done.

Amid this welter of miscellaneous services, there were certain things which they had to do repeatedly.

They insured homeward-bound sugars and the outward-bound stores of their correspondents. Usually they had express orders for this, but some planters preferred to leave them to judge whether to insure or not, and even without this latitude they sometimes took it upon themselves to do so in an emergency, such as the outbreak of war, which could not be known in time at the islands. As they said, nobody was likely to thank them for this; if they insured and the sugars arrived safe, the planter would think them officious, whereas if they did not insure and the sugars were taken, he would think them negligent. On occasion, they insured in peace-time the sugars of such correspondents as were deeply in debt to them; this precaution was one which, fifty years later, the Pinneys considered that every factor had a right to take, but this house only took it seldom and with apology. For this business the house preferred to deal with the public insurance companies, especially the London Assurance, with whom they had an open account and settled once a year. They would only take out a policy with an unknown insurer for a risk which the companies would not underwrite, for example, upon a ship already overdue. Some of these outsiders proved to be bankrupts: when this happened the planter was apt to claim that the house ought to pay his loss, but they always replied that it was not the custom of merchants 'to insure the insurer'.

The house had a lot of trouble in obtaining skilled employees for their correspondents. Here they found repeatedly that the colonies must expect to put up with the second best. When they wanted a plumber they were told 'that he must be a Person in debt, that is a good Workman, to leave this Country where there is good Encouragement, to go to the West Indies'. When they wanted a private tutor, they found 'it would have been an easy matter to have obtained a Clergyman for the business, as he would have had the prospect of otherwise advancing himself in the Island. We have had many Laymen recommended to us, but some we thought too young, others we were told were mere Scholars and not men of breeding, and we think the last qualification as necessary as the former for the tuition of young Gentlemen.' The best they could suggest was to offer a lay tutor an additional encouragement by building a school-house for him and permitting him to take day scholars in order to supplement his salary. When they wanted a doctor, they found 'there is great plenty of such from Scotland and Ireland and these will not do'— I do not know why, since the great age of the Edinburgh medical school was just beginning. They even resorted to a crimp to get them a surgeon and, failing that, they took up with a Scot who brought 'very good Credentials from the professors at Edinburgh'—but he proved to be an idle, worthless fellow.

They had just as great difficulty in procuring a boy of fourteen or fifteen without any professional qualification. The West India planters liked to obtain young boys for book-keepers and overseers from the Blue Coat Hospital. The authorities of the hospital made difficulties; they would apprentice a boy to a planter but not to an agent on his behalf, for there were ugly stories of cruel and neglectful treatment in the West Indies. Pursuing the matter further, George Maxwell found that he had no hope of getting a boy unless he enlisted the interest of Mr. Smith the writing-master. There were two ways of doing this: either one might force his hand by making interest with one of the governors of the hospital such as Sir Hans Sloane, or one might put money into his pocket by sending to him West India lads to be instructed in writing and accounts (this seems to have been a common practice). Maxwell employed both these means, but even then he came up against a further difficulty—he had to have the consent of the parents.

By G. M.'s going often to the Hospital, he became known to some hundreds of Boyes, and it required no difficulty to get the Consent of any of them, for he was encircled by a multitude all crying out, 'I'll go Sir!', and with their own goodwill, if that was all, he might have loaded a ship with them. He took a fancy to one James Lowman, a sprightly boy, whom the Master spoke well of, and got the Consent of his Mother, who keeps a School, after using all his eloquence in expatiating very justly in praise of the Delights and beauties of dear B^dos, in so much that the poor woman was possessed with an ardent desire to go with her son, but there was no need of her.

This embarrassing success was not repeated very often; for ten years on end the house could not get a Blue Coat boy and had to fall back upon Scotland. Even in Glasgow there were rumours of ill-treatment in the West Indies. One agent wrote to know what the lads were to do? 'We answered to be Brought up Planters and See the business of your Plantations carefully and Properly done. It was dreaded by some, that they were to be put to the hard labour of Negroes.' Other boys were afraid of the climate—one actually ran away a few days before he was due to sail because he had heard of Scots boys who had lately died in the West Indies. Nevertheless, the Scots boys did well and the house had to fulfil repeated orders for more.

The partners often had to obtain for their correspondents offices in the customs and seats on the council of the island and to nego-tiate between the secretaries, provosts marshal, &c., of the colo-nies, who seldom left England, and the planters or merchants who wished to rent their offices from them, perform the duties, and receive the profits.[15] In these last cases the house offered its own security for the due payment of the rent and, in return, charged 5 per cent. commission upon the rent itself.

For all this business, some political influence was necessary. The house relied most on the powerful John Sharpe, who was agent for Barbados and for other islands, solicitor to the Treasury, and general factotum for the Pelhams and their friends.[16] The partners once said that most of their business was negotiated through Sharpe. They had some hold upon his goodwill for, besides everything else, he was a solicitor and they could direct to him all the lucrative law business arising out of the appeals which their correspondents sent home from the colonial courts. Besides this, it was usual to make him a present of £50 whenever one of their correspondents was elevated to the council by his means. The house did not, however, rely on Sharpe alone, especially after Henry Lascelles himself became a member of parliament. Writing to Thomas Applewhaite on 31 July 1745, they said that they had paid Sharpe the usual present, although it had been Henry Lascelles who had got the business done, as Sharpe was engaged in soliciting it before Lascelles became a member of parliament. The implication must be that an M.P. did not need to fee agents as he commanded enough interest of his own. But this was not always so. Although Henry Lascelles thought well of his family's political influence, he had to admit at least once that a dozen members of parliament could not have prevailed against Sharpe. The house also used, on occasion, the influence of the governors of the islands. Sir Thomas Robinson, Governor of Barbados, was a fellow Yorkshireman and dined at Henry Lascelles's house even before he accepted the office, probably in order to find out what additional salary he was likely to get from the legislature of the island. He continued to show goodwill but unfortunately he ceased to be a political asset, for he got involved in quarrels and had to be recalled. The house started on very good terms with Henry Grenville, his successor, an even more powerful character since he had at one time brothers at the Admiralty and the Board of Trade and a friend at the Treasury. The favour of both these

[15] See J. H. Parry, 'The Patent Offices in the British West Indies', *English Historical Review*, lxix (1954), pp. 212–14.

[16] For his career as agent, see Lillian M. Penson, *The Colonial Agents of the British West Indies* (London, 1924), passim, especially pp. 167–8.

governors was particularly necessary to the Lascelles family so long as Edward had not been restored to his collectorship of customs. Soon after this happened, the house quarrelled with Grenville for reasons unknown, and found that they could hardly get anything done against his will.

The partners used such political influence as they had for promoting not only the interests of particular correspondents, but those of the island as a whole. George Maxwell, in 1744, lobbied thirty M.P.s in a day against a proposed tax on sugar. Henry Lascelles soon afterwards got a relation, who was surveyor-general of the Ordnance, to expedite the dispatch of small arms ordered by the colony and to ensure that their quality was good. Both partners waited upon Sharpe in 1744 in order to discuss with him the danger from the French at St. Lucia and the necessity of a cartel for dealing with the French and Spanish prisoners of war. The partners were tempted once or twice to use their interest against, rather than for, the wishes of the majority of the island: for example, they tried, apparently without success, to prevent the confirmation of a bill for reducing the rate of interest from 8 per cent. to 6 per cent. As creditors to the planters, they naturally liked to keep the rate high.

From the internal politics of the island they tried to stand clear, for they were likely to lose business by taking one side or the other. Even neutrality did not always satisfy their angry friends. Thus, when Governor Robinson removed Judge Harrison from office, they declined to sign a memorial on Harrison's behalf and he accused them quite unjustly of being 'retained' by his enemies. They had to answer a similar complaint from their friend Gedney Clarke who, as collector of customs, got into a quarrel with the attorney-general of the island.

Don't think [they wrote to him on 28 December 1750] that We are so anxious after the Commissions as you take upon you to represent us. The Gentleman to whom you have so great an invetteracy, offered Us his Business, and in course We accepted of it. We must tell you, that People in the West Indies have their passions greatly inflamed by the heat of the Climate, and are apt to take fire upon every occasion, which they cannot be sensible of themselves, nor will be so, unless they change the Climate and come to a Colder.

No doubt George Maxwell was here writing from his own experience.

Nothing gave the house more trouble than the duty of looking after the children of their correspondents in the islands. If it had been a mere matter of social duty, such as asking them to stay in the Christmas holidays, or taking a post-chaise to Honiton in order to rescue a stranded creole maiden, it might have been tolerable. But the house had to take serious financial decisions, such as that of supplying a young man with money without order from his father, in order to rescue him from the moneylenders or from the sharks who offered to get his life insured, with no good purpose, we may be sure. Worst of all was the supervision of these children's education.

They arrived with a sallow complexion and a sing-song accent, and it was much if they could be got to look and speak like Englishmen. Their book-learning was grossly behindhand and the factors sometimes shrank from putting them to a school where they would have to sit below the smallest boy. It was too late for them to take Latin—French and arithmetic were the most that could be expected, and if they were put upon higher things they complained of being made to waste their time 'learning Greek derivations'. With all this ignorance and, often, ill-health they combined extravagant ideas of their fortune and expectations and a total aversion to discipline. Conrade Adams was always running away from school and had to be placed in an 'Academy' where the discipline was looser. Young Upton Law likewise ran away from the ironmonger to whom he was apprenticed and, when the house spoke of sending him back to Barbados, threatened to drown himself. James and William Dottin Maycock were made of sterner stuff. They were expelled from an academy near London for knocking down the usher who got them a punishment from the headmaster for impudence; in addition they went about to plays and concerts without the headmaster's leave. The house took lodgings for them in London and provided them with proper masters, but the elder boy had high words with his landlady and struck her, then drew his sword upon her husband who took her part. These boys had to be shipped home to Barbados. So likewise did Peers and Tom Alleyne, who were grossly extravagant at Oxford. Peers was at The Queen's College—according to him the most expensive in the university, where the tutor took no pupils, but farmed them out to a certain Dr. Brown, who charged an extra twenty guineas a year. The doctor complained of Peers for 'being continually in Company with a Young Gentleman of the Leeward Islands whom he wrote a very bad Character of'. This undesirable companion left the university, and Peers was, for a time, charged with no more than going to bed and getting up too late. The house tried to persuade him to be 'a good Oeconomist', but in vain: he insisted on drawing a bill of exchange because he 'liked better to be allowed to draw for his allowance himself, as most of the Young Gentlemen do, than to receive it in a Guinea a time from his Tutor, and he alledged also that he could be a better Oeconomist by having the whole under his own management'. How often have undergraduates told that story! His brother Tom, at Magdalen, was just as expensive, and when the two of them were shipped home £2,220 had to be paid in order to get them out of the country.

I could continue for a long time this catalogue of tiresome youths; but let the story of young Sam Husbands stand for the whole. Soon after he arrived at Westminster School he was nearly turned out because his tutor refused to pay the under master a fee which he claimed of right. The boy's father then started complaining of his heavy expenses. The partners replied that they could not be expected to see to these in detail—they preferred that the schoolmasters should pay the necessary bills, subject to an examination of their accounts. In any case, if Sam had too much pocket money, that was the fault of a Mrs. Gordon, who was supposed to be looking after him and doled out his allowance through a milliner. Worse was to come. Sam could not go back to school after the Christmas holidays of 1755, because he had been 'unfortunately drawn into the embraces of a vile wicked Strumpet who gave him the foul disease'. He was reported to be 'a sincere penitent', and when he was cured and ready to return to school 'our G. M.' felt that he owed some explanation to the headmaster. The great Dr. Markham 'expressed a concern for what had happened but said, Sammy was a lad of parts and to be regarded, that he should not take the least notice of it to him nor seem to know of it, and he hoped he would keep the thing a secret from the other Boys at School. He further said, you know, many Lads have met with the same mischance, and afterwards proved and turned out good Men, and this Lad therefore is not to be neglected or lost.' For a time Sam prospered: he reported himself to be on good terms with the headmaster and to have 'executed themes, on two subjects set him, with great applause vizt., one on diligence and the other on prudence'. This good reputation was not to last. A few months later Dr. Markham found himself forced to expel the boy from school. His offence was that of setting a bad example by lying in bed until eight or nine in the morning: evidently head-masters' sense of proportion has changed since the eighteenth century. Sam proceeded to Cambridge, where he continued to give trouble: he went on lying in bed and, on the pretext of living by a 'regimen', he would not dine in Hall—although he paid for his dinner whether he took it or not; he pestered the house to buy him a horse because a doctor had ordered him riding; 'to say truth, we were apprehensive this was only a Scheme, to have a horse of his own, and be like others of his rank, who keep horses'. In the end they became so tired of him that they washed their hands of him. Indeed they were heartily sick of all such business. When the father of Conrade Adams complained of their charg-ing $2\frac{1}{2}$ per cent. on his disbursements, they retorted that the money was dearly earned as this sort of business was so far more troublesome than 'a common cash article'. Before they had done with Sam Husbands they exclaimed, 'When young People will follow their own ways, it is an office more eligible to be a Hog Driver than to have any concern with them.' The worst of it was that they were not even casting their bread upon the waters: as they observed, very few of the young men of whom they had taken charge in this way became or even continued their corre-spondents after getting possession of their estates.

For all the services which I have been describing, the house needed a considerable capital. Even for paying the freight and duties of incoming sugars and accepting the bills of exchange which the planters had drawn on the strength of them, a sum of at least £20,000 was needed. But the matter did not stop there. Most planters expected a fair-sized advance upon account current and many of them wanted loans of a more specific nature.

In chapters xi and xii of *A West-India Fortune* I have de-scribed fully the system of West India finance—the loans on account current; the contract debts fortified, perhaps by a bond to repay twice the sum borrowed, perhaps by a formal judgement in the colonial courts or at least a warrant of attorney to confess judgement; lastly, the mortgages. I refer the reader to that description, nearly all of which holds good for the history of the

house I am now discussing. I shall now concentrate on the differences between the history of the Lascelleses and that of the
Pinneys, many of which are significant.

The greatest of all these differences was this: the planters were
much less deeply in debt in the earlier period than in the later,
and the factors had far more confidence in the ability of the sugar
industry to carry and repay these debts. There were many reasons
for this. Barbados was an island with plantations of moderate
size, whose owners generally resided on the spot. The initial
capitalization had been made—that is, the slave population had
been bought—at the low prices of the seventeenth century, even
though current replacement had to be made at greater cost. In
the decade before the house began business the sugar prices had
been at their lowest, and it was not likely that the factors would
have allowed the planters to get deeply into debt; and these lean
years were succeeded by a generation of higher prices and optimism, which might well be called the silver age of the British
West India sugar industry. Lastly, the house itself was relatively
new, and started with a clean sheet—not that that would have
mattered after 1800, when a new house had to begin by raising
capital to pay off the previous encumbrances of its would-be correspondents.

There are many symptoms of this relative buoyancy. In the
first place, the House of Lascelles was content with much less
security than the House of Pinney would have demanded. The
partners allowed the debts on account current to run into thousands without asking for a bond or a mortgage: one of their
correspondents, John Frere, owed them more than £14,000, and
they still disclaimed any wish for better security. There was little
talk of mortgages: it was generally believed that a planter's credit
was blasted by a mortgage, and the house itself must have acknowledged this to be true, for it more than once refused to pay bills of
exchange for a planter who was believed to be mortgaging his
plantation. The Pinneys could not have taken these risks, and
nearly every big debt on their books was a mortgage debt.
Secondly, the Lascelleses, unlike the Pinneys, never objected to
their correspondents selling their sugars in the island instead of
consigning them home. Indeed they often congratulated their
correspondents on having done so. They could not have held this
opinion if they had looked upon consignments of sugars as the

only means of repaying debts otherwise desperate. They thought only of the commission, and did not even mind very much when their correspondents left them for new factors. This, again, would have been unpardonable in the later age. Lastly, it is clear that Henry Lascelles, at least, was looking for opportunities of investing money in Barbados: he welcomed opportunities of buying judgement debts from good debtors and was angry when others tried to buy good debts owed to himself. When a prospective bond or judgement debtor asked for a 'defeasance'—that is, an undertaking not to demand repayment within a given term of years—he stipulated that the defeasance should be mutual, in order that he might not have his money returned sooner than he wanted it. He sold out of the public funds in order to make these loans, and he wanted, in return, an investment equally permanent. He could not have behaved like this if he had doubted the security of his money.

The greater security and prosperity of sugar business showed itself in another way—in the greater financial independence of Barbados as a community. There were sterling debts and currency debts—that is, debts repayable in England and debts repayable on the island: interest on the former was limited by law to 5 per cent., on the latter to 6 or 8 per cent. Many of the debts which the Lascelles family handled were currency debts. They arose from judgements in the colonial courts. All these 'judgement debts' (often, as I have said, little more than a formal means of registering the debt) were the object of a lively traffic: people bought and sold them. It is clear that, at any rate in the preceding age, Barbadians had owed money not so much to Englishmen as to other Barbadians, and had had some prospect of repaying them; there must have been a class of prosperous planters who could afford to lend to new-comers and the weaker brethren. Probably this class had not altogether disappeared in Henry Lascelles's time.

There was some disadvantage in holding currency debts. Money repaid in the island could only be remitted to England by shipping sugar and standing the risk of the seas, or by purchasing a bill of exchange, at a rate which varied. Often this rate was disadvantageous to the remitter, that is, a lot of Barbados money was needed to buy a moderate quantity of sterling. Henry Lascelles disliked having his currency debts remitted to him at such a disadvantage: sometimes he insisted on leaving the money in the islands, at other times he would stipulate beforehand the rate of exchange at which remittance was to be made. All these difficulties were avoided by making the debt a sterling debt. This was not the only reason why sterling debts tended to supersede currency debts. The latter could only exist on a large scale either where there were still local capitalists or where the debtors readily repaid money on the island and the sum so repaid became available for new loans. Both these conditions were disappearing, and when the only source of fresh capital was England (even if it came from the West India trade itself, that is, from the payment of interest in London by planters to factors), then every important debt would be a sterling debt. This condition had come into existence by the time the House of Pinney and Tobin began business in 1783.

Even in the later pages of the Lascelles letter books there are symptoms of increasing debt. Mortgages were more frequent and excited less repugnance than they had done a generation earlier. Debts on account current were swelling, and the planters with favourable balances were fewer and fewer in comparison with the others. The Lascelleses even began to find that when they got a debtor to sell his plantation the purchaser was no better able to pay for the debt, and, little as they liked it, they had once or twice to threaten that in the end they would take the debtors' plantations to themselves. In fact, they must have done so more than once. In 1836, when the slave-owners were compensated for the abolition of their property in the slaves, the heirs of Henry Lascelles were recorded as possessing four plantations in Barbados, with 933 slaves in all. At least two of these plantations, it seems, must have been taken over from their debtors.

In one important respect the Lascelleses differed from the Pinneys very much: they dealt much more largely with merchants resident in the islands. This kind of business lacked many of the advantages which could be got from dealing with planters: a merchant might have no landed security to offer and, though his business brought in a larger commission on purchases, it yielded much less on returns, since these often took the form of bills of exchange, on which only $\frac{1}{2}$ per cent. was paid, instead of sugars yielding a commission of $2\frac{1}{2}$ per cent. or more. The merchant's debt would carry 5 per cent. interest, but so would that of a planter with better security. Some of these disadvantages the Lascelleses tried to overcome: in particular, when they dealt with a merchant they tried to get some other, better established merchant, preferably one with some landed property, to go security for him. At any rate, a large part of their business was done with merchants, and this is not altogether surprising. Henry Lascelles himself had been a merchant in the island; his brother Edward still was one; his wife's nephew Samuel Carter and many of his closest associates, especially the Gedney Clarkes, father and son, and Thomas Stevenson, still were merchants.

Some of these men had a miscellaneous business in dry goods, and in prize sugars when opportunity offered in war-time. But, as a rule, big business was slave business, especially in Barbados. The reasons for this were largely geographical: Barbados was the first port of call in the West Indies and many a captain threatened with mortality, mutiny, or scarcity of provisions, and ignorant of the state of the markets, would call at Barbados, if only to refresh the negroes and ask for news of commercial conditions. Barbados, therefore, was an island of great slave merchants.

The method of selling the slaves in the islands was changing. In the old days the captain, with or without the assistance of a local merchant, would hold an auction in which the slaves were sold for sugars to be paid promptly and carried home in the ship. This way of doing business had its risks: above all, the captain could hardly know which planters were capable of paying for their purchases in a reasonable time. This difficulty increased when the payments began to be made largely in bills of exchange —a development which came about, perhaps, because, as the price of negroes rose and the price of sugar fell, no slave ship could have carried the entire value of her slaves in sugar. In these new conditions the captain needed the help of a merchant, who seems at first to have acted simply as a factor, selling the slaves on commission. In time, however, the factor became something more. The owners of the slaves would expect him to contract, and even bind himself by a penal bond, to sell the slaves at or above a certain limit of price and to return the proceeds by the ship which had brought them. In these cases the factor insensibly became the real purchaser of the slaves: he paid the limit demanded by the owners, resold the slaves to the planters for payment in six, nine, or twelve months, and compensated himself—indeed, made his fortune—out of the difference between the cash price and the credit price. But as he was to lie out of his money, he had to have either a large capital or a financial backer in London. Gradually his relations with this backer took a more precise form: the Liverpool and Bristol slave merchants would expect the London financier to give security on behalf of the local slave merchant in the colonies. Usually this was a 'specific security'—that is, the financier would bind himself in a penalty of, say, £10,000 that the local slave merchant would comply with the conditions imposed by the owners of the ship. The letter books of the house do not show what return the financier got for this business. The house did not go into partnership with the merchants in the islands, for whom they gave these securities, and it is not certain that they got anything more than the usual 5 per cent. interest on the money advanced.

Much of their business was of this kind. Moreover, besides this security business, which only involved a risk of actual outlay, they advanced money to slave merchants in the islands in large sums. Some of this money was used for outright purchase of slaves to be sent from Barbados to another island or to Carolina; the rest was used in miscellaneous ways, probably in part for buying plantations. At various times Samuel Carter and the Stevensons owed the house between £10,000 and £20,000 and Gedney Clarke, senior, an enterprising, showy man, with all sorts of irons in the fire, owed at his death nearly £50,000, to which his son added a further debt of £25,000, nearly all of which must have been lost when he went bankrupt in 1774.

The biggest business of all was done with the family of the Harvies, and I shall tell this story in more detail, partly because it explains why a family which specialized in the trade of Barbados ended by owning two plantations in Jamaica.

In 1740, one John Harvie was procured by the house to go over to Barbados as a private tutor. He seems to have married a daughter of Thomas Stevenson and in 1744 he was home in England asking for an advance which would enable him to start business as a dry goods merchant in the islands. Fortified by the security which Thomas Stevenson offered, the house agreed to advance £4,000 to Harvie for the purchase of linens and calicoes. He remained in Barbados until 1753, by which time his debt had insensibly swelled to more than £10,000. He then decided to go down to Jamaica with his brother Alexander and enter the business of slave consignments. For the purpose, the house agreed to advance for him a sum which was never to exceed £20,000, and the partners sent their friends in Bristol and Liverpool a letter to this effect. For a year or two all went well, but the Harvies seem to have been plungers. The years just before the Seven Years War were not a good time for selling slaves—the prospects of Jamaica and its industry seemed doubtful. The Harvies, however, rushed in where others feared to tread, and by the end of 1754 their debt to the house approached £60,000. This was too much, and George Maxwell was driven nearly distracted by financial anxiety. But he could do little. The agreement with the Harvies did not expire until July 1757: the house could have denounced it on the grounds that the £20,000 limit had been exceeded, but, lured by promises of repayment from the Harvies and fearing to blast their credit by a violent move, the house did not take this step. Maxwell tried in vain to induce the Harvies to give up slave consignments, but they refused to do this. Their idea was to 'push the business' for a few years and then shut up shop completely and collect their debts. This was not altogether silly; for a merchant, whether dealing in slaves or in dry goods, was apt to find that planters would cease coming to his shop if he asked them to pay their old debts, so he could only dun them after he had wound up his business. But the Harvies trespassed too much on George Maxwell's good nature: even when they had given up the slave consignment business they started it again more than once; besides this, although they promised not to do so, they went into the dry goods business, shipped cargoes to the Spanish colonies, and, worst of all, started buying plantations right and left. Their debt to the house, which had at one time reached £80,000, came down to £60,000 but could not be reduced further. Three Harvies died one after another; although they believed that they had (besides plantations worth £50,000) enough money owing them to pay off the house, most of these debts proved bad, and they were reduced in the end to asking Daniel Lascelles to take over their plantations. This he had no wish to do. He would rather have got them sold to a purchaser who could repay him his money. At this point the story, so far as I know it, stops; but it is easy to see what was going to happen. The Harvies' plantations, already mortgaged to the Lascelles family, were going to fall into their reluctant hands and to stay there. In 1836 the heirs of Henry Lascelles owned two plantations in Jamaica, with 344 slaves in all.

By the middle 1760's, the house was owed at least £120,000 by merchants (though most of these merchants had, in the course of their business, yielded to the craze for becoming planters as well). Probably—although there is no means of knowing this—the debt owed to the house by mere planters was smaller than this; indeed, the partners often complained that if they had not been forced to lend so much to merchants they could have had a much larger consignment business from planters. But it all came to the same thing in the long run. Whether the house lent money directly to planters or lent it to merchants who sold the planters slaves for which they could not pay, the money was, in fact, financing supplies of slaves to the plantations; and it was only just that in the end, directly or indirectly, the moneylender should become the owner of the plantations.

There are two last questions—where did all the money come from, and what did it all amount to?

Clearly the money did not come from George Maxwell. He always spoke as if it was his partners' money that he was lending, not his own, and they often scolded him for the terms on which he lent it. The mainstay of the house was Henry Lascelles. He may have inherited part of his fortune from a father or uncle who had himself made it in the West Indies. He certainly added to it by his career as a merchant in Barbados, and by the profits of the business I have been describing. When he ceased to be a partner in 1750, he handed over to his son Daniel and to George Maxwell the credits which the house had given to the planters up to that date. He continued to invest directly in Barbados by lending to the planters; probably he also advanced to the house much of the money which they lent—in 1752, for example, we learn that when he made a loan he sold securities, whereas when the house made a loan it had to take up money, probably from him. After his death in 1753 the house was much weakened financially, for only one-third of his fortune descended to Daniel, and even that seems to have been held for him on trust. From this time the house frequently complained of the pressure on its means. There had been squeezes even in Henry Lascelles's time—at the outbreak of war with France in 1744, the invasion scare of 1745, the high price of money in 1746–8 and again in 1750–1—but these

squeezes became much worse after 1753, and the house was working on an overdraft at the bank for much of the time. We do not
know the size of this overdraft, but it frequently troubled the
partners, especially at times of financial stringency (above all,
war-time), when much money could be made by investing in the
public funds and holding them for a rise. Evidently the big loans
to the Harvies and the Clarkes, and such loans as were made to
the planters, took the house, and kept it, very near the edge of its
means or its credit. In the end the storm was weathered—we know
that, but we do not know how.

Even if the house had collapsed, something would have been
added permanently to the national capital. When Henry Lascelles made his will in August 1753, he bequeathed, besides annui-
ties, sums amounting to £284,000. (It does not follow that he
possessed all this, but I do not think Henry Lascelles was likely
to make a mistake.) Of this sum, £53,000 was invested in lands
in Yorkshire; the rest seems to have been in the public funds, in
Henry Lascelles's own plantation in Barbados, and, above all,
in loans to the planters. Only one-third of this money was bequeathed to Daniel, who continued to be engaged in the West
India trade. £166,666 went to Edwin, who never had anything to
do with the business. Daniel's share might have been lost—I have
no reason to believe that it was—but Edwin's share was enough
by itself to found one of the noble families of England.

THE WRITINGS OF RICHARD PARES

A SELECT BIBLIOGRAPHY[1]

1930

'Public Records in British West India Islands', *Bulletin* of the Institute of Historical Research, vii. 149–57.

Review of *Calendar of State Papers: Colonial Series, America and West Indies, Aug. 1714–Dec. 1715, and Jan. 1716–July 1717* (2 vols., London, 1928, 1930), and *Journal of the Commissioners for Trade and Plantations, Jan. 1722/3–Dec. 1728 and Jan. 1728/9–Dec. 1734* (2 vols., London, 1928). *History*, N.S. XV. 268–71.

1932

'War and Trade in the West Indies, 1739–1748', *Revue d'Histoire des Colonies*, xxv. 41–74.

Review of *Calendar of State Papers: Colonial Series, America and West Indies, Aug. 1717–Dec. 1718* (London, 1930). *History*, N.S. xvii. 73–74.

1934

Review of C. M. Andrews, *The Colonial Background of the American Revolution* (rev. ed., New Haven, 1931); *Essays in Colonial History*, by Students of C. M. Andrews (New Haven, 1931); L. W. Labaree, *Royal Government in America* (New Haven, 1930); and Helen J. Crump, *Colonial Admiralty Jurisdiction in the Seventeenth Century* (London, 1931). *History*, N.S. xix. 70–72.

---

[1] This list does not include Short Notices either in the *English Historical Review*, of which Richard Pares was joint editor from vol. liv, no. 215 (July 1939), to vol. lxxiii, no. 288 (July 1958), or in other periodicals. It excludes also contributions to such journals as *The Oxford Magazine* and the *New Statesman*. A complete bibliography, compiled by R. A. Humphreys and George Shepperson, is contained in the *University of Edinburgh Gazette*, no. 21 (Oct. 1958), pp. 24–36.

1935

Review of *Calendar of State Papers: Colonial Series, America and West Indies, Jan. 1719–Feb. 1720, March 1720–Dec. 1721,* and *1722–1723* (3 vols., London, 1933–4). *History,* N.S. xx. 276–7.

Review of A. P. Newton, *The European Nations in the West Indies, 1493–1688* (London, 1933). *English Historical Review,* l. 522–3.

1936

War and Trade in the West Indies, 1739–1763 (Oxford, Clarendon Press), xi + 631 pp.

'American versus Continental Warfare, 1739–63', *English Historical Review,* li. 429–65.

1937

'The Economic Factors in the History of the Empire', *Economic History Review,* vii. 119–44. Reprinted in *Essays in Economic History,* ed. E. M. Carus-Wilson (London, Arnold, 1954).

'The Manning of the Navy in the West Indies, 1702–63', Royal Historical Society, *Transactions,* 4th series, xx. 31–60.

'Prisoners of War in the West Indies in the Eighteenth Century', *Barbados Museum and Historical Society Journal,* v. 12–17.

1938

Colonial Blockade and Neutral Rights, 1739–1763 (Oxford, Clarendon Press), vii + 323 pp.

'Barbados History from the Records of the Prize Courts. I. A Slave Ship at Barbados in 1693', *Barbados Museum and Historical Society Journal,* v. 186–9.

'Barbados History from the Records of the Prize Courts. II. The *Six Friends,* of London, 1693', *Barbados Museum and Historical Society Journal,* vi. 10–20.

Review of *Calendar of State Papers: Colonial Series, America and West Indies, 1724–5, 1726–7,* and *1728–9* (3 vols., London, 1936, 1937). *History,* N.S. xxii. 367–9.

1939

'Barbados History from the Records of the Prize Court[s]. III. A Trader with the Enemy, 1702: Manuel Manasses Gilligan', *Barbados Museum and Historical Society Journal*, vi. 59–66.

'Barbados History from the Records of the Prize Courts. IV. The Barbados Prize Court under Judge Blenman', *Barbados Museum and Historical Society Journal*, vi. 117–28.

Review of Brian Tunstall, *William Pitt, Earl of Chatham* (London, 1928), and C. W. Eldon, *England's Subsidy Policy towards the Continent during the Seven Years' War* (Philadelphia, 1938). *English Historical Review*, liv. 735–6.

1940

Review of Basil Williams, *The Whig Supremacy, 1714–1760* (*Oxford History of England*, ed. G. N. Clark, vol. xi) (Oxford, 1939). *English Historical Review*, lv. 136–9.

Review of Romney Sedgwick, ed., *Letters from George III to Lord Bute, 1756–1766* (London, 1939). *English Historical Review*, lv. 475–9.

Review of *Calendar of State Papers: Colonial Series, America and West Indies, 1730* and *1731* (2 vols., London, 1937, 1938). *History*, N.S. xxiv. 353–4.

1941

Review of *Calendar of State Papers: Colonial Series, America and West Indies, 1732* and *1733* (2 vols., London, 1939). *History*, N.S. xxv. 362–5.

1943

Review of A. L. Burt, *The United States, Great Britain, and British North America: from the Revolution to the Establishment of Peace after the War of 1812* (New Haven, 1940). *English Historical Review*, lviii. 240–1.

1945

Review of H. Butterfield, *The Englishman and his History* (Cambridge, 1944). *Economic History Review*, xv. 87–88.

1946

Review of Klaus E. Knorr, *British Colonial Theories, 1570–1850* (Toronto, 1944). *English Historical Review*, lxi. 108–9.

1947

Review of Richard B. Morris, *Government and Labor in Early America* (New York, 1946). *English Historical Review*, lxii. 107–9.

1948

'Recent British Works on Modern British History', *Bulletin* of the Institute of Historical Research, xxi. 116–27.

Review of E. L. Woodward, *History of England* (London, 1947). *Economic History Review*, 2nd series, i. 79–81.

1949

Review of W. K. Hancock and M. M. Gowing, *British War Economy* (History of the Second World War. United Kingdom Civil Series. London, 1949). *Economic History Review*, 2nd series, ii. 211–13.

1950

A West-India Fortune (London, Longmans, Green & Co.), viii + 374 pp.

'Basil Williams, 1867–1950', *Proceedings of the British Academy*, xxxvi. 251–60.

Review of H. Butterfield, *George III, Lord North, and the People, 1779–80* (London, 1949). *English Historical Review*, lxv. 526–9.

1951

'The Work of a Departmental Priority Officer', in *Lessons of the British War Economy*, ed. D. N. Chester (Economic and Social Studies, X. The National Institute of Economic and Social Research. Cambridge Univ. Press), pp. 154–66.

'George III and the Politicians', Royal Historical Society, *Transactions*, 5th series, i. 127–51.

Review of Keith Feiling, *A History of England* (London, 1950).
  English Historical Review, lxvi. 396–7.

1952

Review of W. C. Costin and J. S. Watson, eds., *The Law and
  Working of the Constitution: Documents 1660–1914* (2 vols.,
  London, 1952). *Past and Present*, no. 2, pp. 58–59.

1953

King George III and the Politicians. The Ford Lectures delivered
  in the University of Oxford, 1951–2 (Oxford, Clarendon Press),
  214 pp.

'The Historian's Business', *University of Edinburgh Journal*, xvii.
  32–38.

'Human Nature in Politics', *The Listener*, 17 Dec. 1953, pp. 1037–8.

Review of Vincent T. Harlow, *The Founding of the Second
  British Empire, 1763–1793*. Vol. i. *Discovery and Revolution*
  (London, 1952). *English Historical Review*, lxviii. 282–5.

1954

'A Quarter of a Millennium of Anglo-Scottish Union', *History*,
  N.S. xxxix. 233–48.

'The Younger Pitt', *The Listener*, 13 May 1954, pp. 821–2.

1955

Introduction to Sir Bernard Pares, *A History of Russia* (3rd ed.,
  rev. and enlarged, London, Jonathan Cape), pp. i–ix.

Review of *Calendar of State Papers: Colonial Series, America and
  West Indies*. Vols. xli (*1734–1735*) and xlii (*1735–1736*) (2 vols.,
  London, 1953). *English Historical Review*, lxx. 458–60.

1956

*Yankees and Creoles. The trade between North America and the
  West Indies before the American Revolution* (London, Longmans, Green & Co.), vii + 168 pp.

Editor, with A. J. P. Taylor, *Essays presented to Sir Lewis Namier* (London, Macmillan), viii + 542 pp.

'A London West-India Merchant House, 1740–1769', in *Essays presented to Sir Lewis Namier*, pp. 75–107.

'The London Sugar Market, 1740–1769', *Economic History Review*, 2nd series, ix. 254–70.

Review of Arnold J. Toynbee, *A Study of History* (10 vols., London, 1933–54). *English Historical Review*, lxxi. 256–72.

1957

Limited Monarchy in Great Britain in the Eighteenth Century. (Historical Association Pamphlets, General Series, no. 35. London, published for the Historical Association by Routledge and Kegan Paul), 28 pp.

'The Revolt against Colonialism', *The Listener*, 1 Aug. 1957, pp. 159–60.

Review of Robert E. Brown, *Middle-Class Democracy and the Revolution in Massachusetts, 1691–1780* (Ithaca, N.Y., 1956). *English Historical Review*, lxxii. 122–6.

Review of John Brooke, *The Chatham Administration, 1766–1768* (London, 1956). *English Historical Review*, lxxii. 333–7.

1958

Review of P. L. White, *The Beekmans of New York in Politics and Commerce, 1647–1877* (New York, 1956), and P. L. White, ed., *The Beekman Mercantile Papers, 1746–1799* (3 vols., New York, 1956). *English Historical Review*, lxxiii. 111–14.

Review of *The New Cambridge Modern History*, ed. G. N. Clark, J. R. M. Butler, J. P. T. Bury, and the late E. A. Benians. Vol. vii. *The Old Regime, 1713–63*, ed. Mrs. J. O. Lindsay (Cambridge, 1957). *English Historical Review*, lxxiii. 303–6.

Review of Sir Winston S. Churchill, *A History of the English-Speaking Peoples.* Vol. iii. *The Age of Revolution* (London, 1957). *English Historical Review*, lxxiii. 496–9.

Review of Carl B. Cone, *Burke and the Nature of Politics*. I. *The Age of the American Revolution* (Lexington, 1957). *William and Mary Quarterly*, 3rd series, xv. 397–9.

1960

Merchants and Planters. [The Chichele Lectures delivered in the University of Oxford, 1956–7.] Economic History Review Supplement 4 (Cambridge Univ. Press). 91 pp.

INDEX